Faces *of* Freedom

Profiles of America's Fallen Heroes ~ Iraq and Afghanistan

Cpl. Steven McGowan, Spc. Wade Twyman and Spc. Jason Hagan in Ramadi, Iraq • 1st Battalion, 9th Infantry Regiment of the 2nd Brigade Combat Team
McGowan and Twyman both KIA 3/4/05 • Photo by Sgt. Chris Lambert

Faces *of* Freedom

Edited by Rebecca Pepin

Foreword by Lt. Gen. John Bruce Blount (U.S. Army, ret.)

Afterword by Maj. Gen. Thomas M. Sadler (U.S. Air Force, ret.)

Photographs provided by family and friends of the fallen, except where noted.

Printed in the United States of America

To order more copies, visit: www.rebeccapepin.com

CREDITS

Editorial Director
Rebecca Pepin

Chief Advisor
W. Thomas Smith, Jr.

Design
Galen Bernard

Story Introductions
Written by Rebecca Pepin, unless otherwise noted

Senior Editors
Kit Lange
Marci J. Hait
Gayle Trent
Heather Hudgens Armstrong
Terri Randall

Military Technical Advisors/Editors
W. Thomas Smith, Jr.
Derek J. Pepin
Henry M. Holden

Associate Editors
Sonya Senkowsky
Christine M. French
Scott Nordhues
Annie Oeth
Bill Schwanke
Ann Stoffle

Cover Photo
Cpl. Heath Cobb and fellow Marines at a memorial service in Iraq for Sgt. Mark P. Adams of North Carolina (photo courtesy of Heath Cobb, who was a sergeant when he left the Marine Corps).

Many of the famous quotes featured in this book were taken from the journal of fallen Marine 1st Lt. Ryan McGlothlin.

CONTRIBUTING WRITERS

Jo Anne Allen
Kristin Anderson
Gloria Butler Baldwin
Heather Barr
Adrianna Belan
Heather Brown
Chris Churchill
Kay B. Day
Sophia Dembling
Jennifer Evans
Marci J. Hait
Judy Crausbay Hamilton
Kristin Harty
Nicole Henrich
Lauralyn Duff Hogan
Hannah Horne
Chera Kimiko
Starlyn Klein
Kit Lange
Curtis Lum
Jennifer McCollum
Kara Gormley Meador
Zlati Meyer
Laila Morcos
Valerie A. Nichols
Rebecca Pepin
Tony Perry
Susan Peters
Jay Price
Gene Retske
Keith Rogers
Norman Rudi
Jim Sheeler
W. Thomas Smith, Jr.
Sara Steffens
Lt. Col. Mike Strobl
David Swanson
Monte Turner
Melanie Votaw
Chuck Walsh
Sonu Wasu
Jane Watrel
William Wilcoxen
Leigh Ann Williams
Jennifer Wilson
Cindy Woods
Karen Spears Zacharias

SPONSORS

Battalion Commander's Sponsorship ($10,000)

Food City (K-VA-T Food Stores, Inc.)

Company Commander's Sponsorship – ($2,500 - $5,000)

Alpha Natural Resources
Anonymous

Platoon Commander's Sponsorship ($1,000)

U.S. Tactical, Inc.
Network IP
APPCO of Blountville, TN
Triad Packaging, Inc.

BOOK PURCHASES FOR LIBRARIES

Wal-Mart
All school and public libraries in southwest Virginia
and numerous veterans' organizations

Bristol Motor Speedway
All libraries in Tennessee

OTHER DONORS

New Peoples Bank
Niswonger Foundation
The Joy Foundation, Ltd.

Please contact Rebecca Pepin if you would like to become a sponsor or library donor:
beccapepin@yahoo.com
www.rebeccapepin.com

DONATED BY BARRY CHRYSLER-DODGE-JEEP

This book is dedicated to Medal of Honor recipients:

Army Sgt. 1st Class Paul R. Smith

&

Marine Cpl. Jason L. Dunham

Photo courtesy of Spc. Jason Hagan

Foreword

By Lt. General John Bruce Blount
United States Army (retired)

"Where do we get such men?"
— James Michener, *The Bridges at Toko-Ri*

Since its birth on a Massachusetts battlefield more than 230 years ago, our nation has expanded its borders, prospered, welcomed newcomers, and defended the rights of others through the great sacrifices of the men and women who have worn the uniform in peace and in war.

Today, many uniformed Americans continue to sacrifice for their fellow man, and — as you'll see in the pages of this book, Faces of Freedom — many who have now paid the ultimate sacrifice had dreams, hopes for the future, wonderful memories of the past, and families who loved them just like the rest of us. The difference is that they were — in the words of George Skypeck — the kinds of Americans whom "others did not want to be," who "went where others feared to go, and did what others failed to do."

We are fortunate that we as a nation have produced such men and women since 1775, and we continue to do so in the 21st century.

These young Americans defend us regardless of personal politics. To them it is not about the unfortunate partisanship so prevalent today, but about duty, honor and a sometimes difficult to describe patriotism, love of country and a devotion to the same.

It may be hard for many Americans to appreciate that deep sense of service to one's country. But what we may all appreciate is the fact that without such men and women, this great experiment in representative democracy would be moot, and the world would be a far darker place.

*— **Lt. Gen. John Bruce Blount (U.S. Army, ret.)**, the former chief of staff of Allied Forces Southern Europe, has held every level of command from infantry platoon leader to commanding general of Fort Jackson, SC, the U.S. Army's largest basic training facility. A highly decorated three-star officer, Blount served in combat in both Korea and Vietnam and was awarded a Purple Heart, Bronze Star, Silver Star, and many other awards and decorations.*

From the Editorial Director

On Oct. 27, 2006, I became an American.

At the swearing-in ceremony in Abingdon, VA, Judge Michael F. Urbanski challenged the group of 15 new citizens before him to make a difference in our communities. He urged us not to become complacent and to always remember that we have an "obligation that accompanies the honor of becoming an American."

It reminded me of the men and women in the armed forces who selflessly serve day-in and day-out. I couldn't help but feel emotional as I considered the thousands of military members who were in faraway lands on that day instead of sharing a special moment with *their* families.

My thoughts were particularly with those serving in the current conflict in the Middle East. Would I be an American worthy of their sacrifice? I reflected on Eleanor Roosevelt's wartime prayer, shared with me by a Vietnam veteran friend of mine:

> *"Dear Lord,*
> *Lest I continue*
> *My complacent way,*
> *Help me to remember that somewhere,*
> *Somehow out there*
> *A man died for me today.*
> *As long as there be war,*
> *I then must*
> *Ask and answer*
> *Am I worth dying for?"*

The book, *Faces of Freedom: Profiles of America's Fallen Heroes ~ Iraq and Afghanistan,* is the way in which I have chosen to say "thank you" to those who serve. And through this project, I have seen many Americans who have not forgotten their obligations as sons and daughters of this great land. *Faces of Freedom* was made possible by dozens of volunteer writers, editors and artists.

In these pages you will read about some of the nation's fallen heroes. Some were great warriors. Some served their countries quietly and dutifully. All loved America.

On Dec. 14, 2005, President George W. Bush addressed the nation about the ongoing Global War on Terror. He talked about how the power of freedom will overcome tyranny. "We can be confident because we have on our side the greatest force for freedom in human history: the men and women of the United States Armed Forces," he said.

The president pointed to Marine 2nd Lt. Ryan McGlothlin, from southwest Virginia, as an example:

"Ryan was a bright young man who had everything going for him and he always wanted to serve our nation. He was a valedictorian of his high school class. He graduated from William & Mary with near-perfect grade averages, and he was on a full scholarship at Stanford, where he was working toward a doctorate in chemistry."

The president went on to explain that Ryan was killed while fighting along the Syrian border in Iraq in November of 2005.

Not every soldier, sailor, airman, Marine or Coast Guardsman will be recognized in a speech by the president. In fact, many will barely get a mention in their local newspapers. The primary purpose of this book is to raise money to benefit veterans, through Fisher House and Wounded Warrior Project, and to heighten awareness about the sacrifice and selflessness of our troops. These men and women are not just numbers. They were our friends and neighbors, and the loved ones of our fellow Americans. While only 52 fallen heroes are featured here, *Faces of Freedom* is a tribute to all who have made the ultimate sacrifice so that we — and our future generations — may live in peace, security and freedom.

— Rebecca Pepin

Acknowledgements

The efforts of many individuals have helped bring this labor of love to fruition. Those efforts include the work of volunteer writers and editors (many of whom are full-time professional journalists and authors), the Wentworth Printing team, the art director and the families of the fallen.

I will be eternally grateful for the time and talent of nationally acclaimed writer and military expert W. Thomas Smith, Jr., who served as chief advisor for this project and always made himself available.

The tireless dedication of Jane Watrel, Derek Pepin, Bobby Griffin and Don McGlothlin is truly commendable. They have been my greatest allies in getting the word out about Faces of Freedom and have been instrumental with fundraising.

I am sincerely grateful to those who have generously provided financial support as shown in the list of sponsors and library donors. Many individuals have made personal contributions, and each has made a difference.

Special acknowledgement is given to Steve Smith, president of K-VA-T Food Stores, Inc., and the Food City team for selling the books in Food City stores and contributing all proceeds to this effort to help wounded veterans.
Thank you to Mike Lewis, Wal-Mart Market Manager in southwest Virginia, for getting behind *Faces of Freedom*.

Marci J. Hait should be recognized for her quick responses and "bring it on" attitude no matter how much work I sent in her direction during the writing process. I also appreciate the press releases and promotional support.

Thank you to Kit Lange — a dependable go-to writer, editor and blogger.
Thank you to Galen Bernard for the incredible vision.

It has been a pleasure to work with the benefactors of Faces of Freedom, Fisher House and Wounded Warrior Project. Among the many others who were an important part of this book are Jim Weiskopf, Ramona Joyce, Terri Randall, Gayle Trent, Heather Hudgens Armstrong, Henry M. Holden, Sonya Senkowsky and William Guenon.

A special thanks to Wentworth Printing (Jimmy and Kyle Doar, Adam Geerts, Will Connolly, Reney Gissendanner, John Kemmerlin, Ray Camacho and Eddie Shannon), Jeff Byrd, Kevin Triplett, Gene McNeill, Angelo Falcone, Melanie Votaw, Ruth McGlothlin, the Fox Tri-Cities news team, Loree Hirschman and Ryan Boyd with www.military.com, Tim Smith, Sherri Jessee, Ann Stoffle and Adrianna Belan.

The steadfast support and unwavering belief of my husband, Derek Pepin, means everything to me. Thank you, Derek.

Recognizing our Afghanistan and Iraq veterans — as well as those serving, and who have served, in the Horn of Africa and throughout the rest of the world — is of the utmost importance.

Table *of* Contents

Lance Cpl. Bradley Michael Faircloth
February 19, 1984 — November 26, 2004

Lance Cpl. Bradley Faircloth was wounded twice in the two weeks before his death in Iraq. Both times, he was hit by grenade shrapnel. He received two Purple Hearts.

To Brad, being wounded was no big deal. "He was talking about it like it was a big inconvenience more than anything," said former Marine Sgt. Nate Fox, who served with Brad in Iraq. "He was a true warrior. He was the way a Marine is supposed to be. Dedicated, tough and fearless ... ready to be the first man on the stack."

Being the "first man on the stack" meant being the front man when it came to clearing houses. "When you're the first through the door, you've got a chance to die, and he wasn't afraid to volunteer. He'd blow through any door like a linebacker," said Nate, who considered Brad a "real tough kid."

Former Cpl. Evan Matthews will never forget Brad's gallantry. "He was intense, and a hard worker and he cared about his friends," he said. "I had a rotation set up for who would be the first to go in the houses, but Brad always wanted to be the one to go first."

Off the battlefield, Brad's buddies say he had a good sense of humor, and he always talked about home and friends. "He was pretty much real about everything — genuine," said Nate.

"What he was doing was what he wanted to be doing," Evan continued. "He wanted to be a Marine, he wanted to be in the infantry and he wanted to serve his country."

— *RP*

The Final Letter

"If you are getting this, you already know that I'm not alive. Don't worry, I said my prayers. If there's some way I could be remembered by everyone, I'd like that."

Lance Cpl. Bradley Faircloth wrote those words in a letter to his mom. He was serving in Iraq with the 3rd Platoon, Alpha Company, 1st Battalion, 8th Marines. If he was killed in action, a fellow Marine had instructions to send the letter to Kathleen Faircloth.

She received the letter a month after Bradley's death.

At only 20 years old, Bradley died in Fallujah, Iraq. He was known as "Freddie the Barbarian" because of his courage in leading the front-line searches. On Thanksgiving Day, 2004, during one of these door-to-door searches for insurgents, machine gun fire greeted him inside one of the buildings and took his life.

Kathleen Faircloth fears she might have taught Bradley those early lessons of strength and determination. As a single parent, the mother and son pressed through hard times and uncertainty.

"I taught him, don't be afraid of anything," said Kathleen. "Now, I may regret that." Kathleen encouraged his desire to reach out and help others. The two were active in their church and went on foreign mission trips. Kathleen said, "He was a rebel with a cause." However, his decision to join the military surprised his family and friends. Before then, football was always his focus.

"I miss home a lot sometimes. I think about it rarely, but when I do, it makes me sad. I wish about playing football and all of my friends that came from it," he wrote.

Bradley made quite an impression and name for himself on the field. The 6'2", 220-pound defensive lineman for the Murphy High School Panthers wore the number 44 jersey. After years on the sidelines, Bradley worked to gain the muscle, strength and brawn he needed to be a starter. He got coach Robert Curtis' attention early on.

"Someone with his character and determination will make it," Curtis remembers telling the other coaches. "He's gonna play."

"Brad was always the first one on the practice field and would spend extra time running sprints. He wanted to get faster," said Curtis. By his senior year, Brad was a starting linebacker for the Panthers. His team went to the Alabama state playoffs that year.

Curtis often tells his young students about Brad. He remembers the night of the playoff game; Brad broke his finger during warm-ups. He wanted to play so badly that he set his own finger with tape and went into the game without complaining.

"I've been coaching for 31 years and only a few students do what he did," says Curtis. "You had good kids, but few were above and beyond like Brad." The young man's attitude won him the Murphy High School Coach's Award his senior year. The award was created especially for Brad and has since been named in his honor.

Following high school, Bradley played football for Delta State University in Cleveland, MS. After only one year of college, he heard the call of the armed forces. Coach Curtis worried that the same determined, fearless attitude on the football field would get him hurt or killed in war.
"He wasn't going to sit in a hole. He was going to be the leader," Curtis says. "Everything he did, he had to be first. That's what worried me."

"This is my calling. I love my country," Brad told his coach on his last visit. "Besides football, my country is most important to me. If I see you, I see you. But God bless America."

Curtis remembers, "The last time I saw him, I had tears in my eyes when he left. He was like a son to me. He'll be missed."

Bradley's mom, Kathleen, believes the events of September 11, 2001, strongly influenced her son to join the Marines. Bradley was a senior in high school when the terror attacks happened. She remembers Bradley came home that day and said, "I'll fight for my country."

Bradley deployed to Iraq in June of 2004. In the five short months he was there, he was wounded twice with injuries to his face and leg. He was awarded Purple Hearts both times. He died on November 26, 2004, and was awarded a third Purple Heart for his sacrifice.

Bradley wrote, "I thought I would do something great one day. Maybe I'll get a special medal or something. My worst fear is being forgotten by people who knew me."

In his letter, Bradley requested a tribute for his Murphy High School football team. A bronze statue of the school's mascot, a Panther, now sits in front of the school. It was funded by donations made in Bradley's memory.

"I wanted to be talked about when I was alive and missed and remembered when I was gone," he said in his letter. "I love you and the family and my friends very much, remember that. I hope I made you proud cause I tried."

Kathleen vividly remembers the day she heard the news of her son's death. She was away from home when her cell phone rang. She drove back thinking, "I'm going home to hear my son is dead."

During Bradley's memorial service, friends and family paid tribute to his heroic life. He asked in his letter that the funeral be "more of a celebration of my life with lots of pictures and lots of people." And as a final request, "Put my #44 jersey on the coffin."

"I lost a son, but gained a brotherhood," Kathleen says now. "I now have children all over this country." Amazingly, Marines who currently serve in Brad's battalion traveled to Mobile, AL, after Hurricane Katrina to help Kathleen. The Marines blitzed the home, making needed repairs because they believed in "taking care of their own."

Since Bradley's death, Kathleen has received letters, cards and condolences from across the country. But in the end, it is her son's letter that is most haunting and heartfelt:

"We got this cadence that we sing that goes like this: 'If I die in a combat zone, box me up and ship me home. Pin my medals upon my chest. Tell my momma I did my best.'"

Bradley is buried at Mobile Memorial Gardens, Mobile, AL.

— Hannah Horne
News anchor for WIS-TV in Columbia, SC

U.S.ARMY

CW4 Chester William Troxel
October 8, 1961 — January 7, 2006

"Chet" Troxel could fix anything — from a watch to a helicopter. And he was generous about sharing his talents, always helping friends who needed a dishwasher repaired or anything else fixed. Before he left for Iraq, he even replaced the alternator on a neighbor's car.

In his civilian job, he was a helicopter mechanic who eventually became director of rotary-wing maintenance for Era Helicopters. One of his National Guard crew members, SFC Brad Quigley, called Chet an "outstanding pilot" who knew the aircraft extremely well. He was also someone who never took his crew for granted. "Often, long after the other pilots had gone off to the bar or to bed, he would show up with a stack of pizzas for us crew chiefs who were working late to ready the birds for the next day's mission," said Brad.

Chet also did his best to be there for his family, even when he was far from home. "He would tell the kids 'Call daddy's cell phone anytime,'" said his wife, Sheree. She said he may not have been much of a romantic, but there was never any doubt about how much he cared. While away for several months in Croatia for his civilian work, he bought a fax machine for Sheree. "In the mornings I'd wake up to notes that said 'I love you,'" she said.

One of the things she'll miss the most is reuniting after he'd been away. Sheree explained the sense of comfort she always felt: "It was like a sigh of relief. He'd give me a big hug and say, 'It's OK, I'm home now.'"

— *RP*

Legacy of an Arctic Cowboy

"Icy three-three coming around on your left!" Those were the last words anyone heard over the radio from CW4 Chester "Chet" Troxel before his powerful Black Hawk went down – for reasons unknown – in a remote part of the desert in northern Iraq near Tal Afar. It was January 7, 2006. Earlier, the evening sky was somewhat cloudy when the helicopter, with call sign, *Icy 33*, lifted off from the Q-West Base Complex for a classified mission.

Chet was a veteran pilot flying the second aircraft in a two-ship formation. They were helping to carry out a night assault mission by providing airlift for the 101st Airborne "Screaming Eagles" Division. Four civilians and seven other soldiers were on board when the tragedy struck. Those individuals included three of Chet's fellow Alaska National Guardsmen. They were a close, cohesive unit. Their deaths were the first Alaska National Guard combat losses since World War II.

During a memorial ceremony in Iraq, the company commander declared Chet's call sign "Icy 33" officially retired in honor of his ultimate sacrifice.

"Chet was one of those individuals who was rock-solid, nothing would get him riled,"

said his buddy and fellow guardsman Maj. Darrin Dorn, who also attended the same church as the Troxel family. "He could always be counted on to do the right thing. He never forgot where he came from as an enlisted soldier and went out of his way to make sure the young soldiers were taken care of."

Darrin describes Chet as a "true aviation professional" who loved to fly. "He used every excuse he could to get in the cockpit. In the summer of 2004, Alaska had the worst fire season in its history. Chet was one of the first to volunteer for the firefighting effort and stayed until the last day, several months later. He would fly all day and work at his computer most of the evening to make sure he stayed on top of his civilian job," he said.

Chet earned the nickname "Corporate" because he was always glued to a cell phone or a laptop, keeping up with his many responsibilities. He was determined to give 100 percent in whatever he did. In fact, Chet was so devoted to his unit and his flying duties with the guard that, after knee surgery, he worked overtime to recuperate quickly so he could make the deployment to Iraq.

Chester Troxel's intense aviation career spanned a combined 26 years in the Army

and Army National Guard. During his service to the country, this patriotic arctic cowboy was also a loving husband and a father.

Sheree Troxel met Chet when she was 17 years old. He was 20. The pair married six months later. "I thought he was the smartest, wisest man on earth. He had it going on, and he knew what he wanted to do with his life."

At the time, Chet was a Chinook mechanic at Fort Wainwright. His ultimate goal was to become a military pilot. Going to flight school would have taken him away from Sheree for one year. That's when he made her a deal she couldn't turn down. "He knew I wanted to have kids but he wanted to wait. So he told me, 'If you let me go to flight school, we can have a baby!' Needless to say, flight school changed my life forever," she said.

Although flying was his passion, what Chet loved most in life was spending time with Sheree and their two children, Hollis and Summer, who are now 17 and 15. "He was gone six to eight months of the year with his job, but when he was home he was home with us," said Sheree.

She and Summer have a disability that Chet made sure never interfered with quality family moments. "It's called HSP, Hereditary Spastic Paraplegia," explained Sheree. "This affects our muscles from the waist down. We are just like ya'll, except we walk like ducks. But, we do it with a smile!"

The disability meant Sheree was left behind during Chet's winter runs in their South Anchorage neighborhood. But he decided to change that. "He went online with a baby jogger company and found a special-needs jogger and he ordered one so I could go with him," said Sheree. "That was just great. I thought, 'Wow' ... He was something else,"

When the kids were younger, Chet and Hollis would often bond by spending afternoons hiking a rugged mountain called Flat Top. Summer, who was 8 at the time, insisted she should be able to go, too. Despite the HSP, Chet found a way to make that happen for his little girl. He fashioned a gurney-type device, laden with pillows, and strapped it to his back so he could carry a gleeful Summer as he trudged up the mountain. When they neared the peak, Chet let her down and watched proudly as she climbed to the top on her own.

Summer is now a spunky teenager who has many memories of days like that spent in the Alaskan outdoors. "I am not a frilly, lacy-type girl and that was fine with my Dad. He enjoyed showing me how to fish or to shoot a gun or change a tire," she said. Summer spent a recent school break recovering from yet another extensive surgery to both of her legs. But she doesn't let her physical condition slow her down. Her father taught her to dream big. "He always encouraged me to believe I can do whatever I want when I grow up. He also taught me to count my blessings, such as my family and those who love me and for God's hand on my life."

Hollis, a runner like his father, says his dad taught him to always be accountable. "My Dad and I were really close. He was always responsible for his actions. This is a part of him that I want to carry on in my life. Dad taught me that if I made a mistake, do whatever it takes to fix it and to not lay the blame on someone else," said Hollis, who had plans to go to France with his father to visit Normandy. It was important to Chet that his children understand the sacrifice of the nation's veterans.

"Every Memorial Day we went out to the veterans' cemetery here [in Anchorage] and looked at the names. It was sacred to him," said Sheree. "When there were protestors in town, Hollis would get angry but Chet would explain that it's OK. He told him 'they have a right and the freedom to do that because of what we've done.' He was very proud to be an American."

Sheree says her faith in God is helping her find peace. She shared this personal note she wrote to the soul mate who was taken from her all too soon. Bronze Star recipient Chester Troxel was 45 years old:
"My Darling Chet,

One of the hardest things about this whole thing was leaving you so far away in Arlington. But I am comforted by the fact that you are not really there. You are with your Lord. And you are in my heart and in the face, eyes and actions of your amazing children. I love you so very much and miss you so. I have peace, because I know you are at peace. I will see you in my thoughts and dreams. You are my hero, not just because you gave your life for your country, but because you also gave yourself to our children and me for 23 years. You have been my Hero for 23 years and you will be my Hero forever."

— Lt. Judy Crausbay Hamilton
Army Nurse Corps and Vietnam veteran

"If there must be trouble,
let it be in my day,
that my child may have peace"

— Thomas Paine

Cpl. Michael James Halal
May 19, 1982 — September 13, 2004

Marine Cpl. Michael Halal of Glendale, AZ will always be remembered as "Mikey" to his mother Jacque Mikkelson. A loving child who adored camping and the outdoors, Michael was a free spirit. He turned into an outgoing, and often rebellious, teenager who didn't have the patience for discipline or education. At one point, he even dropped out of high school. It's ironic that he would be remembered as a great teacher by his fellow Marines.

Dennis Medina of Florida writes, "I knew Michael for the last three years because I, too, was a member of 1/8. One of the things I remember about him the most was his leadership ability. He was a young Marine well beyond his years. I remember one training exercise that we were at, and he was the instructor for the 240G shooters. He taught that class as if he had been in the Corps all his life and like that weapon was just another piece of his gear."

After a rocky start in the Corps, Michael became a highly skilled machine gunner and dedicated Marine. He was known for his ability to motivate those around him and to "break down" complicated lessons, making things easier for his Marines to do their jobs efficiently. Michael was serving his second tour of duty in Iraq when he was killed. He and another Marine lost their lives in a vehicle accident in Al Anbar Province. Michael, 22, was a trusted advisor and a loyal friend.

Now a quilt made from pieces of Michael's clothes, like his old Boy Scout uniform and graduation gown, keeps his life close to his mother. Every patch represents a special memory. So many people now possess "patches" from Mikey's moments with them.

— RP

The Consummate Teacher

Like his grandfathers, great-great grandfather and great-uncle before him, Marine Lance Cpl. Michael Halal felt he could make a difference in this chaotic world. In fact, he *was* making a difference the night of September 13, 2004, when a Humvee accident in Al Anbar Province, Iraq, took his life.

Michael Halal, born May 19, 1982, in Phoenix, AZ, was always a rough and tumble, in-your-face kind of boy. Growing up, he loved Dungeons and Dragons, computer games, laser games and music groups like Linkin Park. He especially loved to go shooting with his mom out in the Arizona desert.

"He was always a fun-loving personality," mother Jacqueline (Jacque) Mikkelson remembers.

"He loved having fun; he was a giving person who didn't have to 'go out' somewhere to enjoy himself."

Michael loved his family deeply. Besides his mother, he was very close to his sisters, Jessica and Chrissy; his brother, Robert; and stepmother, Bonnie Halal. He also stayed on good terms with Grandma Beverly in Sun City because, as he'd always say, "I can smell those sugar cookies from miles away!" On his last leave home — Christmas 2003 — Michael ate an entire pan of those sugar cookies as soon as they came out of the oven.

Michael's life was not always easy. His parents divorced, his enthusiasm for life often got him in trouble and he ended up dropping out of school.

After much soul searching, Michael decided to join the Marines as both his grandfathers had done. He hoped he could add to the proud family tradition. By gaining discipline and professional training, he knew he could forge a promising future.

Though accepted into the Marines with a GED (general equivalency diploma), before Michael could continue his training the Marines required him to earn his high school diploma. After fulfilling that requirement, he completed boot camp and the School of Infantry, becoming an infantryman with 1st Battalion, 8th Marines at Camp Lejeune, NC.

For someone who disliked school, Michael became quite a student in the Marines. His mother's scrapbook is full of certificates stating his accomplishments. Ironically, according to friend and fellow 1/8 Marine Benjamin Czap, who is now a sergeant, Michael became the consummate teacher in his unit.

"Michael was very confident. His perception of combat situations, and people in general, was amazing," he said. Ben shakes his head and smiles ruefully, remembering Michael's talents. He speaks of Michael as someone who consistently demanded the best of himself, but who also was able to inspire others to reach for the best in themselves as well. Ben says one mission in particular sums up the kind of person Michael was.

"During one mission, Mike and I were the 'kill team' for a 1,000-meter IED [improvised explosive device] sweep ... outside of Fallujah, Iraq," he remembers. "Our mission was to take out any snipers and/or IED triggermen who were planning to ambush the company." Ben says the temperature was 147 degrees Fahrenheit already — at 10:00 in the morning.

"The mission's warning order allotted for a six-hour mission completion time," he continues. The mission was crucial.

"I was 500 meters out and 500 meters ahead, maintaining a constant 45 degree advanced lead of the company. Mike was my designated marksman, situated 200 meters out and back from my location. Mike was to stay out of sight while maintaining mobility. He was capable of 700-meter shots and was to cover the company and me in all directions.

"We were two of the most capable Marines for these harsh conditions due to our bond of competitiveness," Ben remembers proudly. "We would not let each other falter ... Once we reached our designated stop point on the mission, we had to link back up with our company. Because I was closer to the company, I arrived first — 30 seconds before Mike. Upon his arrival he looked at me, grinning, and said, 'What's the matter? You couldn't stay out as long as me?'"

Ben laughs at the memory, but becomes serious quickly when he talks about the night that Michael was killed.

On September 13, 2004, Michael's mission was to deliver heavy equipment that would help construct a mortar shelter for Bravo Company. On the return, around 2100 hours — riding in the dark with no lights — the Humvee that Michael was riding in rolled over. He and one other Marine were killed. Less than two weeks later, Bravo Company was mortared heavily, but the shelter that had been built with that equipment saved many lives.

Although he had been notified earlier, Lance Cpl. Michael Halal was promoted to corporal officially the day he was killed.

Michael left quite a mixed legacy in his 22 years. He will be remembered for his cocky self-confidence, his genuine love of family and children, his sharp shooting skills — in the deserts of both Arizona and Iraq — and his strategic mind, whether playing Dungeons and Dragons or guarding fellow Marines on foot patrol.

Cpl. Michael Halal joined the Marines to make a difference, and that he did. Perhaps Sgt. Ben Czap summed up Michael's influence best: "He changed how I will act the rest of my life. He opened my mind to be analytical, to look at all the options quickly, and then choose accordingly. I will think of him every day of my life as I push myself to become my very best."

— Valerie A. Nichols
Author, English teacher, creative writing instructor
valerieanichols.com

Greater love has no man than this, that he lay down his life for his friends.

— John 15:13

Airman 1st Class Jesse Monroe Samek
January 3, 1983 – October 21, 2004

Jesse Samek was known for putting others first. In fact, it is because of his actions that others are alive today.

Senior Airman Calvin Paquette picked up on Jesse's giving nature when they met during training in 2004. Jesse was becoming a flight engineer; Calvin an aerial gunner. Jesse's courses were incredibly rigorous academically. Although he had to work hard to stay in the program, Jesse still managed to take time out of his intense study schedule to help a classmate who was struggling with part of the curriculum.

He did things like that "without a moment's hesitation," said Calvin. "Jesse was a level-headed, easy-going, good guy; and he was a lot of fun to be around. You didn't have to put on any pretenses around Jesse. You just had to be who you were."

Jesse's buddies nicknamed him "Spewy" during training because of a problem he had with air sickness. But instead of letting it slow him down, Jesse worked that much harder to prove himself.

In Afghanistan, as Jesse was preparing to leave for what turned out to be his final mission, the trip got postponed. Jesse took the rare opportunity to grab some dinner and a haircut. Well, almost. The crew got called back before the barber was through. Calvin recalls, "He came up to me and asked 'Dude, are we going?' and when I told him we were, he laughed and told me he just got half a haircut. He thought it was pretty funny." Calvin will always remember Jesse as a courageous person who never hesitated when called to duty.

Jesse was posthumously awarded the Air Medal with Valor for his selfless acts during that fateful flight.

— RP

Touching the Face of God

"Mom, I decided to take out as much life insurance as I can before leaving for Afghanistan this fall."

"Why spend the money, Jess? You're single and have no debt."

"It's not very expensive, and nothing is going to happen to me. But if it does, you and dad will be able to get the house fixed."

Little did the Sameks know that just a few months later, Jesse's planning for them would come to pass. Life and death happen, and none of us gets to choose when. For Airman First Class Jesse Monroe Samek, it was two weeks into his first overseas deployment, on the night of October 20, 2004.

Jesse Samek was born on January 3, 1983, to Gavin and Julie Samek. Three years later, his brother, Ben, arrived. They were a close family that truly enjoyed being together. The love that strengthened Jesse throughout his growing years became integral to his success as an adult.

Jesse was a young man who spent his free time discovering the awesome wonders of the outdoors rather than the glitter and glitz of city lights. To Jesse, a dream vacation was spent camping, hiking, fishing and boating. Of course, going deer hunting with his dad and brother were some of the best times of his life, too.

"He had a quiet soul and enjoyed experiencing the beauty of nature that God imparted to us," his mother said.

He was an avid sports fan and loved all the St. Louis teams — even in the years they were lousy. He was particularly fond of hockey, and played both roller and ice hockey throughout his childhood. When he was 11, he and his brother invented a game that became a favorite pastime for an entire neighborhood of boys who would show up for "tournaments" in the family's basement. They played one-on-one on their knees using a small foam ball or a wadded-up piece of paper. There were no sticks, just their hands to shoot the "puck."

Music was also important to Jesse. As an adolescent, he learned to play the guitar but never seemed to find the time to play as often as he would have liked. He enjoyed many kinds of music and used to say that he loved having parents "who knew how to rock".

According to family and friends, his heart was full of all that is good: integrity, honesty, love, compassion, humbleness and an indomitable spirit.

He lived a life of significance. He believed in treating people with care and respect and greeting them with a smile. To those who knew him, he could never be forgotten. They say a man's worth is measured by how much he was loved in his lifetime. Apparently, Jesse was among the richest of men.

Blake Johnston, one of his best friends, said, "Some of the best times of my life were spent with Jesse. One of the things that I never told Jesse was how much I admired him. People were always happy around Jesse. He was the type of guy that people were drawn to. I admired him for being an all-around guy. He was the friend you find once in a lifetime."

Joining the Air Force was the biggest decision in Jesse's short life. After one year of college, he decided to enlist before completing his degree. He chose to be a flight engineer, which at the time was being offered to a limited number of newly enlisted personnel. Since only about one percent of the people in the Air Force actually have an "in the air" job, Jesse was excited. He thought of the job as a stepping stone to becoming a pilot.

Jesse was surprised, however, to discover how difficult the training was for his job. On average, only nine out of 100 candidates who begin the program end up graduating. He had never been an exceptional student, so the grueling curriculum proved to be quite the challenge. Jesse had to study for several hours a day and was in training for nearly two years. In the beginning, he would often call home with doubts about his abilities, but with the unfailing support of his family, he quickly acquired an intense determination to succeed. And Jesse not only succeeded, he excelled.

Because of the difficulty of the program, the Air Force allowed each student to fail three individual courses and still pass. Jesse was one of the few newly enlisted students to pass without a single failure, and he finished the course in half the average time. One of the instructors who had been flying for more than 20 years commented to Jesse's parents, "He was the best flight engineer I have ever flown with, bar none."

Jesse absolutely loved to fly. Several of his crew members commented that he was usually smiling when he was in the air, even when he was on a difficult and extremely stressful training flight. He graduated from the program with confidence and pride. He was subsequently assigned to one of the elite Air Force Special Operations Rescue Squadrons — the 66th. The motto of the Rescue Squadrons is "That others may live." Isn't that the definition of a hero?

During his last rescue mission, Jesse diligently did his job. At risk to his own personal safety, he prepared for a rescue hoist by himself. Rather than allowing the others to help, he directed two pararescuemen to secure themselves in the cabin of an HH-60 Pave Hawk helicopter until the craft was in a stable hover. This one heroic decision saved the lives of the pararescuemen when the helicopter became engulfed in dust, impacted with the terrain, and rolled down the side of a mountain east of Shindand, Afghanistan. Jesse, in the least secure position, was the only crew member to lose his life.

"Regardless of the tragedy that took Jesse's life, Jesse wanted to be in the Air Force. He wanted to rescue people, and he loved being in the air," Julie said Both Julie and Gavin find it comforting to picture Jesse while reading the poem "High Flight," written by pilot John Gillespie Magee, Jr. in 1941:

Oh! I have slipped the surly bonds of Earth
And danced the skies on laughter-silvered wings;
Sunward I've climbed, and joined the tumbling mirth
Of sun-split clouds, — and done a hundred things
You have not dreamed of — wheeled and soared and swung
High in the sunlit silence. Hov'ring there,
I've chased the shouting wind along, and flung
My eager craft through footless halls of air ...

Up, up the long, delirious burning blue
I've topped the wind-swept heights with easy grace
Where never lark, or ever eagle flew —
And, while with silent, lifting mind I've trod
The high untrespassed sanctity of space
Put out my hand, and touched the face of God.

Memories from the summer of 2004 are also comforting to the Sameks. The family took its last vacation together while Jesse was home on leave before heading to Nellis Air Force Base in Las Vegas, NV, for his permanent assignment. The family had not taken a traditional river float trip in years, so for old times' sake, they ventured out together, creating life-long memories jam-packed with shared laughter and love. To spend such a special time together shortly before Jesse died was truly a gift from God.

— Jo Anne Allen
Author
mysonisamarine.com

Pfc. Karina Sotelo Lau
January 2, 1983 — November 2, 2003

Karina Lau may have been a soldier in the United States Army, but her passion was the stage. "She wanted to act and sing," said Karina's older sister, Martha Rivera. She describes Karina as a quiet teenager who spent a lot of time alone in her room, but someone who blossomed when there was an audience. "The last play she did, 'The Wiz' ... she was a bad witch. Oh my God, when we went to see the play and she was on stage I couldn't believe it was the same person," said Martha. "She just shined. And that voice she had ... it was amazing."

Karina's voice was an incredible gift that, given her small stature, took many by surprise. After leaving behind college and a music scholarship to join the military, Karina's songs were a welcome reprieve for her comrades in Iraq. "Her friends in Iraq told me she'd sing in the church — 'Amazing Grace.' I got e-mails from strangers telling me they missed that voice that they heard," said Martha.

Through tears, Martha explained Karina's reason for enlisting. "She wanted to see the people [of Iraq] have the same freedom that we have in this wonderful country."

Karina's older brother, Luis Lau, is a chief in the United States Navy and says he is "very proud" of her. Her great aunt, her *tia*, Delfina Gastelum, remembers Karina fondly as a "very special girl who loved her family and her country."

"She felt like she was making a difference," added Martha. "I just want people to know what kind of person she was and that she *did* make a difference."

— RP

Karina's Song

Ruth Lau opens the first photo album and her daughter Karina's face is everywhere. Karina had a smile that could light up a room, or a stage, and it often did.

Amid the smell of tortillas grilling and a background of comedy and commercials from a Spanish language television station, Ruth talks of her daughter in the past tense.

"She was so happy," her mother says. "She always wanted to do everything perfect." Ruth turns the pages to a photo taken from her front door. Across an open field is the elementary school that Karina attended. "If she was late, she would run all the way to school crying," Ruth adds.

Born in Livingston, CA, "Kari" had the graciousness of a small-town girl and the heart for something more. As she looks at the photos, Ruth comes to an image from high school where Karina is very beautiful. But in it, her eyes have lost their sparkle. Karina looked forward to college, yet she often spoke of serving her country and sometimes felt sad she couldn't do both.

"She was always doing things for other people, for her friends,"

Ruth says. She tells of the time Karina made gingerbread cookies for a friend and how Ruth still has one in her freezer as a reminder. Karina was an excellent student and a gifted musician who loved the saxophone. She played 10 instruments, including the guitar, flute, trumpet, "a little piano" and xylophone. She also loved to sing."She sang every day," says her mother. "She was in musical plays at school, in the jazz band and she played the guitar." Karina, who loved Judy Garland, was thrilled to sing the national anthem at her graduation from Livingston High School in 2001.

She performed in school musicals, including "Grease" and "The Wiz," and often sang around the house by herself or with her father. She dreamed of becoming a star and joked about opening a musical theater with her family. "She would say, 'Daddy and Luis can cook, and I will sing'," said Ruth.

Her parents, Ruth and Agustin Lau, met in Mexico. She was a native; he was the son of a Chinese father and Mexican mother. Their eyes met, and it was love at first sight. They married after two years and later immigrated to the United States with her children, Jose and Martha Sotelo.

The Laus moved to Livingston where they had a son, Luis. And on January 2, 1983, their last baby, Karina, was born.

Karina's grades and musical talents provided her with a full scholarship to the University of the Pacific in Stockton, CA. She would have been the first person in either of her parents' families to graduate from a four-year college. But after only two months, she called her parents to say she wanted to come home. "She said it wasn't enough," Ruth remembers. "We tried to tell her it would get better, but she said she wanted to do something that made a difference."

So Kari left college. A few weeks later, she enlisted in the Army.

Karina was sent to Fort Jackson, SC, for basic training; to Fort Gordon, GA; and finally, to Fort Hood, TX, where she completed communications and switchboard training with her usual good marks. Shortly before Karina was deployed to Iraq with the 16th Signal Brigade, her parents drove from California to Texas to see her.

Her father cooked her favorite dish, chicken with pineapple, and they had a brief but happy time together. The videotape from that visit is one of her parents' most prized recollections of their daughter. Karina came home for three weeks before shipping out. Somehow, no one thought to take photos of her before she left.

"We didn't take any pictures of her when she was home," her mother remembers with a catch in her voice. "I don't know why. We never expected anything would happen to her."

Karina apparently kept making music once she was deployed as part of Operation Iraqi Freedom. "The other soldiers, they wrote about her and said she was always singing and dancing, that she made them laugh," says Ruth. That was no small contribution to life in a war zone. The notes also said they would miss her giving spirit and enthusiasm.

In a last e-mail to her half-sister, Martha Sotelo Riviera, Karina said that she loved what she was doing, that she would be careful and that she would write again soon. She signed it "Love, your baby sis."

The message was sent just hours before Karina and other soldiers were scheduled for rest and relaxation time away from the fighting. She would have been back in four days, ready to handle the important communication for her troops and to have them laugh at her antics and be entertained by her singing and dancing.

On November 2, 2003, the helicopter arrived, but there were not enough seats for everyone in line. Karina would have been the first passenger for the next flight. Perhaps that dazzling smile prompted the soldier ahead of her to give up his seat. So, Karina boarded the CH-47 Chinook Helicopter in his place to head out for four days of R&R. They could not know that just minutes after takeoff, the chopper would be attacked by missile fire and shot down near Al Fallujah, Iraq. In the crash, 20 soldiers were injured and 16 were killed.

Pfc. Karina Sotelo Lau was among the casualties. She was 20 years old, and the first woman from California to die in action in Operation Iraqi Freedom. Her mother stops turning pages in the photo album to reflect. "My husband used to sing every day," she says. "But now he does not sing anymore, not since Kari died."

More than 500 people crowded into St. Jude Thaddeus Church in Livingston for Karina's funeral. "The line of cars was so long," says Ruth. "They had to close the freeway, there were so many cars. People had to stand outside because they could not all fit in the church."

In her memory, the town of Livingston has declared November 2 "Karina Lau Day" to honor a remarkable young woman who died doing what she loved — trying to make the world a better place.

Karina was buried with full military honors at a cemetery in Turlock, CA, not far from her parents' home. Her mother visits her grave nearly every day. Her father prefers to remember her in photos and his memories.

Over a soccer match on the television, commentated in excited Spanish, Ruth Lau quietly opens her last album. Photos of Karina's room show the purple walls she painted herself, the triangle-folded flag, her Purple Heart and Bronze Star upon a quilt made by a woman who has created one for each of the fallen.

The final picture is of Karina's headstone with the notes of a song she loved to sing and an inset brass saxophone. Her official Army photo is mounted permanently beside her name and dates. In it, Karina is smiling broadly, and her eyes are forever alive.

— Cindy Woods
Independent writer, poet, webmaster

bca
B+ NKA

Petty Officer 2nd Class Danny Phillip Dietz Jr.
January 26, 1980 — June 28, 2005

Navy SEAL Danny Dietz of Littleton, CO was the kind of person you'd remember forever, even if you'd only met him once. His roommate from the Basic Underwater Demolition/SEAL (BUD/S) course says Danny "wasn't average." During the challenging training, Danny was one of the top performers in every physical task. "No matter what the instructors did to him he would persevere and succeed," said his roommate Mike, whose last name is withheld for security reasons. Danny, a high school graduate, was very focused on improving himself both physically and mentally. During BUD/S, he would often study things like geometry after a day of grueling field work. He also could be found sketching. Danny was an amazing artist.

He knew how to make others laugh, too. "He was kind of an entertainer and a class clown but he could get away with it because he had the abilities to back it up," laughed Mike. He remembers Danny sneaking his pet chinchilla into their barracks and not getting caught. One of his favorite memories from BUD/S is of Danny and another classmate breakdancing — in camouflage pants, combat boots and a t-shirt — on flattened cardboard boxes out in the sand. The instructors had gotten wind of their skills and, while blasting music from a truck-based, public-address system, demanded the two SEALs perform. "They were laughing the whole time," said Mike of his buddies.

When it was time to leave BUD/S, Danny chose the toughest assignment. "Most people get volunteered for it, *they* don't volunteer," explained Mike, who was not surprised by Danny's decision. "He was strong, and he was a fighter."

GM2 Danny Phillip Dietz, 25, was posthumously awarded the Silver Star and the Navy Cross for valor in Afghanistan. The Navy Cross is the nation's second-highest military honor for valor.

— *RP*

A Hero's Footsteps

"I wouldn't be a bit surprised if with his ... *ability* ... he's still around. His body may not be here, but his spirit certainly is."

Danny Dietz's father has no trouble expressing pride in his son. He uses words like amazing, intelligent, dedicated, athletic, determined and brave. These are words Danny's mother also uses, adding to the list, "a piece of my heart," awesome, driven, giving, and kind. "His heart was very, very large." But the one word Danny's parents both come back to again and again to describe their son is ... *hero*. Danny was a hero. And Danny died a hero's death.

"I can honestly say Danny is my hero,"

says his father. "What he did ... I wouldn't have had the nerve. Unbelievable. This kid had no fear, no fear."

Danny Dietz — "DJ" to his parents — lost his life in the Kunar Province of Afghanistan in June of 2005. He was nearly three months into his third deployment, and just two weeks from coming home. A highly trained Navy SEAL, Danny was part of a four-man, counter-terrorism reconnaissance team working in hot and harsh conditions and moving through extremely dangerous mountainous territory. Ambushed by a "much, much larger" Taliban force coming over the hill in droves, the four men didn't stand much of a chance.

Mortally wounded from the hail of gunfire, Danny just kept fighting. He never made it back from the mission, but he never gave up. Because of Danny's bravery, and the bravery of his buddies, one member of their team ultimately survived the attack. Danny Dietz fought for his fellow SEALs, for his country, for his family and for himself with every remaining second of his life. He was wounded 16 times and shot nine times before he died.

"I know my son and I know he was fighting for everything," says his proud father. "You've got to have the courage, the will. When you sacrifice everything ... *that's* hardcore reality."

Who was this brave hero? According to his parents, Danny was an achiever, someone who pushed himself to be his best. Danny was a fighter. He walked at nine months. He was rambunctious. He was determined to learn.

While learning to ride a bike, "he'd take some major spills and say, 'Come on daddy! Come on!' and I'd say, 'OK, are you sure?' And he'd say 'yes!' so I'd push him and he'd take off and fall and get up and do it again! He was a tough little kid. I'll never forget that."

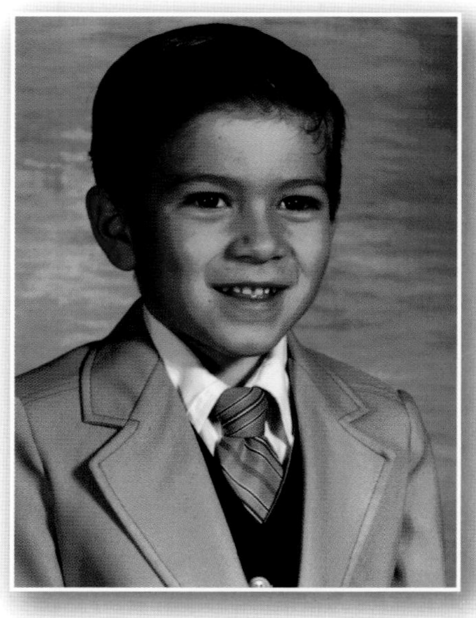

His mother remembers that Danny always had a way with animals. "One time he brought home a basket of wild kitties. 'Look what I got! Look what I got!' I didn't know they were wild and I opened up the box and all I saw were balls of fur ... just hissing and hissing ... so I dropped the basket. And I remember him being so mad at me!" She laughs at this memory. Then says quietly, "But how he caught them, I'll never know." Danny had a gift.

And Danny was gifted. He tested two points above "genius" and was enrolled in the gifted and talented programs at Centennial Elementary School and Goddard Middle School. But while in middle school, he decided to start nurturing more of a bad-boy image instead.

"Danny was bored. He wanted excitement," his mother says fondly. At one point, Danny even had dreams of becoming a ninja. "We were instructors and taught him martial arts. He was a very good little fighter." And he was an incredible athlete, excelling in every sport he played. Once Danny found out about the Navy SEALs and all of the dedication, athletic ability, skill and intellect it required, "*that* was his ticket," says his father. "He decided he wanted *that* excitement."

With this new dream came an unwavering determination that put Danny right back on the path to success.

"Once he got his mind into something, no one was gonna get it out," says DJ's father, while his mother nods in agreement. "I don't know whether I should say it was stubbornness or determination. But if he wanted to do something, he was gonna do it ... he wasn't gonna change his mind."

Shortly before Danny went to Navy boot camp, a friend of his father's kept asking him what he wanted to do when he graduated high school. "Danny would be sitting there eating raw oatmeal to train himself," says Danny's father, "and every time he'd answer, 'I want to be a Navy SEAL.'"

Danny went straight from Navy boot camp to BUD/S (Basic Underwater Demolition/SEAL), an extremely intensive training that pushes people both mentally and physically, far beyond what they think their limits are. Only a small percentage of those who get in have what it takes to finish. Danny graduated from BUD/S on his 21st birthday.

"Once he got in, this ... *man*, he was going straight up," says his father with pride. "There was no stopping him. He was so determined. He was hard on himself because he expected a lot from himself."
Just as he said he would, Danny had become a Navy SEAL.

Danny touched so many lives. His sister, Tiffany, and he were very close and even had their own language growing up. He babied his little brother, Eric. He married his soul mate, Maria. Danny's parents find comfort in that.

"That was a fairytale affair … all the other couples watched them … wondered 'what *is* it with them, what makes them so perfect?'" says DJ's father. "They were two peas in a pod … believe me, they were meant for each other."

"I want the world to know that Danny was not just my husband, but he was my other half, my friend, my role model, and my hero," wrote Maria Dietz in a tribute to her husband. "Although I was not ready to let God take him away from me, I know my husband gave all he could to make his way back to me. He probably wouldn't have wanted to die any other way, but only trying to protect his fellow teammates and his country. I have lost my soul mate, but truly my soul mate is not lost, he is waiting to see me one day again."

Both Danny and his wife were deployed by the Navy for much of their two-year marriage. But they had plans and dreams, and they had each other. Danny's mother aches for her daughter-in-law. "She's a strong person … but she's terribly lonely for him. They were just starting out," she says.

Memories are precious and for Danny's parents, remembering their brave and loyal son is both wonderful and painful. There have been a lot of tears and there has been a lot of anger, but they are determined not to let it destroy them. On the night they learned of Danny's death, this grieving father said to his youngest son, "Whatever we do, don't let Danny's name down. Keep your head up. Be proud. Pay a good tribute to your brother."

At Danny's memorial service, there was an eagle soaring overhead. Danny's father finds comfort in that memory. "I was so proud of that. What a symbol!"

Petty Officer 2nd Class Danny P. Dietz, a highly-decorated Navy SEAL, a brother, a friend, a husband, a son.

"DJ was my first-born. He taught me so much about what a mother is … the strength he had … the beauty of him. A piece of my heart is gone forever. I thank God every day that he gave me my son. I don't understand why he's gone, and I don't like that he's gone, but at least I can be happy and proud that my son died a hero's death. He was an awesome person … a true hero. I am proud that he became one of the best of the best."

"He was amazing," says his father, quietly. "I can look back now, and I salute him. I salute him."

— Lauralyn Duff Hogan
Senior Features Producer for Classical Public Radio Network

Petty Officer 3rd Class Nathan Brandt Bruckenthal
July 17, 1979 — April 24, 2004

Coast Guard Petty Officer 3rd Class Nathan Bruckenthal was a "natural born public servant." His mother, Laurie Bullock, explains that Nathan truly wanted to do good in the world. "He was as masculine as 'The Rock' but as gentle as a lamb," she said.

Laurie remembers chaperoning a field trip while Nathan was attending junior high school in Ridgefield, CT. "I was at the front of the bus and all I could hear was 'Nathan, Nathan, Nathan!' coming from every direction," said Laurie. "One of his teachers explained to me that was because *everyone* liked him. She said he was nice and kind to everybody from the jocks to the unpopular kids. He was a very noble young man."

Nathan also loved to have fun. He enjoyed dressing stylishly, dancing at clubs and jamming with his band in his mother's basement. "They played at his high school graduation — he was the lead singer ... I should say he was the lead screamer ... they weren't very good but they had a good time," laughed Laurie.

Nathan wasn't afraid to "put himself out there." He did stand-up comedy at small clubs in New York and, at age 16, he bared his soul by reading an emotional poem he wrote to a crowd of Laurie's friends. She says that Nathan always had a depth beyond his years. "I have four books of his poems that he wrote throughout his lifetime."

Laurie says it is fitting that her son joined the Coast Guard. "He loved the sea. He once said 'If you miss me, just go to the water and that's where I'll be.' He believed that his spirit would live on."

— *RP*

His Spirit Lives On

Two-year-old Harper Bruckenthal frequents an unusual playground. She spends much of her time at Arlington National Cemetery scouring the ground for stones to give to others, while her mother, Patti, visits her father's gravestone.

The light-haired little girl was born about seven months after her dad, Coast Guard Damage Controlman Petty Officer 3rd Class Nathan Bruckenthal, was killed.

"Patti takes her there all the time," said Nathan's father, Ric Bruckenthal, the police chief in Northport, NY. "It is as close as she can get to her daddy. They go almost weekly to pray and picnic."

Harper's relatives told her that when a stone is placed on a grave it shows someone was there visiting, said Ric. Now, she likes to put stones on graves that are seemingly lacking them, and at the very end, she collects all the stones and always brings them back to her daddy.

At 24, Nathan Bruckenthal was stationed aboard the USS Firebolt, which was patrolling the northern Arabian Sea and was involved in maritime "intercept" missions. He and other servicemen and women were protecting the oil pump stations from suicide bombers who were traveling in boats. On April 24, 2004, the sailors were attempting to board a suspicious vessel which had failed to terminate its voyage at a "no-boat" zone. The boat exploded, killing Nathan and two of his comrades. Nathan was the first U.S. Coast Guard member killed in action since the Vietnam War, according to military reports. On May 7, 2004, he was buried in Arlington National Cemetery.

He had been in the Persian Gulf since February of 2004, and was supposed to be released the following month to go home to be with his wife, Patricia "Patti" Bruckenthal. The couple, who lived in Dania Beach, FL, near Miami, had just celebrated their second year of marriage the month before. "I saw him become a loving husband," said his father.

Nathan's mother, Laurie Bullock, who now lives in northern Virginia, remembers her son as a stylish young man who was humorous and uninhibited.

"Nathan had confidence and a pureness about him ... he was not afraid to share his raw emotions,"

said his mother. "He did stand-up comedy at small clubs in New York, and he would read his poems at poetry night in the coffee houses. He was not shy, that's for sure." Nathan had been serving as a member of the Tactical Law Enforcement Team (TACLET) South since 2002 at the Coast Guard Air Station of Opa-Locka, FL.

His missions included counter-drug operations, counter-terrorism and maritime-intercept operations. These were often dangerous and harrowing tasks that put him face to face with major drug dealers and hardened criminals.

"He was an outstanding team player, an invaluable team member," said Cmdr. Glenn Grahl, commanding officer of TACLET South. The officer recalled one mission where Nathan and the board team on the USS Boone seized 8,000 pounds of cocaine from a ship.

"We called him the Batman of the 21st century," said Chief Warrant Officer Mike Tumulty, a commanding officer in Neah Bay, WA, where Nathan was stationed from 2001 to 2002, prior to TACLET South. "Twenty- to 25-foot seas and howling winds, he would be out there." In Neah Bay, Nathan was the station's maintenance expert for boarding enforcement and recreation boating safety.

Even when he wasn't on the job, he felt the need to serve. He was a volunteer firefighter, emergency medical technician, reserve police officer and high school football coach. "He was a sensitive, big guy ... He was more put together than others his age," said his mother.

"He was a warrior, a humanitarian and had the core values of honor, respect and devotion to duty," said Tumulty. "His integrity was unsurpassed." He remembers that, after the Sept. 11, 2001, terrorist attacks, Nathan took some time off to go back home to be with his family and friends. He assisted with funeral services for the firefighters killed in the attacks. In October, 2001, he volunteered to pass out food to firefighters and other workers at Ground Zero. In May of 2002, he went back to help again. Seeing there was no shrine from the Coast Guard of Washington state, he took off his Neah Bay Coast Guard shirt and put it up as a shrine.

"It was important to him to go in there, to be a part of the war on terrorism," said Tumulty of Nathan's service in Iraq. "He would not have had it any other way. It was his calling."

Nathan learned the military way early in life. After his parents got divorced when he was young, he lived with his mother and her new husband, who was in the Army. "I married a military officer and that made a big impression on him," said Laurie. The family moved often, living in Hawaii, Virginia and Ridgefield, CT, where Nathan attended middle school and part of high school until 1995 when he graduated in Herndon, VA.
"He was just a special person," said his close friend Chris Gust, 25, of Norwalk, CT. "He was a hero to his family, to his friends, to everyone."

At Ridgefield High School, Nathan played football and served as a firefighter for the Ridgefield Volunteer Fire Department. While attending Herndon High School, he was in the Naval Junior Reserve Officer Training Corps.

"He was one of a kind," said Rob Graziano, who went to Ridgefield High School with Nathan and joined the Coast Guard a year after him. "He was probably the main reason why I joined."

It was December of 1998 when Ric Bruckenthal took his son to Battery Park in Manhattan to sign up for the Coast Guard. After basic training, Nathan's career began at the U.S. Coast Guard station in Montauk, NY, on the U.S. Coast Guard Cutter Point Wells where he spent two years.

In Nathan's honor, the station renamed its housing barracks "Bruckenthal Hall" in October, 2005. Nathan's older sister, NoaBeth Bruckenthal, helped unveil the bronze plaque in his memory. In addition, Nathan's awards — the Purple Heart and the Bronze Star with Valor — are displayed in the hall, along with pictures and other memorabilia.

At the dedication ceremony, NoaBeth, helped Nathan's daughter, Harper, kiss the plaque with her father's likeness. Nathan's widow, Patti, is vigilant about showing her little girl pictures of her father so she knows who he is. "It is a living legacy," said Ric Bruckenthal of the tribute.

Other tributes to Nathan include a plaque placed in April of 2005 on the oil platform that he was protecting in Iraq. In April of 2006, the U.S. Naval Patrol Craft Center of Excellence in Norfolk, VA, was dedicated to Nathan and the two other sailors who died during the same attack.

Ric Bruckenthal has his own way of remembering his son's military service and the games of football the two would play together. He has turned a room in his home into a library with pictures of Nathan and other items that remind him of his son."Everything in life reminds me of him," said his father.

Looking out at his front yard, Ric sees the United States flag pole that was erected after Nathan's death. He always wears a black and aluminum bracelet that says "DC3 Nathan Bruckenthal, USCG TACLET SOUTH, KIA [killed in action] 4/24/04." His sons, Nathan's half-brothers, Matt, 17, and Mike, 15, wear similar bracelets.

For Nathan's mother, the image of the sea is a calming reminder that his spirit lives on.

— Heather Barr
Reporter for the News-Times in Danbury, CT

MICHAEL
BOYD
STACK
SGM
US ARMY
IRAQ
APR 5 1956
APR 11 2004
SILVER STAR
BSM PH
NATHAN B
BRUCKENTHAL
DC3 USCG
JUL 17 1979
APR 24 2004
BRONZE STAR W/V
PURPLE HEART
IRAQ
TACLET SOUTH

MCGOWAN
U.S. ARM
Meet the Oldest American
ZIG-ZAG

Cpl. Stephen Michael McGowan
October 11, 1978 – March 4, 2005

Stephen McGowan made everyone feel like family.

"He was definitely a guy you'd instantly become a brother or a buddy with," said former Spc. Jason Hagan, who served with Stephen in Iraq. Jason remembered the endless ribbing between them and the late-night talks that lasted forever.

"He was really intelligent," Jason said.

Stephen would do anything for his friends, including putting his career on the line. "One night one of our buddies came back from leave, and he was pretty trashed coming through the gates. The Army MP was about to bust him when Stephen came walking up. He pretended he was the guy's captain and said he'd take care of him from there, just to bail out his friend. But Stephen could have been in *big* trouble."

Stephen, an airborne-qualified medic, was also really good with the Iraqi children. "He was a big, strong guy; but he had a softer side to him," said Jason. "One day as we were about to drive away in our Humvees after a mission in Ramadi, we saw a family crying and sobbing. They pulled us inside their compound where their young boy had apparently just had a seizure. Stephen got the child back to being coherent. Then the family brought out x-rays they'd gotten in Baghdad and it looked like the boy had a brain tumor. Stephen wanted to get him flown out of there for medical attention, but he couldn't because he wasn't a casualty of war. It really bothered him that he couldn't do more," remembered Jason.

Stephen believed in his mission, and he believed he needed to do all he could for the Iraqi children as well.

"We were their hope," said Jason. "We could see it in their eyes."

— RP

To the Fullest - To the End

When an exhausted Army recruit struggled to finish the obstacle course at Fort Jackson, SC in the fall of 2002, Stephen McGowan was the guy who trotted back to help him. Strong and fit, Stephen had already finished the race. Instinct compelled him to encourage the one who hadn't.

That's just the kind of person he was.

"Stephen had a deeply spiritual side, even in high school," said Father Greg Corrigan, counselor at St. Mark's High School in Wilmington, DE where Stephen graduated in 1996. "He would come in and talk to me in my office about the meaning of life."

A Delaware native, Cpl. McGowan died March 4, 2005, when an improvised explosive device destroyed his Humvee near Ramadi. He was 26.

A rugby player and world traveler, Stephen joined the Army in the summer of 2002. Moved by the 9/11 terrorist attacks, he wanted to do his part to protect the United States. Stephen trained to become a medic so that he could also save lives.

Describing his job to a class of second graders, Stephen wrote that soldiers were "getting all the bad guys" so that Iraqis might live in freedom and peace.

"He loved this country so much," said Stephen's mother, Bobbie McGowan, of Newark, DE. "He wanted to be a good soldier.

He wanted to be a great medic. He wanted to help those children have a better future. He believed in this country so much that probably the best gift he could have given them was democracy...he felt he was participating in something that was just huge."

At 6'1" tall and 215 pounds, Stephen was among the toughest soldiers. He spent countless hours in the gym.

In the summer of 2004, he deployed to Iraq with a scout platoon from the Army's 2nd Brigade Combat Team, Fort Carson, CO. The scouts would be in the middle of the most intense fighting. That's right where Stephen wanted to be.
In Iraq, he turned down a promotion to sergeant because it would have moved him from his platoon to the medical aid station on Camp Ramadi. The 2nd Infantry Division, 2nd Brigade Combat Team, 19 Infantry, Scout Platoon didn't want to lose Stephen either.

"It talks volumes of who he was. Because of the tough physical and mental challenges and types of mission we would be tasked to perform, not just any medic could be chosen for this position," said Stephen's comrade and former Spc. Jason Hagan. "It had to be someone who was highly motivated, physically strong, who adapts quickly to the always changing environment. He had to be basically a scout 99 percent of the time…until one of us went down…then he had to be the best at what he does – giving medical aid."

"He was an adventurous kid," said Father Greg, a pacifist, who tried to talk Stephen out of joining the Army. "He was ornery. He liked to push things to the edge."

Stephen was the guy who said he would go skydiving and then did it. He was the guy who hiked in New Zealand and climbed mountains in Korea just because he could – the guy who wasn't afraid to talk to girls. "Here's my number," he told a prospect who was already involved. "Call me when it doesn't work out."

One Halloween, he dressed as a kissing booth and made money. At Mardi Gras, he did naked pushups for beads. "He was a sinner," laughed his best friend, Adam Freilich.

A fellow rugby player and mischief-maker, Adam met Stephen on the field during a practice at the University of Delaware. Friends referred to the pair as "fire and gasoline." "We were the ones that always did the craziest stuff but never got in trouble," said Adam, now a realtor in Orange County, CA.

He had a beer with Stephen at the Deer Park Tavern in Newark the day Stephen decided to join the Army. When Stephen was deployed to Korea, then Iraq, the friends remained close.

Stephen was to be the best man in Adam's wedding in the autumn of 2005. Instead, Adam placed a photograph of Stephen on an easel. "I tell Bobbie that Stephen outgrew this world," said Adam. "He needed to do the same work somewhere else. He always wanted to be the best he could. He was never one to turn down a challenge."

Despite his tough exterior and freewheeling antics, Stephen had a gentle soul. Raised Catholic, he read about Buddhism and Hinduism and mythology, trying to find a God he could understand.

When he learned he was going to war in the summer of 2004, he gave his mother power of attorney and a living will and told her not to worry. "Have faith that the universe, whether or not it is clear to us, is unfolding as it should," he wrote, paraphrasing the Hindu epic, Mahabharata.

In the winter of 2005, Stephen asked his mother to send Beanie Babies from Delaware so he could give them to Iraqi children he met on patrols."Not everyone here is the enemy," he wrote to his mom, a high school teacher.

Students at Charter School of Wilmington brought hundreds of Beanie Babies to school so Bobbie McGowan could send them to her son. The Beanie Baby drive continues in Stephen's name through the RGW Foundation (www.thergwfoundation.org).

"His focus was on the children – trying to make a better future for those [Iraqi] children," said Bobbie, who wears a necklace with Stephen's photograph on the pendant. Stephen's younger sister Michaela, 23, wears her brother's dog tags around her neck. She also wears his Army PT jacket, and his old PT shirts.

"I'm his little sister," she said, noting that her thick navy blue sweatshirt also belonged to Stephen. "I used to always steal his clothes. Nothing's changed."

For Mother's Day, Michaela unveiled for her mother a display case containing some of Stephen's belongings: his medals, goggles, combat boots and leather gloves. She believes her brother died an honorable death.
"Sooner than I wanted him to," said Michaela, who graduated from college two months after Stephen died.

She works as a teacher's aide at a day care in Pennsylvania. "I was so proud of him. I told him every chance I got how much I love him and that he's my hero." Stephen's father, Fran DiDomenicis, also lives in Wilmington, DE, but the family is estranged. They came together briefly at Arlington on March 15, 2005, to lay Stephen to rest.

A year later, scouts from Stephen's platoon traveled from across the country to honor him at Arlington and support his family. At the cemetery, they gathered to pray with Bobbie's family and friends in a large circle at the foot of Stephen's grave. "Stephen, he loved life," Bobbie said. "That's what he was about."

His legacy endures at Charter School of Wilmington, which in June, 2006 awarded a $1,000 scholarship in Stephen's name.

The CPL Stephen McGowan Award is not based on academic performance. It will be awarded each year to the young man or woman who exhibits some of Stephen's finest qualities: enthusiasm for life, concern for others, and curiosity about the world.

— Kristin Harty
Reporter for the News Journal in Wilmington, DE

Lt. Col. Kevin Michael Shea
September 14, 1966 – September 14, 2004

Kevin Shea, of Washington, D.C., died on his 38th birthday. He leaves behind his wife, two children, his parents and two brothers. He was up for an award for his heroism a month before he was killed, but he never told anyone in his family.

"He was very humble," said Lt. Col. Dave Bellon, who served with Kevin in Iraq. "When you first meet him, you think he's just this big, laidback guy who'd probably be great to go out and drink beers with. But he's one of the most brilliant people I've ever met. He had a problem-solving mind and an exceptional degree of curiosity."

Kevin was a communications officer and an engineer. He wanted to be in the infantry and closer to the action. His buddies knew that and decided to play a joke on him.

They enlisted the help of a Delta Force sergeant major to "recruit" Kevin for a secret mission. The condition was that he had to shed some pounds. Kevin wasn't overweight, but he loved to eat. However, the "mission" motivated him to make changes. For days, Kevin's friends watched him eat nothing but salads and hit the gym regularly, even going for evening runs. When it came time for the guys to fess up, Kevin laughed at himself with an "Okay, you got me," despite everything they'd put him through. He was just that good-natured.

"He was never malicious, never in a bad mood, never not willing to help. He had a degree of personal strength and he never gave in to frustration. I never saw him snap at anyone – not even in the worst conditions," said Dave.

Ask anyone who knew him and they'd say "that was just Kevin."

– RP

He Didn't Have to Stay

It is painful to interview a widow about her husband, a man that took a different path than most men of my generation do. One of a few, they say.

"I want all of my men to come home alive," Kevin M. Shea told his wife, Ami, before leaving for Iraq. In the end, he was the only one from his unit who didn't. The sentiment sounds like a line from a script, but there are men who still think like this way, who still believe in something greater than themselves.

As a young man, Kevin fought in Desert Storm as a second lieutenant. As a major, at age 38, he was still serving his country.

An officer with 1st Marine Expeditionary Force, he was deployed to Iraq during one of the bloodiest periods of fighting. He was stationed in Al Anbar province in the central to western part of Iraq between the land route from Jordan and Baghdad. Fallujah and Ramadi had become common places mentioned nightly on the news as hotbeds of Sunni insurgency. Daily mortar and rocket attacks haphazardly rained down on American strongholds, while improvised explosive devices (IEDs) impregnated roads that Marines and soldiers had to navigate daily.

Earlier, in March of 2004, independent contractors for the Blackwater Security Company were ambushed by small-arms fire while they were driving through Fallujah. Their two cars were set on fire, and the world later watched the video of the occupants' burnt torsos hanging from a pale green bridge that spans the ancient Euphrates. The Marines held back from entering Fallujah in April of 2004, after an uprising that left the province, as well as the country, in turmoil. Fallujah would be a matter dealt with by the Marines later in November. Kevin was stationed at Camp Fallujah while all this happened.

Kevin had an awesome presence shaped by his 6'4" muscular build. He had a stern look and strong, prominent jaw, but his crystal blue eyes reflected a softer man.

He met Ami at the Beachcomber in San Diego while out with cohorts. Ami and her friends were heading to a B-52s' concert. He ditched his friends and bought a last-minute ticket to chase the love of his life. Wearing jeans and a black rugby shirt, he asked for her number and ultimately found a girlfriend, wife and the mother of his two children.

They became best friends, and could talk all day about anything. They would make each other laugh while doing dishes together, Kevin often faking a French

accent from the little French he thought he knew. He wrote his parents to tell them that he was going to marry Ami because she was a strong woman. They were engaged seven weeks later.

"He was not like anyone else I have ever met. He was the most gentle man I have ever known," Ami said.

As much as he loved his new wife, Kevin lived and breathed the Marines.

He attended the Air Force Academy in Colorado Springs, CO. He cross-commissioned into the Marines from there and earned his master's degree in electrical engineering at the Naval Postgraduate School in Monterey, CA. He went on to teach Electrical Engineering at the Naval Academy in Annapolis, MD. He also coached the academy rugby team. He was so popular among the midshipmen that they named him an honorary graduate of the class of 2003.

Kevin's voice had a Texas flavor that remained from the state in which he lived as a child. One hundred percent Irish, his taste was for that of steak, potatoes and a Guinness. Maybe the Monte Cristo cigars he smoked gave him his loud, deep laugh.

His loves in this world were running, rugby and his family. Kevin would take his children fishing at the beach on the eastern shore for the stripers that ran in the cool currents of the Chesapeake.

Kevin told Ami to buy a dog after he deployed. It was a diversion, something to keep her mind off him. He said to wait two months, then buy the dog, and she did. A black Scottie named Molly became the best dog she ever knew. He wanted something to bring her comfort while he was gone. He wanted her to get settled in.

During his deployment, what he didn't tell Ami was that he was nominated for a Bronze Star with a Valor Device for his heroic actions in Fallujah. He and his sergeant were thrown from their Humvee during a firefight and the driver slammed into a building. While the sergeant lay injured and the driver immobilized, Kevin stood in the middle of the street shooting, doing all that he could to protect himself and the other men until the Marines could rescue them.

After seven months, having completed his tour in the blinding light and dry summer heat of the desert of Iraq, Kevin could have come home. Instead, he volunteered to stay longer to wait for the replacement communications officer at Camp Fallujah. He wanted to wait so his men would be safe. The decision would cost him his life.

On his 38th birthday, on Sept. 14, 2004, an enemy rocket slammed into his firebase and killed him. According to Ami, three Marines have professed that they were the ones who closed Kevin's eyes and that they were there with him during his last minutes. That describes the impact he had on his men.

In an earlier e-mail, Kevin had included a picture of himself. Ami said it was then that she knew he wasn't going to return. In the photo, Kevin was not looking at her, but at something off in the distance.

In the city of Temecula, which from the missionaries translates into "the land where the sun shines through the mist," Ami Shea, her daughter, Brenna, 12, and her son, Michael, 9, continue to live in honor of Kevin's life.

They have planted a sapling, a five-foot oak tree that they decorate with balloons on Kevin's birthday. They visit the tree with their dog, Molly. Ami is learning how to fish now, just enough to take her son and daughter out for an afternoon, but she admits she would have no idea what to do if they actually caught a fish.

"When he died, something changed in the world. I am so proud he died a Marine," she said.

Kevin is credited with developing a new communications system that was implemented in Iraq. "It has directly saved the lives of thousands of our soldiers and Marines. As of now, all the armed forces are using this system," explained Ami.

Kevin was posthumously promoted to lieutenant colonel and was finally awarded the Bronze Star for which he'd been nominated after the firefight in Fallujah.

I was in Iraq, in Ramadi, and in Fallujah as a journalist when Kevin was stationed there. I knew a lot of Marines like him, some living and some now dead. I would have liked to have met Kevin Shea. Maybe I did.

Kevin was a husband, a father, a son and a brother. He is buried in Arlington National Cemetery.

— David Swanson
Staff photographer for the Philadelphia Inquirer

HAYNES
CROSE

Sgt. Bradley Stephen Crose
August 4, 1979 – March 4, 2002

United States Army Rangers are considered to be some of the best-trained light infantry soldiers in the world. They are mentally and physically tough, often engaging in unconventional warfare in faraway lands around the world. It's not uncommon for their missions to be classified as they fight terrorism, gather intelligence or otherwise engage the enemy. Their motto is "Rangers Lead the Way!"

Army Sgt. Bradley S. Crose served with Alpha Company, 1st Ranger Battalion, 75th Ranger Regiment out of Hunter Army Airfield in Savannah, GA. He traveled to Washington, DC with his unit shortly after 9/11. Brad was able to see the immediate effects of the attack on our nation. He was provided a personal tour of the Pentagon and was told amidst the rubble and debris, "When you get there [Afghanistan] – this is why you are fighting."

Less than a year later, Brad was among eight American servicemen killed outside Gardez, Afghanistan during a nine-hour firefight trying to rescue a Navy Seal. Those who knew Brad remember him as quiet and unassuming. When tested, he was known as someone who had guts. On the one-year anniversary of Brad's death, his father, Rick Crose, wrote:

"Today the honor of your sacrifice and magnitude of your life looms ever large. Even though our hearts still ache and our eyes mist in remembrance of you, our hope is rooted in the knowledge of your steadfast faith and the assurance of your eternal security. Thank you for being a Christian warrior, Patriot and Ranger. America remembers, we will never forget. RLTW." Brad is also survived by his mother and stepfather, Sheila and John Maguhn; stepmother, Diana Crose; brother, Aaron; and stepsister, Hannah Higginbotham.

— RP

A Ranger Who Lead the Way

Bradley Stephen Crose, born in Orlando, FL, in August of 1979, heroically gave his life to his country. He was killed in action on March 4, 2002, during Operation Anaconda in Eastern Afghanistan as part of America's response to the September 11, 2001, attacks on our country.

Brad's father, Rick Crose, described his son with tremendous pride, mentioning that Brad had the physique of Michelangelo's "David." At 5'10" and 185 pounds, Brad was all muscle and all Ranger. He was 22 years old when he died alongside his fellow Army Rangers.

Military service was certainly not unfamiliar territory for Brad. As the youngest of two brothers, he and his family moved frequently up and down the East Coast as his father was sent from one Navy duty station to the next.

"Brad and his older brother, Aaron, looked forward to the moves," Rick recalled. "They were excited to make new friends, make new adventures." The two brothers were the best of friends.

At age 11, Brad was one of the most talented players on both his Pop Warner football team and his competitive, premier soccer team. The fast pace and demands of these sports left 11-year-old Brad eager for a break from team competitive sports, but he found his passion in Tae Kwon Do, training under 1984 Tae Kwon Do Olympian Ron Berry. It became apparent within a few weeks of training that Brad had a special and unique talent for the sport, as he was able to fight competitively with black belt-rated fighters his own age. Brad was soon ready to get back into the world of competition, but for the first time he managed his own successes rather than placing dependency on others. By the age of 12, Brad placed third at the Tae Kwon Do Junior Olympics in Ohio. Just two years later, at the age of 14, he was invited to participate in the Men's Nationals in Houston, TX. Accepting this invitation to represent the state of Florida, Brad challenged and fought full-grown men in his art.

During Brad's sophomore year of high school, older brother Aaron enlisted in the Marine Corps. The following year, Brad signed on with the Army and received a rare Army Ranger appointment guarantee. It was shortly after graduating from Orange Park High School in a suburb of Jacksonville, FL, that Brad officially began his journey toward becoming a U.S. Army Ranger. It was exactly what his father had raised him to be.

"I raised warriors," Rick said. "I did that on purpose and did it without apology." Brad's Tae Kwon Do studies formally came to an end upon entry into the Army.

He did not want to completely disclose his black belt status and kept a relatively low profile. He did, however, actively use his Tae Kwon Do training as a Ranger. In addition to Olympic style fighting, Brad was also trained in a form of street fighting, making his skills of martial arts well-suited for his role in the U.S. Army Special Forces.

Brad's parents agree he was a risk taker. If there was a ramp you could jump a bike over, Brad was flying through the air. Reflecting on a much more innocent time, Rick recalls the first time his youngest son vocalized his eagerness for a career full of adventure.

"Dad, when I grow up, I want to jump out of airplanes," 8-year-old Brad told his father. Brad knew early in life that he wanted to go into the Army and by the time he was 12, he knew he wanted to be a Ranger. When he was 16, he asked his Dad if he could have skydiving lessons for his birthday, but his wish would have to wait. It was too dangerous a sport for a 16 year old to take up.

"If something happened to you," his dad remembers saying, "I would blame myself eternally. When you are 21 and responsible for yourself, you can take your own lessons." He jumped out of a plane at 18, as a United States Army Ranger. Brad used to say that he thought he had the best job in the world.

"I get to jump out of airplanes, I get to blow stuff up, I get to shoot guns and I get to drive motorcycles with night vision goggles and I get paid for it," his family remembered him saying. "It is just the best thing in the world."

Brad's sense of service to his country was solidified when between his junior and senior years of high school he traveled with his family to Washington, D.C. While on this family trip, Brad was able to experience the museums, the rich historical spots and the sacred ground of our memorials. During a visit to Arlington Cemetery, he vocalized a clear understanding and reverence for the men and women who gave their lives for our country; he felt that it was on their backs that we are free people in a free nation under a free democracy. He was proud of his heritage and of the legacy of our nation.

Just a few short years later, our nation would be attacked and many things about our way of life were forever changed. Sgt. Brad Crose and his family were no different. Rick had a frightful thought that fateful September morning.

"This could cost my son his life," Rick remembers thinking. "I knew that those weren't just random happenings, we were being attacked."

While stationed in Savannah, GA, not long after Sept. 11, Brad was given the opportunity to lead a group of Rangers, in uniform, to a Redskins football game in Washington, D.C., as part of a military demonstration.

Gen. Doug Brown, the commanding general for all Special Forces, met Brad at the game. Pressing a coin into Brad's hand, the general told him to take it into battle and bring it back bearing enemy blood. Brad carried the coin with him to Afghanistan.

While deployed, Brad had an ongoing relationship with a fourth-grade class from his church's elementary school. Though he only had one opportunity to write them while away, he wrote in his letter that he was planning on coming to see them when he returned home. Brad never made it to their classroom, but the teacher and parents from that fourth-grade class have all visited with the Crose's since Brad's death to share the impact their son had on the 8- and 9-year-old boys from that class.

One of the fourth-grade boys came into the funeral home during visitation prior to Brad's funeral, where Brad's medals were on a small table in the chapel. This young boy took one of his very own medals that he had earned not long before and began to say a prayer for Brad, out loud and uninhibited. He was there to give back to Brad as much as he knew how to give.

The boy left his medal behind as he walked away.

Many lives were touched by a hero named Bradley S. Crose. He gave more to his country than his life and a legacy of freedom. Brad has provided many people — more than those who had the honor to know him personally — with the motivation to reach for and obtain all that they aim to achieve.

The coin Brad received from Gen. Brown was found after the young Ranger was killed. The blood on it was from a man who loved his country enough to give everything he had in her defense. It was his own.

— Jennifer McCollum
Advocate on Capitol Hill for fellow war widows

"The Ranger battalion is to be an elite, light, and the most proficient infantry battalion in the world; a battalion that can do things with its hands and weapons better than anyone. The battalion will not contain any "hoodlums" or "brigands" and if the battalion is formed of such persons, it will be disbanded. Wherever the battalion goes, it will be apparent that it is the best."

— Gen. Creighton W. Abrams, Jr.
U.S. Army Chief of Staff, 1972-74

Sgt. 1st Class David James Salie
June 12, 1970 – February 14, 2005

"If you're looking at this, then I'm not coming home," David Salie said to his family from a videotape. The "suck" video, as he called it, was something he hoped his wife and children would never have to see.

But the Columbus, Georgia native wanted to make sure he was always there for his children, so he made videos for them to watch during his deployment, and some for if he never made it back. In one tape, he made up silly stories to entertain them. In others, he encouraged his children to live a good life. For his daughter Chyna, he reminded her that she can do and be anything she wants and tried to inspire her to be an independent woman who thinks on her own. For his sons, Luke and Hunter, he offered his formula for what it takes to be a good man.

It may have seemed the towering man, who stood nearly six and a half feet tall, was invincible. But he was killed in a bomb blast on Valentine's Day in Baqouba, Iraq.

His wife, Deanna, watched the "just in case" videos shortly after he died.

On the tape to her, David tells her, "You are without a husband in person, but I am always with you."

— RP

A Daughter's Story

Chyna Salie's father had a nickname for her.
"He called me Lovey," she said. Now, it's just her mother yelling out, "Lovey!" across parking lots and at home. Sometimes, it embarrasses her but she knows it's her mother's way of reminding her how much her father loved her.
Not that 13-year-old Chyna has forgotten.

"He loved me a lot," she said.

Sgt. First Class David J. Salie was in killed in Iraq on February 14, 2005, just four days after he led the troops of 2nd Platoon, Bravo Company, 2/69 Armor, 3rd Infantry Division in Iraq to begin a year-long tour.

Chyna's favorite memory is of the day that David Salie adopted her when she was 9 years old. "I woke up early," Chyna remembered, "and Mom said we were going to the courthouse so Daddy could adopt me." David Salie was the only father Chyna's ever known. She was two years old when her mother married David. "It was like he'd always been my father. Being adopted just changed my last name," Chyna said. But David was so excited he could hardly contain himself. Adopting Chyna was his way of letting others know what he felt in his heart; she was his precious girl. "He was happy and excited because, finally, in other people's eyes, he was my dad," Chyna said

That day, Chyna stood confidently before the judge in a flowered dress with lace on the bodice. When the judge asked her why she wanted David Salie to adopt her, Chyna smiled and told him, "He's my dad. He's there to hug me when I'm sad and to kiss my knees when they get scraped."

And he was there to hold her the day her grandfather was killed in a car accident. Distraught over the abrupt death, Chyna was in her room crying when her father came in and curled up on the bed next to her.

"Sometimes," he said, "when God needs people, He takes them. Your Papa is in a better place."

David may have known when he was headed for a better place. Even though he'd served in previous conflicts and survived, this time he told his wife he thought his luck was up. He started doling out his clothes to friends. And he made videotapes for the children and his wife to watch after he died.

Deanna dismissed his worries. At six feet, five inches tall and 225 pounds, David just looked invincible. What could kill a man that big and strong? Deanna couldn't imagine anything snuffing out her husband's engaging smile or his electric embraces. But on Valentine's Day, 2005, Chyna remembers when Army officials knocked on the door of their Fort Benning home.
"My mom started freaking out," Chyna said. "She was screaming, 'They're here! They're here!'"

Her mother's behavior confused her and scared her brothers. "I'd seen movies where soldiers came to the door dressed in mailman-like outfits — blue ones. These guys were dressed in green uniforms. That confused me. But as soon as they said 'We regret to inform you' I knew who they were.

"Mom was on the floor crying — crying hard. Grandma was on the floor beside her, trying to pick her up, trying to comfort her. My brothers were crying. I was crying. I couldn't hear half of what the soldiers said, we were all crying so hard," Chyna remembered. She also remembers the false hope. "I kept hoping it was all a prank — that they had the wrong guy," she recalled. Chyna fell asleep, hoping it had all just been a bad dream. But when morning broke the next day, she realized her father really was dead.

The next year after David's death, the Salie family had to move off-base and into civilian life. They moved into a new home, went to new schools, found new friends and began a new way of life.

Chyna says she not only misses her father, but the military life centered around him, with all its adventures and challenges.
"I liked moving around, getting to meet new people, going to places like Alaska and Hawaii. Plus, in the military, everyone was on the same level," Chyna said. "People didn't look down on you if you didn't make a lot of money. Nobody made a lot of money."

Now, Chyna tries to be brave for her mother, who she hopes will one day be as happy as she was before her father died, and for her two little brothers, Luke and Hunter.

"I purposely try not to cry because it upsets my brothers. Hunter says stuff like 'When is Daddy going to wake up?' Mom can only deal with one thing at time, so I don't want to be a burden. And I'm afraid that my crying will make my mother more sad than she is already," Chyna said.

So she tries to be the best girl she can be, because she knows her life choices will validate her father's sacrifice. What good is freedom if you use it to self-destruct?

"I want everyone to know that my father was a really good person. He didn't go to Iraq to be a hero. He went because he believed it was the right thing to do," Chyna said.

After David's death, Deanna discovered her husband's videotapes, and found he had tried to cover all his bases: a tape for Chyna for the day she got married, videos for the boys about growing up to be good men. On a tape for Deanna, David reminded her to be strong for the children.

"Hold our kids tight for me," he said to the camera, "and make sure they know who their Daddy was and what he stood for."

— Karen Spears Zacharias
Author, journalist
heromama.org

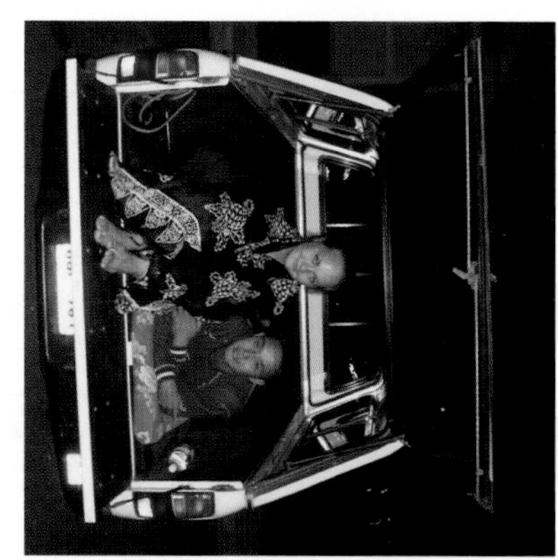

DAKINE

7UP

Sgt. Deyson Ken Cariaga
July 28, 1984 — July 8, 2005

Born and raised on the beaches of the Hawaiian Islands, the ocean was Deyson Cariaga's first love. At a young age, he learned to ride the waves of the Pacific on a surfboard.

Later, he discovered another passion — helping others.

At first, he thought about becoming a firefighter. But instead, the Honolulu resident joined the U.S. Army, quickly becoming a member of a military intelligence unit.

It was a decision that didn't surprise his mother. Theresa Inouye says her son had a caring disposition. She affectionately nicknamed him the "Pied Piper" because children and animals were always drawn to him.

Once based in Iraq, one of Deyson's missions was to find the source of mortars and roadside bombs. His fellow soldiers say Deyson cared deeply about trying to make conditions safer for his brothers-in-arms.

He was killed by a roadside bomb just 20 days shy of his 21st birthday in Balad, Iraq on July 8, 2005.

Deyson was the first Hawaii citizen soldier to die in Iraq and the first to be killed in combat since Vietnam.

He was awarded the Hawaii Medal of Honor, as well as a Purple Heart and Bronze Star, posthumously.

He is now laid to rest within view of the Pacific waters he held so dear.

— *RP*

The Pied Piper

Deyson Cariaga knew how to take charge, barely out of his diapers. His babysitters even gave the tot a nickname: the "Super Superior" because he already knew how to lead others. He wasn't a bully; he just wanted to help.

"To any new kid they had coming in he would say, 'You gotta put your shoes over here, you gotta roll out your mat,'" said Theresa Inouye, Deyson's mother. "He always took charge and cared for the younger ones."

As Deyson grew older, his leadership skills and compassion grew for others. He was a junior leader with the YMCA and later helped train students in the Junior ROTC program at Roosevelt High School in Honolulu. He worked after school at a private care home for senior citizens. His service as a food server often was requested by the seniors who enjoyed his company and ability to make them laugh. They would even offer him tips.

Soon, he got a new nickname: the "Pied Piper."

His mother dubbed him that because children and adults were always drawn to him. Sometimes Deyson would complain about always being around children, but Inouye said she knew that privately her son loved it. "You take him into a crowded situation, he'd always be the one that the kids went to. Kids know who they can play around with, and he always ended up with the kids," she said. Deyson loved the ocean, sports and anything to do with the outdoors. He played the violin and the saxophone in middle school and the clarinet in Roosevelt's band. He also earned a letter on the school's junior varsity track team. One year, his schedule was so crammed, he had to choose between JROTC and track. He chose the military program, because he knew it would be a test of strength.

"He just loved challenges — physical challenges. It just provided him with a program he liked, something that would challenge his physical ability.

He knew exactly where to go, what was required of him. He liked that," Inouye said. Deyson received his mother's permission to join the Hawaii Army National Guard soon after graduating from high school in 2002. He finished among the top 10 of his class of 1,500 during boot camp.

"He was doing it for what I felt were good reasons. He knew I didn't have money being a single parent; and it would help pay for his college education." Inouye said. "He could go to college, finish college and get to participate in the military games that he liked. So I signed him up. I allowed him to go. I felt it was better to send him off with my blessing and support."

Although he now had to live the life of a military man, Deyson never stopped helping others. He was assigned to the 229th Military Intelligence Battalion and was deployed to Kuwait in January 2005. In early February, the 229th departed for Iraq.

As the medic for his unit, "Dice" (as he was called by his fellow soldiers) was never without his medical bag, just in case a child needed a band-aid or a fellow soldier required assistance. Deyson would ask family back home to send candy so he could hand it out to Iraqi children. He often carried a large bag of toys for the children.

Inouye said that her son would call at least once a week and always asked her what she wanted him to bring back from Iraq.
"He was so funny, talking about, 'What do you want from here?' I would say, 'Deyson, you're not on vacation.' But that was him. He was always thinking about the other person. In fact, he had a list of things and he was gathering things — gifts to bring back," she said.

But on July 8, 2005, less than three weeks before his 21st birthday and a long-awaited leave to visit home, Deyson was killed when a roadside bomb exploded near the Humvee he was driving. Three others in the vehicle were injured.

Deyson was Hawaii's first citizen soldier to be killed in the Iraqi conflict. His death shocked the many people whose lives he touched.

"It was pretty tough for everybody. As a unit, everybody felt it," said Sgt. Jared Chong, Deyson's team leader and roommate in Iraq. He said Deyson got along with everybody and that his JROTC background and positive attitude prepared him for his life in the National Guard. "He fit right in with the rest of the guys — local boy who could get along," Chong said. "He was always giving. He was always there trying to help. He was one of those guys you would never have to ask him to help you out. If something needed to be done, he was there."

In their spare time, Chong and Deyson would work out together. The two were preparing for a triathlon when they returned home. "He was my running buddy. It was a partnership. I'm not going to do any triathlons. My workout buddy is gone," Chong said.

Inouye said her son was always surrounded by people who loved him. A single parent, she and her son lived with her parents who treated him like their son.Haruko Akatsuka would talk to her grandson often when he was in Iraq and said he always seemed happy.

"He felt he had a lot of things that the Iraqi kids didn't have, and he wanted to share what he had with them. He was a very caring person," she said.
During their phone conversations, grandmother and grandson talked about his eventual homecoming and eating at his favorite Japanese restaurant. She told him that his dogs and plants were doing well. She told him that she kept his room clean, but wasn't touching anything.

Akatsuka last spoke with her grandson a few weeks before his death.
"He sounded good. He was anxious to come home. I was so happy because he was not sick or anything. I could feel his happiness in his voice and that made me happier and I was waiting for him," she said.

Since his death, Haruko and her husband Roland visit Deyson several times a week at the National Memorial Cemetery of the Pacific at Punchbowl, where thousands of veterans are buried. Haruko Akatsuka said she's accepted the fact that her grandson is gone, but she misses him dearly.

"I took him like my son and I can thank my daughter for leaving him with us," she said. "He was there for us. I needed someone, he needed me. We needed each other and he brought joy to us because he was such a good son, a good grandson."

But even in death, Deyson continues to be a pied piper, bringing people together. On a sunny morning at his former high school, dozens of family and friends gathered to commemorate his 22nd birthday by planting a tree and dedicating a bench in his honor. The guests reminisced about the person who brought so much joy to others.

"Having something like this ceremony, I think he would really appreciate it," Chong said. "Family. That's what it's all about."

— Curtis Lum
Staff Writer for The Honolulu Advertiser

"To laugh often and love much; to win the
respect of intelligent persons and the affection
of children, to earn the approbation
of honest critics; to appreciate beauty;
to give of one's self, to leave the world a
bit better, whether by a healthy child,
a garden patch or a redeemed social condition;
to have played and laughed with enthusiasm
and sung with exultation; to know even one
life has breathed easier because you have lived
— that is to have succeeded."

— Ralph Waldo Emerson

TITUS
U.S.ARM

Spc. Brandon Thomas Titus
December 12, 1983 — August 17, 2004

Army Spc. Brandon Titus of Boise, ID was the son of a decorated Vietnam veteran and the great-great nephew of a Medal of Honor recipient. Calvin P. Titus was with the U.S. Army's 14th Infantry Regiment when he received the nation's highest military award for being the first to scale the city wall at Peking in 1900 during the China Relief Expedition.

Brandon Titus, 20, was determined to make his mark in the military, too.
"He gave it everything he had every single day of his life, and he never asked for anything back," said former Cpl. Kyle Angelini, who'd known Brandon since basic training and served with him in Iraq. "When new guys came in, they'd put them under Brandon; because they knew if the guys learned half the work ethic of Brandon, they would be great soldiers."

Brandon didn't sweat the small stuff and, as Kyle said, "He didn't sweat the big stuff either!" Stress just seemed to disappear around him. Perhaps it was his oddball sense of humor or his ability to make others laugh without even trying. Kyle remembers the time his family took Brandon out to dinner in New York. "He ordered a burger and the waitress asked if he'd like fries. He made her check to see if they were made from Idaho potatoes. I think he was going to have coleslaw if they weren't," laughed Kyle. "He was dead serious. He wasn't trying to be funny — that was just him."

And Brandon was never more serious than when it came to serving his country. "Before he found out he was being deployed he was going to try to transfer units so he could go to Iraq," said Kyle. "He was all about the Army, and he wanted to make his dad proud."

— RP

In His Father's Footsteps

On Aug. 30, 2004, Brandon Titus, a member of the Army's elite 10th Mountain Division, got his final wish. Nobody ever wanted it to come true. Brandon became the first veteran to be buried in the Idaho State Veterans' Cemetery, a casualty — like so many other veterans — of a roadside bomb in Iraq.

Brandon always looked to his father, Tom, as a role model. Growing up in Boise, Idaho, he was constantly reminded of his father's heroic efforts during the Vietnam War. Tom suffered severe wounds during two highly decorated tours of duty in Vietnam, earning him two Purple Hearts.

When his parents divorced, Brandon decided he wanted to live with his father. Tom instilled in Brandon a passion for living life to its fullest. As a single parent, Tom raised his son with the morals and values that he practiced: respecting women and giving more than 100 percent to whatever you do.

Tom was later diagnosed with cancer, causing Brandon to grow up faster than a typical teen. He always stood by his dad and spent countless hours at his bedside.

Those who knew Brandon well, however, were familiar with his prankster side. "You always knew if he was saying something sarcastic or joking about something because he had a smirk on his face. And if you saw that smirk it meant Brandon liked you," said Brandon's dad. That was just one of the many characteristics Tom passed on to his son.

Tom recollected hearing one day about how some girls in one of Brandon's classes were planning on going around to certain houses to toilet paper them. When Brandon learned his house was on the list, he and his guy friends came up with a plan of attack. As the girls showed up one night, Brandon and the boys were laying in wait on the roof with water balloons and water guns. It was quite a funny ambush. Brandon was always on the defensive, and he knew how to get the job done.

After the Sept. 11, 2001, terrorist attacks, Brandon decided it was time to follow in his father's footsteps. "I realized I was being very ignorant and that before I could take all the freedoms that this country gives me for granted I should probably earn them. I decided four years of my life isn't that much at all and I should give them to my country," Brandon told his dad just a few days before he was deployed to Iraq.

Brandon had dreams of teaching someday. It was another way he wanted to give back. But instead, he put those plans on hold and enlisted in the Army. After

Airborne and pre-Ranger training, he was assigned to the 10th Mountain Division based at Fort Drum, near Watertown, NY.

"I'm happy because I'm going with some guys I know. The way I look at it, the sooner I go, the sooner I will get back," Brandon had continued in his conversation with his father.

Unfortunately, 20-year-old Spc. Brandon Titus gave his all and lost his life on a distant battlefield. The aspiring teacher was killed in Baghdad on Aug. 17, 2004, when an improvised explosive device (IED) detonated near the checkpoint he was manning. Brandon posthumously received the Combat Infantryman Badge, a Purple Heart and the Bronze Star.

Tom remembers when the military officials showed up at his door to give him the news about his son "like it was yesterday." "I froze," said Tom.

Tom recalled what his all-American boy had said to him before he left for Iraq. "He said, 'I will give you a detailed letter that I want you to read if I don't make it home.'" Tom had hoped that he would never have to read it.

Tom said that in the letter Brandon talked about how his time had come and how he didn't want anyone to be sad. A part of the letter read, "I joined the Army because I realized this line of work was in my blood. I wanted to do this to make my dad proud."

Tom said reading the letter was the hardest part of dealing with Brandon's death because he felt guilty that his son wanted to be like him. "A lot of combat Vietnam vets have had to deal with survivor's guilt and this threw me right back in it," said Tom, whose cancer has now been in remission for six years.

In the letter, Brandon also specified that he wanted to be buried in the new Idaho State Veterans' Cemetery. Idaho had been the only state in the country without a veterans' cemetery. Burials were not supposed to take place in the cemetery until construction was complete, but because Brandon died in active duty combat and that was his wish, a special exception was made.

Idaho Gov. Dirk Kempthorne, who knew Brandon personally, spoke highly about the young hero to the hundreds of people who turned out to pay their respects at his funeral service. Friends and family described the soldier as selfless and compassionate, offering help to anyone who needed it. Not only was he a good talker, he was also a good listener.

"He was such a great guy, a great athlete and he always made people laugh," said Andy Villegas, a high school friend of Brandon's.

Brandon's younger sister, Libby, said growing up with her brother was not always easy. He always acted like the typical older brother — protective and doing things to annoy her. When it came to dating, she spoke of the "fear factor." "You get past dad; you got to get past big brother," she said.

Tom remembers Brandon and Libby as being normal siblings who argued. In fact, he said one time he walked into a sporting goods store and asked for a loud whistle and a black and white referee shirt. The guys at the store asked what sport he needed it for and Tom replied, "For my kids!" This is another example of the humor Tom passed down to his son.

Looking back, Libby said she would take all those arguments back just to have another day with her "big bro," who later became her best friend.

The members of Brandon's troop said the mood drastically changed after Brandon was killed. They didn't have Brandon standing in line making little comments that were oftentimes sarcastic, but funny. He was respectful and took the job seriously, but he also knew when he could play.
"He worked his heart out to do what he needed to do," said Tom. Officers even acknowledged that if you heard some sort of crack, you knew it was Brandon. You could always count on him to make you smile. In fact, he was responsible for naming his platoon "The Outlaws."

Brandon and his dad were often considered "outlaws" while riding around town on their motorcycles. It was a passion they shared and time well spent together. Now Tom's time is spent honoring Brandon by riding in his memory, raising awareness and support for fallen soldiers and their families.
Brandon Titus was the sixth Idaho soldier to make the ultimate sacrifice during Operation Iraqi Freedom. Killed on patrol, he left behind a message saying he wanted to make his dad proud. Brandon's dad says he is the proudest father in the world.

— Starlyn Klein
News anchor for KBCI-TV in Boise, ID

Lance Cpl. Jonathan "Kyle" Price
April 23, 1986 – January 13, 2006

Marine Lance Cpl. Kyle Price, of Woodlawn, IL would call his fiancée from Iraq and tell the expectant mother to put the phone to her belly so he could talk to his little girl. "She would sometimes kick, and it felt like they were bonding even though he was so far away," said Brea Tate. "He would tell her to be good to mommy. It was so sweet it made me cry, but I was smiling at the same time. He couldn't wait to be a daddy and would've been the perfect one, as well."

His military buddies call Kyle a "friendly guy" who got along with everyone. "That was one of the coolest things about him. He liked all kinds of people, and he didn't judge anyone," remembered Marine Lance Cpl. Ben Desilets, who met Kyle during training in Oklahoma and served with him in Iraq. "We used to sit up at night and talk a lot. He gave me relationship advice and helped me stay away from drugs." Ben says Kyle was "all about the Marine Corps" and planned to be a career Marine.

He continuously strived to better himself. "We were over there, and he learned the Iraqi language so good that he was able to interrogate [some of the most wanted terrorists]."

The day Kyle was killed, he had taken Ben's place on a patrol. Ben returned to the United States distraught and angry; but in Kyle's honor, he decided to turn that negative energy into something positive. Now he helps young Marines the way Kyle mentored him. Kyle Price had a way of inspiring people to be their best.

— RP

A Price for Freedom

John Hunsell knew the words before they were spoken. There is only one reason the military comes to your door when your son is serving in the war. The conversation is still a blur; yet, it remains almost frozen in time. The boy John had raised from a toddler fell under enemy fire and, at 19, lost his life while fighting for the freedoms in which he so boldly believed.

Cheryl Price-Hunsell can pinpoint the exact moment when her life became a self-described "living hell." The boy with the never-ending smile who lived his life by a golden rule taught to him by his mother long ago was gone. Her tears began to flow and continue to this day.

"My daughter asked me if there would ever be a day when I didn't cry, and all I could tell her is that I don't know," Cheryl said. "I started crying that day and I've cried every day since."

Lance Cpl. Jonathan Kyle Price – Kyle to those who knew him – and his unit were guarding a team of Marine engineers on January 13, 2006, in Ar Ramadi, Iraq when they came under small-arms fire. The dedicated Marine took a position between the enemy and the team he was assigned to protect.

"Kyle died doing what he believed in," John said. "He died a hero.

He felt strongly about what he was doing, and he felt strongly about his country." Kyle signed up for the Marines at a time when he knew his primary assignment would lead him to Iraq, but he never wavered in his commitment. He was not motivated by the politics of war. He had never even stepped into a voting booth. He was prompted by a sense of honor, duty and the right to freedom. He was a Marine.

He was a Marine at heart long before he put on his fatigues or stepped into his dress blues. He entered the brotherhood of the Corps already possessing the values of honor, courage and commitment by which every Marine lives his life.

"He always wanted to be in the military," said his mother, "from the time he was a little boy." His love for the Corps was possibly born from serving in the Heartland Young Marines in his hometown of Woodlawn, IL. Or perhaps it was his dedication to the Boy Scouts, where he earned the rank of Eagle Scout. It was during his time in Boy Scouts that a young Kyle went along on a camping trip to help supervise the younger scouts. Soon after the tents were pitched and the equipment unpacked, the boys' weekend outing fell under the cloud of Mother Nature. The storms began to roll in and over the group of young boys who, scared and panicked, began to cry and run for shelter. Kyle immediately

took charge. He calmed the fears of each child, gathered them together, and bravely led them to safety.

Cheryl remembers speaking to Kyle after the weekend storm and praising him for taking action to protect the children under his care. "He really didn't see the big deal," she said. "He said, 'Mom, somebody had to do it.'" Kyle was the boy with the contagious smile — the coy smirk following an ornery deed, the confident grin of accomplishment, and the ear-to-ear smile that both greeted people and put them at ease was his trademark.

He motivated everyone around him to be a better warrior, a better person, and to always give their best. He reached out to Iraqi children and carried candy with him in order to provide sweetness during a life lived to the backdrop of war.

His dedication extended well beyond his military career. He was devoted to his family, had found the love of his life and was expecting his firstborn child.If Kyle had apprehensions about becoming a father, he hid them from his parents and his fiancée Brea Tate. He carried a sonogram picture of his daughter tucked inside his jacket nearly every day he spent in Iraq and declined evenings out with his friends in the Marines, opting to save his money, instead.Slightly less than two months after Kyle was killed, Madison Kay Price entered the world on the birthday of her Grandma Cheryl, with a picture of her father at Brea's side and members of his Marine unit anxiously pacing in the waiting room.

"It felt like he was there. I know he was there," Brea said of that day. Madi inherited her father's nose and, through a gift of divine nature, that amazing smile. "Sometimes even the way she moves her hands is exactly like him," Brea said. The young mother said it is sometimes bittersweet to look into her child's face and see the smile of the love she lost. More often than not, she finds comfort in the tiny smile that mirrors Kyle's expression. Brea described the father of her child as funny, goofy, smart, caring, ambitious and the man who, above all else, made her feel safe in the world. She felt safe by his side, in his arms, or with his hand gently wrapped around her own. "I just knew when I was with him that nothing bad would ever happen and everything was going to be okay," she said through streaming tears. The weekend Kyle died would have been the anniversary of the couple's first date. Knowing he would be in the field and unable to talk to his fiancée, he programmed a voice mail to be received on Brea's phone. The devastated young girl had already been told the news of Kyle's death when the message came through.

"I was still sort of numb and just saw that I had a voice mail. It was Kyle. He said he loved me and wished me a happy anniversary," she said. "It was hard to hear him, he was already gone. But I feel so lucky now to have had that. It was a blessing."

Kyle shared his joy of becoming a father with three of the most important people in his life — the same people who now fill the roles of aunts and uncle to baby Madi. He and his sisters, Krystal (Price) Martin and Rachel Hunsell, and his brother, John R. Hunsell, were a close-knit group that always looked out for one another.

Growing up, Kyle was typical in many ways. He could be the characteristic little brother always ready to reach into his bag of tricks to annoy big sister Krystal or the big brother playing video games for hours with John R. Hunsell and never once letting him win. Many weekend evenings would find Kyle and little sister Rachel in front of the television watching wrestling or simply hanging out and laughing.

As Kyle grew older, his relationship with Krystal transformed from sibling to friend — a change they both cherished. Kyle shared many special moments with his sisters and brother and was always willing to share that trademark smile.

As family and friends work toward a way to move on without him, Kyle's parents have found comfort in the legacy left behind by their beloved child. John Hunsell said he sometimes sits and thinks about all Kyle was able to accomplish in his 19 years and always ends with the same thought. "I hope that I can accomplish half as much in my life as he did in his," John said proudly. "I look at everything he did, and it makes me so proud of the man he became. He was only here with us such a short time but he never let a minute of that time go to waste."

Looking around her living room at the pictures and pieces of Kyle's life that serve now as reminders and memorials, his mother, too, is filled with an overwhelming sense of pride. "I am so proud and so lucky he was my son," Cheryl said. "I'm proud that I'm Kyle's Mom."

When asked what she will miss the most about her son, a warm grin shines through the tears on her face as she remembers. "I'll miss his smile," she softly replied. "I'll miss his smile."

— Leigh Ann Williams
Staff writer for the Morning Sentinel in Mt. Vernon, IL

Cpl. Antoine Jay McKinzie
February 25, 1981 — March 21, 2006

Army Cpl. Antoine McKinzie was assigned to the 4th Battalion, 27th Field Artillery Regiment, 1st Armored Division. The 25-year-old from Indianapolis was killed when his Humvee came under enemy small-arms fire during combat operations in Baghdad, Iraq. He was a son, a big brother and a friend. "He's my inspiration, really," said Antoine's stepfather, Dwight Adams. "I mean, I don't know anyone who is more courageous than the men who are over there." His best friend, Jerry Henson, told one reporter that Antoine was a "quiet, well-spoken and intelligent" person who could be somewhat reserved until you got to know him.

"I just remember his laugh. He had one hell of a laugh," Jerry said. "He had a hearty, tall-guy laugh. It is one of those things that I will miss a lot."

Antoine's younger brother and sister looked up to him. Olivia Adams, 11, put her feelings into a poem:

My Brother Antoine

I have some secrets, I'd like to tell
About my brother, you knew so well.
Yes, he was tall,
And yes, he was brave,
But, I could beat him at video games.
We would watch TV,
Especially wrestling.
But when the Patriots played,
Their losses would be depressing.
He could be fun,
Like trick or treating,
Just to share the candy-eating.
Once he took me to my Sweetheart Dance
And, I got to see him swing and prance.
Although he was a soldier to you-
Brave, strong and true,
He will always be my big brother Antoine, you see;
And with love
Will always be in my memory.

— *RP*

Proud to Have Served

Four simple words, carved in stone, can't capture the life of a humble young man and dedicated soldier struck down in his prime by a sniper's bullet in Baghdad. But somehow, for the family of Army Cpl. Antoine J. McKinzie, of Indianapolis, IN, those words offer some solace and understanding and a good place to start telling his story.

Antoine's life, and the many challenges he overcame in his 25 years, still resonate strongly in the daily lives of his family: his parents, Zyvonne and Dwight Adams; his brother, Will, 17; and sister, Olivia, 11.

"Antoine will always be remembered for his gregarious spirit, fun-loving nature and can-do attitude," said his mother, Zyvonne. "His friends and family used to like to call him the 'Gentle Giant.'"

Antoine also made a big impression on his stepfather, Dwight, who welcomed the very active, fun-loving, yet sometimes pensive little boy into his life as his son from the age of six.

"Antoine helped raise me as much as I did him," Dwight said. "In many ways, he helped me to grow into the man I am today."

As a young man and student, Antoine not only had to outgrow the natural awkwardness of youth, but he also had severe learning disabilities that he had to overcome before graduating from high school, including a speech impediment, attention deficit disorder and dyslexia.

While he sometimes spoke a bit too slowly and deliberately — probably a lingering result of his speech troubles as a youth — Antoine grew up to become a calm, articulate and intelligent young man whom others naturally listened to and looked to for leadership.

His commanding officer, Lt. Col. James W. Danna III, said Antoine was a favorite of his comrades in the Delta Battery, 1st Battalion, 40th Field Artillery. Because of his impressive physical appearance — Antoine was 6-foot, 3-inches tall and 220 pounds of hard muscle — his fellow soldiers liked to call him "Big Mac" and "Mac Ten."

Stationed at the Baumholder Army Base in Germany, Antoine made two trips home after entering the service: once at Christmas in 2003, shortly after graduating from boot camp, and later — his last visit home — in October 2005, after serving one tour in Iraq and while getting ready to go back for a second stint in combat.

He shared a few stories of his last tour in Iraq that left no doubt that he would be going back into harm's way. Antoine had a look of apprehension when talking of returning to Iraq, but he strongly believed in his mission. He genuinely liked the Iraqi people, and he was eager to rejoin his comrades.

As a teenager learning how to drive, Antoine had experienced more than his share of fender benders. When his stepfather joked with him about the Army letting him drive one of his unit's costly M109A6 Paladin mobile howitzers — basically a large, armored cannon on tank treads — Antoine responded simply with his wry sense of humor. He said, "Hard to hit anything out there, Dad. It's mostly just sand; sand to the east, sand to the west, sand to the north, sand to the south."

As a testament to his skill with weaponry, personal bravery and the confidence of his peers, Antoine was given the dangerous and crucial job of manning a 50-caliber machine gun atop a Humvee in the lead vehicle of a motorized patrol through Western Baghdad on March 21, 2006.

Shortly after noon, while traveling on a street called the Irish Road, Antoine's patrol came under heavy insurgent fire from the rooftops and street. Antoine quickly ducked into the Humvee, radioed in the coordinates of the gunfire as the bullets were striking his vehicle and steeled himself to rise up into the fire, man his machine gun and help draw off fire from his comrades. In a matter of moments, he was fatally wounded by a sniper's bullet to the head.

Even though they are all still struggling with Antoine's loss, his family and comrades in arms were deeply touched by the story of Antoine's sacrifice, and he later was awarded a Bronze Star and Purple Heart for his heroism.

His military family gave Antoine three separate memorial services: in Baghdad; in Kuwait, where some of the unit was stationed, and in Baumholder, Germany.

The Army sent his family a videotape of the Baghdad services with fellow soldiers lining up solemnly to salute Antoine's boots and helmet and to place military service coins beside them, as is traditionally done.

In a letter sent to his parents by his commanding officer, Antoine was described as "more than just a good soldier, he was a good friend, one who was always there for his comrades."

"Antoine McKinzie was a true hero ... whose spirit will live on forever," Lt. Col. Danna said.

Antoine probably would be embarrassed by all the attention he received at his hometown funeral from local officials, friends and members of the community. Motorcycle riders from the Patriot Guard — mostly former veterans who provide security at the funerals of service members killed in Iraq — showed up to provide Antoine a memorable send-off by giving him a procession and lining both sides of the entrance to Crown Hill Cemetery in Indianapolis, where he is buried.

His parents will always remember Antoine as that little boy who loved playing with his Transformers, his G.I. Joes and his He-Man action figures. His brother and sister undoubtedly will remember the big brother who always looked after them and loved to watch pro wrestling on TV — especially his favorite character, The Rock.

And many of Antoine's friends will likely remember him as an average guy who loved football and playing video games. He always followed his favorite team, the New England Patriots, and he loved playing the latest version of "John Madden Football."

Antoine was an aspiring artist who was always drawing as a teen and studied graphic design in college. He will never get a chance to pursue his dream of working for a software firm designing computer games.

But he will always be remembered in the prime of his life as a shy, young man who joined the U.S. Army nearly two years to the day after the September 11 attacks to grow into a more confident, more dynamic young man.
His mother, Zyvonne, gave a fitting description of Antoine; one that helps sum up the ultimate sacrifice that one human being can give for another.

"Oftentimes, when we think of heroes, they are larger-than-life personalities with big ideas, accomplishing big dreams," she said. "What most people don't realize is that most heroes are everyday people doing extraordinary things. They are unassuming and quiet. They succeed when they think no one else is watching and in doing so, they inspire others to succeed. Cpl. Antoine J. McKinzie, my son, was one such hero."

— Jennifer Evans
Independent writer

2nd Lt. Richard Brian Gienau
August 21, 1975 — February 27, 2005

Twenty-nine-year-old "Brian" Gienau, of Tripoli, IA loved being around people. He loved hanging out with his son Keenan, and he loved the military.

"The military allowed him the adventure he craved," said Brian's father, Richard Gienau. Brian, a second lieutenant with the Army National Guard, began his military career in the Navy.

"He wasn't afraid to try different things and go different places. While he was on the USS Enterprise, they ported in Australia and Brian went bungee jumping," marveled his mother, Debbee Way. She explained that Brian was the type of person who wasn't really great at sports, but he tried out for numerous teams because he thoroughly enjoyed the camaraderie.

"He made the best of every situation. He probably even found positive things about being in Iraq. He was a very positive person," explained Richard.

Brian was also always looking out for others. "The number one thing that bothered him about going to Iraq was having people at home worry about him," said Richard. Brian knew his soldiers felt the same way about leaving their loved ones behind. So, he made sure they were taken care of during their deployment. He packed a television and a video game system; and he even tried to acquire a sophisticated phone mechanism but discovered the cost was way out of his league.

Brian's mom called him a natural leader. "He was not one to sit in the background — he wanted to be upfront. But he didn't belittle the people he led. He felt like an equal to everyone," said Debbee.

"I'm honored to be able to say I was his father," said Richard.

— RP

In Each Other's Hearts

Brian Gienau was someone you could instantly feel comfortable around. "His smile was so friendly that if you walked by, it would just make you feel good. He had such charisma that he was able to talk with his face," said Brian's father, Richard Gienau.

And Brian could talk to anyone. From high-ranking military officers to children in the Sunday school class he taught, he always knew how to relate. It was a gift that endeared him to so many.

"He was always laughing. He had such a carefree attitude that very few things could bring him down," said his mother, Debbee Way.

"Second Lieutenant Brian Gienau was more to me than just one of my soldiers, he was one of my friends. Brian was an outstanding soldier and officer. His platoon always looked to him for guidance and wisdom," said Brian's Company Commander, Capt. Jason Wisehart, who addressed the congregation at his memorial service.

"Brian possessed leadership skills that all company commanders would love to have in their lieutenants. More important than Brian's leadership and soldier skills was the type of person Brian was. Brian always brought a smile to my face and would make me laugh even during the most stressful time. I used to tell everyone that Brian was always full of piss and vinegar....Brian is truly a soldier who will be missed by all....."

Brian's path to serve his country with distinction was not an easy one. Born in Cedar Falls, IA on August 21, 1975, he was the first child of Debbee and Richard. While in the first grade, his parents' separation forced Brian and his younger sister Amanda to leave behind their school, their church and their friends as they moved in with their father. Because Richard worked long hours, Brian and Amanda grew extremely close, depending on one another for support.

In high school, 16-year-old Brian's world was shattered when he lost his beloved sister in a car accident. "I knew they didn't fight much, but I didn't realize how close they were until after Amanda died," said Richard. He took his son to a counselor and confirmed what he already believed: Brian was mentally and physically strong and was coping with the tragedy.

Although he struggled with the loss for a long time, Brian persevered. He was an excellent student and only fell off the honor roll once – the semester after Amanda's death. His upbeat demeanor continued to shine through and he was always

observed as a "good-hearted, hardworking young man, and a very conscientious, goal–driven person."

"He was an adult as a teenager – responsible and independent," said Debbee.

Upon completing high school, Brian enlisted in the Navy and spent four years as an avionics technician. After Navy basic training, he married his high school sweetheart, Cara. They were blessed with a son, Keenan Christopher Gienau, on November 2, 1995. Brian's extended periods at sea were extremely stressful for his young bride, and they separated after his military service.

Following his discharge from the Navy, Brian returned to care for Keenan in Iowa, where he also enrolled in college — something he'd always wanted to do. He joined the National Guard Unit in Waterloo to help pay for his education. In order to become an officer, he also signed up for ROTC at the University of Northern Iowa at Cedar Falls. While getting his degree in Management Information Systems at the University of Northern Iowa, he was able to spend some quality time with Keenan, who is now 10 years old.

"He played with me and did fun stuff like shoot paintball guns, and we went to the water park in Waterloo and played games on the X-box. Stuff like that," said Keenan. He remembers his dad as a friendly person who "wasn't shy."

Of course, there are a lot of sad times. "When I think about him I start crying," said Keenan. But he says he is proud of his dad for always following through on his goals, including joining the military, "because he followed his heart."

Not long after starting a full-time job in 2004, Brian received word his unit, the 224th Engineer Battalion, was to be deployed to Iraq. Brian would join his unit as a platoon leader of A Company. Before shipping out, he made the most of every precious moment with his parents, Keenan, and his girlfriend, Katie Allen.

At a Prairie Lakes Church gathering in Cedar Falls, Pastor John Fuller called Brian to the front of the congregation and said a prayer for him. "We cheered for him," recalled Fuller. "Our whole church stood and clapped for almost a full minute!"

When Brian reported to his company, his positive outlook rubbed off on those around him. "Lieutenant Gienau had a great attitude, a great sense of humor. He listened to his platoon. When a private said, 'Let's try this…' they would work together to see why it did or did not work. Brian was a computer whiz, he was offbeat, and he listened. He did everything he asked his men to do. He was phenomenal. He could talk to anyone. He was a soldier's soldier, rather than a command soldier — something you don't always see in officers," observed platoon sergeant David Zulaica.

The National Guard Unit flew to Kuwait, and the Battalion moved north to the Forward Observation Base Duke, between Karbala and An Najaf, Iraq, on January 15, 2005. They were to integrate with the 11th Marine Expeditionary Unit, which had command and control of the area. First missions were performed in Karbala and An Najaf preparing for the elections.

One of Brian's first tasks in the transition with the Marines was to be in charge of a detention facility. These detainee facilities were in terrible condition and under excruciating observation, visited frequently by ranking officers. Brian took charge and improved conditions, exceeding everyone's expectations. When complimented, he answered with his favorite expression, "Sweet!"
Since the battalion's main mission in Iraq was route-clearance operations, they soon expanded from one clearance team to four . The traditional concepts of engineers included removing physical obstacles, finding and reducing minefields, constructing protective positions, and repairing bridges and roadways. In this conflict, they were also performing infantry activities, detonating improvised explosive devices (IEDs), tending prisoners, serving as scouts and forward observers, and performing other activities that demand adaptation to the military environment.

The area around Camp Duke was quiet compared to areas to the north. On February 27, the unit was to move to Camp Ramadi, further north in Al Anbar Province — a hotly-contested area at that time. Advance elements of the battalion were to head out, with other contingents to follow the next day. Brian was to lead the second mission and decided to accompany the first convoy so as to understand the terrain and route at ground level, which is sometimes difficult to comprehend from a map.

Leaving the compound, Brian was riding next to the Humvee driver in the last vehicle in the convoy. As they sped along the route at 50 m.p.h., the Humvee hit an IED, located directly under Brian. The vehicle left the road, flipped several times, and landed on its side.
Four of the passengers were seriously wounded, and Brian was killed instantly.

The last time Richard Gienau spoke to Brian, he reminded his son of some wise words that came from then nine-year-old Keenan before Brian left for Iraq. "I told him 'Remember what Keenan told us: 'we're all in each other's hearts.'"

— Norman Rudi
Author, U.S. Army veteran

MILLSAP
U.S.ARMY

1st Sgt. Timothy James Millsap
November 17, 1965 – April 25, 2005

Nine months after his first year-long deployment to Iraq, Tim Millsap was sent to the Middle East, again. Although it meant leaving behind his wife and daughter, he knew it also meant he would finally become a first sergeant. That was the reason he had remained in the Army.

Tim, a veteran of more than 20 years, was a born leader.

"When I started in the military, I was really young and inexperienced. Tim was older than me and much wiser," said Capt. Terry Alvarez, Tim's friend of six years. "He helped me with a lot of challenges, and he made a point of looking out for me. He didn't have to do all that. Even when I was in Kansas and he was in Iraq, he would always respond when I asked him for advice – he even called me once from over there to help me. I miss him most when I find myself in those situations."

Tim also knew how to make people laugh. One day his parents, Kenny and Rosie Millsap, were in a tiff and Rosie swatted her husband with a dishrag. Tim managed to lighten the mood by picking up one of Rosie's homemade biscuits and acting like he was clunking it on the counter. "He said 'If you wanted to hurt him, Mom, you should have hit him with one of these!'" laughed Rosie.

Now Kenny connects with his son when he mows his gravesite. "I water it and keep it dressed up, and I wear a button all the time with his picture on it. I just can't let go of him," he said.

– RP

A Born Leader

Kenny and Rosie Millsap live across the street from the school where their son Tim graduated (actually, he was "Timmy" back then). Kenny says at times he can still see him as the young, optimistic, energetic boy kicking a ball around on the soccer field. That soccer field now bears the name of Kenny's only son.

"I don't know if I could express the value for me to get up in the morning, walk out into my front yard and look down the street and know that field belongs to my son," Kenny said through tears and a smile.

Tim Millsap was supposed to own the Wichita South High School soccer field in a different way. After serving for more than 20 years in the Army, Tim was making plans to retire soon. He wanted to go back to his second love – his first being the military. He wanted to coach high school soccer and would have loved to do it at his alma mater. He never got to live out his retirement dream. Just a few months before he was to leave the Army, Tim Millsap was killed by a roadside bomb."That is the one thing that hurts the most," said Tim's mother. "The night those three guys came to my door. He was so close. He was so close." Tim had prepared his parents for what it meant when three military men came to your door. No words were necessary. Rosie says she will never forget the night or the feeling. "All I did was just scream. Kenny came running in the house. When he saw the three guys, he just hit the floor."

The Millsaps are now on a mission – a mission to make sure their son is never forgotten. That's why the soccer field means so much. That's why it meant the world to them when a local television station decided to honor Tim as the "hometown hero" during the city's Independence Day celebration. They want the world to know their son as they did ... a natural born leader. "From the time he was a toddler, you never saw him follow anyone," said Kenny. "Everyone was following him." Kenny says that's why his son joined the military. He knew he could lead.

Tim's mother knows there's a more noble reason he joined the Army. At age 19, while enrolled locally in college at Newman University, Tim enlisted without telling his parents. "I asked him, why did you join the Army? You have it made at home. You go to school. You don't work. We give you money. You don't do chores around the house. You've got it made!! And he looked at me and he said, 'Mom *that* is why I am doing it.'"

Tim just plain wanted to help other people, and he was successful at it. He quickly moved up the ranks of the Army until finally, at age 39, his dream of being a First Sergeant came true. Six months later, Tim died.

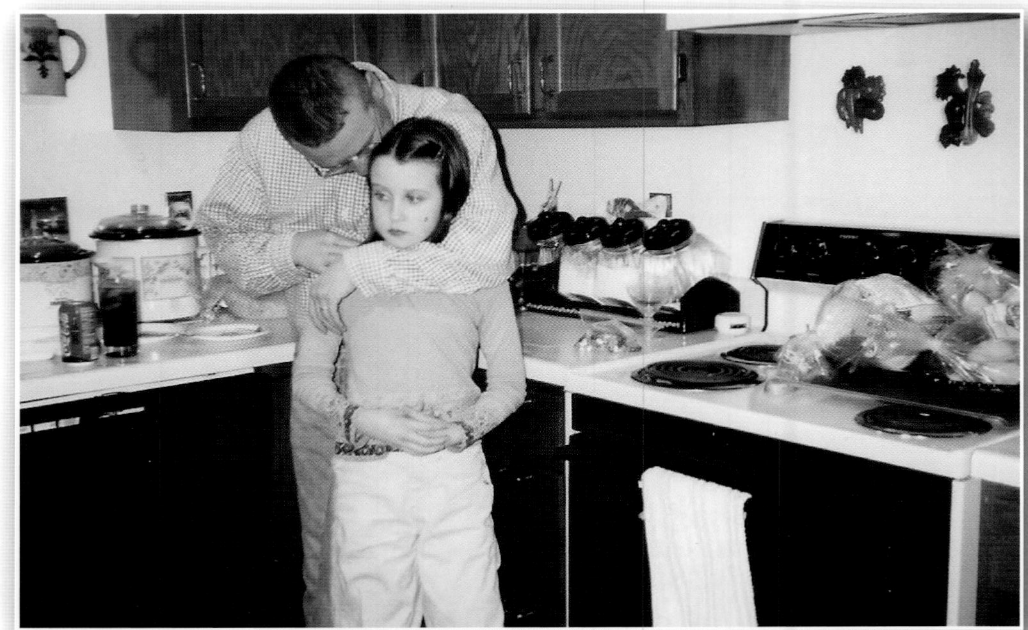

It was a simple thing that killed him. He was returning a tow bar to another company. He left the safe zone — "outside the wire," they call it. While there, he thought he would just go ahead and check on the troops. He was riding in a vehicle on a road outside Baghdad. That's when the bomb went off. It killed Tim instantly. The two soldiers with him survived.

Tim's wife, Alyne, knows that if someone had to die, Tim would have wanted it to be him. "Whenever there was a soldier he knew or worked with, especially ones he counseled to stay in the Army, he was devastated if they were hurt or injured," Alyne said. "I think he would have done it all again ... as long as those two other soldiers were okay."

Alyne and Tim had been married 20 years. They were high school sweethearts. Both sets of parents tried to talk them out of getting married at age 19, but Alyne would hear none of it.

"Everybody wanted to hang out with Tim because he was such a cool guy. I certainly did. I followed him all over the world."

She says Tim wasn't a "touchy-feely" kind of guy. "He was straight-up, what you saw is what you got. He was a stoic person and he didn't smile or grin in most of his pictures, but he had a great sense of humor," his wife said. "I always knew, when you could see those dimples, he was up to no good."

Tim's Army buddy, Terry Alvarez, will never forget the time he forgot his glasses at Tim and Alyne's house after being there for dinner. "I called Tim and asked him to bring them to work the next day and he told me 'No problem.' The next day he walks into the office where about 15 people were working and started screaming at me at the top of his lungs. 'Do you mind telling me what your glasses were doing on my wife's nightstand?!' I turned bright red and stuttered for a couple of minutes ... then he started laughing. I was the butt of most of his jokes," chuckled Terry.

Alyne enjoyed both the adventure of being married to Tim and the life of an Army wife. She never thought twice about a deployment, except this last time. "For whatever reason, I was way more emotional than I had been previously. It struck me as odd because I had never been clingy or emotional about these things." Now she knows why. Through her tears, Alyne said, "I come home and I want to get him on the phone. I mean, everything else is just kinda secondary to the day-to-day conversation."

This was to be Tim's last deployment. He told his parents that. He told his wife that. His only child was counting on it. When asked what she misses most about her dad, Tim's 15-year-old daughter, Deanna, can't get the words out. Her head immediately drops.

Minutes later, she begins to wipe away her tears. "I miss everything about him. I miss everything."

Deanna does have a favorite memory. Her father would take her on hunting weekends — just the two of them. "I loved doing that because it was just the two of us the entire time. It was funny because on our hunting trips we would talk about what we would do on the next hunting trip!" She laughs. "Just let people know we miss him. A lot."

Tim's sister fights back tears as she remembers a brother who always wanted to help somebody who was not quite as fortunate as he was. "That's one reason he would have loved the soccer coaching," Sherry Henry says. "Because he could mold someone, help someone establish their way."

Tim helped a lot of soldiers establish their way during his 20 years of duty. His father knew he would be that way from the day he was born. "I saw it in the wee hours of the morning on November 17, 1965 when the doctor came down the hall carrying this little bundle of boy screaming at the top of his lungs," said Kenny Millsap. "I knew then, he wanted to go out and start leading."

— Susan Peters
News anchor for KAKE-TV in Wichita, KS

Lance Cpl. DeShon Otey
March 25, 1980 — June 21, 2004

Marine Lance Cpl. DeShon Otey — 2nd Battalion, 4th Marines — and his sniper comrades were highly successful in Iraq. In fact, their exceptional accuracy led to the enemy placing a bounty on their heads while they were serving in Fallujah.

DeShon, a highly trained marksman, lived for the Marines. He was the consummate professional. "He had a good head on his shoulders, and he always did the right thing," said DeShon's younger brother, Marine Lance Cpl. Ronald Otey, 22.

DeShon was like a father figure to Ronald and their younger brother, Dominic. "Basically, he was there for us all the time. We looked up to him, and he led the path for us. He was a good role model — he stayed out of trouble, and he taught us right from wrong," said Ronald, who remembers DeShon's affectionate nicknames for the boys. "He called me 'Squabitt' because I sort of had buck teeth, and he called Dominic 'Mud-Duck' from a movie he saw. It was all in good fun."

Ronald says DeShon always put his family first, often calling home from Iraq to check on them. He misses having his big brother to turn to for advice. Their mother, Robin Mays, remembers their last phone conversation: it ended with them both saying "I love you."

DeShon and three other Marine snipers were gunned down in Ramadi. They were found dead in a walled compound, stripped of their body armor. The military still does not know the exact circumstances surrounding their deaths. DeShon was 24 years old.

— *RP*

Big Shoes to Fill

On April 6, 2004, Marine Lance Cpl. DeShon Otey was the sole survivor of his green Humvee when he was among those ambushed in Ramadi in the Al Anbar Province west of Baghdad. The Iraqis began firing with machine guns, and DeShon jumped out of the vehicle to fire back from behind a low wall.

"He could see the bullets dancing around him. One went through his pant leg, but it didn't hit him," DeShon's mother, Robin Mays, says. "They threw a hand grenade at him, and it landed at his feet but didn't go off."

He called his mother to tell her he was okay, and people walked up to him repeatedly during their conversation, congratulating him for a job well done. One of the writers of the film, "We Were Soldiers," flew in to meet DeShon and told him some of his story might become part of a movie. This helped to cheer him when he was faced with the seven empty bunks of his buddies, many of whom had become trusted confidantes.

DeShon had wanted to be a Marine for about as long as he could remember. While in high school, his tests for the U.S. Marine Corps and the U.S. Air Force were outstanding; and before long, he was chosen to be a sniper. DeShon aspired to be a sniper and always wanted to be in the middle of it, never cowering in the face of danger. Eventually, he was promoted to lance corporal of 2nd Battalion, 4th Marine Regiment. He was never formally pinned, however, because he was too busy fighting in Iraq. His battalion was known as "The Magnificent Bastards" and suffered some of the greatest losses in the Iraq War.

DeShon joined the Marines just a few days after his graduation from North Hardin High School in Radcliff, KY. As you might expect of a Marine, he was involved in sports that required strength. An avid amateur boxer with bouts in nearby Louisville, he was also a lineman for the North Hardin High School football team. "[He was] the one who knocked them down," his mother says, chuckling at the memory. As a teenager, DeShon helped an Elizabethtown funeral director prepare bodies for funerals because he simply wasn't afraid of death.

After meeting an FBI agent on an airplane, DeShon hoped to become an agent himself someday. He also had a creative side. He was a talented poet/rap artist who had been asked to join a well-known rapper's group in Los Angeles. But DeShon had already committed to the military.
He participated in jungle operations and survival training in Guam, where he was left in the wilderness for two weeks. The Marines had to eat crabs, snakes and snails. "The snails were the nastiest," he told his mother. She says his group performed best in the survival course, which led to their deployment to Iraq.

On Monday, June 21, 2004, Robin went to work as usual and remembers that she was wearing a brown sundress. Late in the day, she felt sudden shooting pains through her torso. "It felt like it was going to kill me," she says. She tried to call her other son, Ronald, who had just gotten married and was stationed at Camp Pendleton, preparing for deployment. "Come back home" was her message. When the Marines came to her door that evening, one of the papers they gave her said that 24-year-old DeShon had been shot multiple times in the torso.

Only minutes after learning of her son's death, Robin turned on the television set to see film of his body on a rooftop. "That's my son right there!" she shouted. It was only then that she realized what the Marines in their dress blue uniforms had told her was true. DeShon and three other elite snipers had been in Ramadi once again, this time operating without backup anywhere nearby. They were found shot to death — their body armor taken from their bodies. No one knows exactly what happened. Less than three months after the incredible luck DeShon had experienced on April 6, his buddies were faced with the sight of *his* empty bunk.

"I fell on the floor, and I felt like I wanted to die," Robin says. "But I knew I had two other kids. I had to get Ronald home." After DeShon's death, Ronald was reassigned to Camp Lejeune in North Carolina where he remains stationed today.

At first, it was beyond fathoming that DeShon could be gone. Robin had just spoken to him the morning before. "I talked to him about three o'clock our time Sunday morning. He was outside. I said, 'Isn't it dangerous?' He said, 'No, I'm okay,' but he didn't want to get off the phone."

Eventually, he said, "I think I'm going to die. I think it's my time. I don't want to die." But when his mother questioned him about why he felt he was going to die, he quickly changed his tune in order to keep her calm. "Don't worry about me," he told her. "I'll be safe. I always am. I'm going to call you tomorrow." Their last words to one another were "I love you."

While you never get over the loss of a child, Robin says she is comforted by the fact that her son died a hero. "I go and put flowers on his grave. He's buried at Cave Hill Cemetery in Louisville next to a World War II veteran and Korean War veteran and 10 graves from my mother," she says.

If you ask DeShon's friends to describe him, you'll hear words like "friend," "brother," "teacher" and "natural-born leader."

DeShon's memory lives on in his namesake — the son of his brother, Ronald, who was born on July 3, 2005, one year to the day that DeShon was buried. Someday, little DeShon will learn all about the big shoes he's filling.

— Melanie Votaw
Author, journalist
RuletheWord.com

"You may never know what results come from your action. But if you do nothing, there will be no result."

— Gandhi

Staff Sgt. William Francis "Bill" Manuel
February 27, 1970 — January 10, 2005

Army National Guard Staff Sgt. Bill Manuel was the fourth of five children. Damian, Anthony, Tammy, Bill, and little Kermit were a close-knit bunch. Bill was the quiet one.

"He always kept to himself. He didn't brag or boast about anything he accomplished," said Bill's mother, Shirley Manuel. After he died, Bill's family discovered medals and awards they never knew he had.

Kermit Manuel, Sr. says, although shy, Bill was a bit of a wild child, getting into some trouble as a teen. But he says the National Guard helped Bill grow. "He just loved the Guard, and he loved those Bradleys [tanks]," said Kermit. Bill matured and he took on more responsibility, earning his own money for college through the Guard and other jobs.

"During one of our long talks, I just realized, 'Wow, he has certainly grown up to be quite a man,'" said Shirley. She treasures memories of Saturday afternoon visits with her son.

Bill was a devout Catholic. Although he couldn't always make Sunday service, he would stop by the church to pray during the week. Kermit recalled through tears the last time he saw his son. "I said, 'Here, you take my rosary and I'm going to take yours and you be sure to bring me back mine.' I told him that I was proud of him and that I loved him and that I'd be thinking of him every second of every day. Then we grabbed each other and hugged."

Shirley is now holding tight to an old key she found in Bill's briefcase as a reminder or her son's unwavering faith. "It's a key to heaven. The verse I found along with it reads 'What does it profit a man to gain the whole world and lose his own soul?'"

— RP

Brotherly Love

Cajun cooking is a staple in Shirley Manuel's household. For years, her five grown children — Damian, Anthony, Tammy, Bill and Kermit — have flocked home to fill their bowls and bellies with Louisiana favorites like shrimp and okra gumbo. Bill liked his overflowing with seafood and always used his favorite big white bowl to ensure heaping amounts. On this day, the menu is red beans and rice, but Bill is here only in spirit and in the many pictures spread across the table.

One snapshot shows him with family, "smiling loudly," as they say in these parts, at a picnic around Mother's Day 2004. That was the going-away barbecue for Bill and other National Guard soldiers. There were also images of Bill overseas, smiling and laughing with children on sandy desert roads. The children are holding an American flag.

Then there's another, more somber image, taken less than a year later in Baton Rouge: Bill's coffin, draped with the flag.

On Jan. 10, 2005, Louisiana National Guard Staff Sgt. William Manual, 34, was killed in Iraq with a fellow guardsman when a roadside bomb blew up the Bradley Fighting Vehicle he commanded.

Bill grew up in the small town of Oberlin, planted smack in the middle of the "heel" of Louisiana. It's where he played high school football and track, and where he came to love Zydeco music. A favorite song, by friend Keith Frank, was a Zydeco remake of the theme music to the 70s sitcom "The Jeffersons" — a song called "Movin' on Up."

In a town where fewer than 10 percent of adults over 25 have any college degree at all, Bill moved himself on up to McNeese State University, earning two bachelors degrees, in criminal justice and social science. He took a job at Coushatta Indian Casino in Kinder, LA, just south of Oberlin. That allowed Bill to stay near family and continue to enjoy this "sportsman's paradise," where he hunted squirrel and fished for bass.

Bill quickly climbed through the ranks to casino management. And one weekend a month, he performed his duty to his country in the National Guard.

In the early 1990s, Bill became one of the first Louisiana National Guard soldiers trained on a Bradley at Fort Polk and came to train many others — including Louisiana National Guard Gen. Bennett Landrineau and Brig. Gen. John Basilica, Jr.

Bill's family says the National Guard helped mold him. When he first joined the Guard, briefly overlapping the service of older brother Anthony, he didn't always seem to take things seriously. Anthony, now 39, recalled one weekend when it was time to show up for duty. The soldiers were lining up, but Bill was missing. A short time later, he saw Bill running, uniform out of place and boots untied, to make it in time for duty. "They had military time and Bill's time," said Anthony. "He was always out of uniform, he was always late."

That lackadaisical attitude changed as it became clear the unit would be activated. The entire family noticed the transformation. He made it his role to be sure the younger men were OK, and he served as a sounding board for their fears, said his mother. "He really took care of those boys."

In the spring of 1998, Bill became a husband and step-father when he married Nicole Willis from the nearby town of Oakdale, LA, and took in her son, Ricky, 12, as his own. The wedding was at Kermit Sr.'s house. "They laughed the whole time," he said. "The justice of the peace had to quit the wedding and say, 'Stop laughing. It's getting hot. We gotta finish this.'"

In 2004, Bill prepared for deployment at Fort Hood and at the National Training Center in California. Anthony recalled one emotional day when, driving down some country roads, Bill began playing a Keith Whitley and Earl Thomas Conley song called "Brotherly Love."

There's a bond that brothers know,
And it gets stronger as they grow,
A love that time and miles can't come between.
We disagreed, but in the end,
There will never be two closer friends,
And Brotherly Love is something we all need.

There were lighter moments, too. Before his deployment, his father said, Bill went on a fishing trip and caught an 80-pound blue catfish. "We took a picture. It reaches from the ground up to our shoulders. You ought to see the grin on his face."

During final good-byes at England Industrial Airpark — Alexandria (LA) International Airport, formerly England Air Force Base — Shirley hugged her adult son close. "I told him, 'I love you,' and all I heard was a choking sound," she said, holding back tears. "He hugged me real tight."

With Bill in Iraq, the family kept in touch daily by Web-cam and Instant Messaging. "I couldn't live without the phone or computer," said Kermit Sr. Bill told his family he saw the good he was doing in the eyes of grateful Iraqi children and their parents. But there was much about his work Bill had to keep to himself. As a Bradley commander, Bill had a dangerous job. "Their mission was basically clearing improvised explosive devices [IEDs]," explains Bill's younger brother, Kermit, 35. Extremely hard to detect, such roadside bombs have been called the single greatest casualty-producer in Iraq. After six other Louisiana National Guardsmen died in a single bomb blast, family members' concerns intensified. Bill knew the situation was getting bad, said Anthony. "That week before he got killed, I really started worrying," said Bill's father. "On Sunday at nine o'clock, I got to see him [via the Internet]. He looked tired. Then he had to go back out on patrol. We said our good-byes. That Monday, he was killed."

Word of Bill's death came first from other Southwest Louisiana soldiers, many of them younger ones he'd befriended and taken under his wing and spread rapidly through the small town. "You got cell phones, computer, Internet, so everybody was finding out already," said brother Kermit. The brothers went to be with their mother before casualty police showed up to confirm the news.

When the family went to pick up Bill's body from Baton Rouge later that month, recalled Shirley, the roads in the small towns the family rode through were lined with veterans and others. "I don't know how they knew," she says, still in wonderment. "People were out there saluting. It was amazing." "And when we got to Kinder, everybody was kneeling down and praying — all of Allen Parish, all of Lake Charles," adds Anthony.

"Every town we went through — highway 1-90, all the way down to the curb, from city hall to Ardoin's funeral home — people were kneeling down with candles lit when we came through," said Kermit Sr. "It was probably nine or ten o'clock that night when we got home from Baton Rouge. And it was cold, and they were kneeling in rocks and on the sidewalk to show their love and respect for Bill."

Bill's funeral was a packed house of family, friends, coworkers, soldiers and even more veterans on hand to give their strength to the Manuels. "After he died, I found out Bill had friends I never knew he had," said Shirley.

Mourners included shift workers from the casino. "Each one of them almost had the same story," said Anthony. "They said, 'You know? He was the only manager who ever said, 'Thank you.'"

Later that night, members of the Honor Guard stayed by the brothers' side. They told them, "We just want you to know what a privilege it is to stay with you and honor Bill." They passed the time telling stories about Bill, and listening to his favorite music, Zydeco.

— Laila Morcos
News anchor for KPLC-TV in Lake Charles/Lafayette, LA
and WWL 870 AM in New Orleans, LA

Spc. Thomas John Dostie
February 25, 1984 — December 21, 2004

Tommy Dostie didn't know a stranger
.
"He had a way of just making friends easily. He'd sit down with you and he'd start talking with you and, before you knew it, you'd be talking uncontrollably," explained his older brother, Timothy Dostie. "It was just his personality. He absolutely brought out the best in people."

Perhaps people relaxed around Tommy because he never seemed to judge anyone. "He took people as they were — good, bad or indifferent," said Timothy.

The brothers grew up in a small, rural community in Maine. Tommy loved the outdoors, and he especially loved the winter weather. In fact, Timothy is still in awe of Tommy's tolerance for the cold. "Twenty degree weather was comfortable for him — that was basically flannel shirt weather for him. He did not like the heat whatsoever!"

Tommy was also a bit of a daredevil who liked to push things to the limit, including his brother's patience. "He had the ability to make you laugh so hard you were ready to cry, or make you so mad you were ready to just go after him," laughed Timothy.

— RP

"He Was a Soldier"

Towns don't come much smaller than Somerville, Maine. This is a place with no stop lights, no stores and fewer than 500 residents. This is a place where long stretches of road are lined with little more than trees and oncoming cars are few. This is the place that produced Maine Army National Guard Sgt. Thomas J. Dostie, a young man who died while serving in Iraq.

Tommy grew up in a two-story, shingled house set amongst piney Maine woods, with a unpaved road running by its front and a gloriously blue lake named Long Pond out back. It was an environment most any kid would likely love and it particularly suited Thomas, his family says. It was, and is, a quiet place to grow up — at least until he went roaring by.

In the winter, when the central Maine snow can pile many feet deep, Tommy, as he was usually called, would roar around Somerville on his snowmobile, zipping through the woods or zooming over the hard, frozen lake. When the long winter gave way to spring, and when the lake's water went from white to blue, Tommy would simply change his mode of transportation. "He loved to go out in his boat," says Michael Dostie, Tommy's father. "The first chance he got, as soon as the ice was out, he'd be going up and down this lake."

See, almost from the beginning, Tommy was interested in the mechanics of motors. He took his first engine apart when he was 5, and the thrill never faded. And the faster he could make the engine, the better. "Everything he had, flies," said his father. "We built a snowmobile together. You should see that thing go."

Tommy's engines may have been loud, but he was not. He was mostly as quiet and unassuming as the town in which he was raised. He wasn't flashy. He didn't brag. At 112 pounds, competing as a lightweight, his high school wrestling coach said he remembers him as a modest and respectful athlete who followed instructions, practiced hard and didn't say a whole lot.

Tommy's family is well-known in central Maine, because concern for others comes naturally to the Dosties. Michael Dostie, a warm and friendly man, is the Somerville code enforcement officer and the chief of the volunteer fire department. Margaret Dostie, Tommy's mother, takes in foster children, volunteers to raise money for area schools and helped organize the region's chapter of Heart to Heart, a support group for the families of deployed servicemen and women.

For that reason, it didn't surprise many people when Tommy decided to serve too, when he joined the Somerville Fire Department at the age of 16 or decided to join the Maine Army National Guard while still in high school, completing basic training in the summer between his junior and senior years. His motive for joining the military, however, wasn't purely selfless; he joined because he wanted to learn. "He liked the idea of school being paid for," Michael Dostie said. "He wanted to be a diesel mechanic."

Tommy was just 19 when he learned he'd be going to war, and his unit, the 133rd Engineering Battalion departed for Iraq on Feb. 25, 2004, on his 20th birthday. The 133rd was charged with rebuilding the war-torn nation's infrastructure, with giving Iraq the simple things most nations take for granted: running water and passable roads.

Tommy served as an engine mechanic. And though his mother says he hated Iraq and couldn't wait to return home, by all accounts his character remained the same. He was a quiet and calm soldier, a young man who rarely complained and a steady friend who loved to joke — traits that made him well-liked in central Maine, but became even more valuable among the stresses and horrors of war.

"He was a soldier," says Ron Cyr, a family friend, "but more than anything he was just another guy trying to do something good in this world."

Ten months after Tommy arrived in Iraq, two months shy of his 21st birthday, a suicide bomber blew up a dining tent at a base camp in Mosul. The tent was filled with hundreds of American and Iraqi soldiers and civilian workers having lunch, and Thomas Dostie was one of 22 people who died that day.

His death rocked Somerville, where many people considered Tommy a friend. His death brought public grief, including an impromptu candlelight vigil. Eighty people stood in eerie silence outside the Somerville Fire Station, including many in quiet prayer.

The Dostie family asked those wanting to show support to forgo flowers and cards and instead send donations to the fire department. In a part of the nation with more than its share of poverty, the response swamped the department. When the checks were counted, the department had $14,000 in hand. The money funded a 680-square-foot addition to the station, giving the department new comforts: running water, a kitchen and a bathroom.

On an inside wall, there's something else: a plaque commemorating Thomas Dostie's sacrifice and noting that his firefighting number — Somerville 8 — has been retired from service.

Everyone knew Tommy would return to Somerville when his time in Iraq ended. In fact, he planned to build a cabin across the dirt road from his parents' place. It's likely that his children, too, would have grown up riding snowmobiles through the piney Maine woods, and they, too, would have had Long Pond as their playground.

"The plans of his cabin, that's what we put on his headstone," Michael Dostie says. "It was a project we were going to do together."

— Chris Churchill
Staff writer for the Times Union in Albany, NY

C
CROSS AMERICA
FREDERICK
U.S. ARMY
ans @ Quick As A Wink Printing-Lima, Ohio

Sgt. Kendell Kioma Frederick
August 17, 1984 — October 19, 2005

Army Reservist Kendell Frederick — born in Trinidad — died trying to become an American. He was killed by a roadside bomb after completing one of many steps in the naturalization process at an immigration office set up in Iraq. His 16-year-old sister, Kennisha, says Kendell always looked out for all three of his younger siblings. "One time he was going to fight a boy who was messing with me in school. He was really protective, like a best friend," smiled Kennisha. She went on to describe a young man who helped her with math homework, always called or sent a card on her birthday and never failed to Instant Message from Iraq. "He'd ask me how I was doing, if I was keeping out of trouble, and if I was doing good in school."

Kennisha also remembers Kendell as truly joyful. "He was always laughing and smiling and joking," she said. On the website *fallenheroesmemorial.com*, it is clear that Kendell's laughter touched the hearts of many. "He always had a joke or some funny dance to make you laugh," wrote one soldier. "I will never forget his great, big smile and his laughter that he brought to everyone. He was a joy and I will never forget him," said another.

A staff sergeant from North Carolina wrote a note directly to Kendell telling him it was an honor to have served with him in Iraq: "Your humble ways, love of life, family and the U.S. made you an even better soldier than most in my eyes."

— *RP*

The soldier who died trying to become an American

Like so many scheduled interviews in my work as a journalist, I was originally slated to chat with Mrs. Michelle Murphy – mother of a soldier killed in Iraq – on what was otherwise, to me, an insignificant day in early July 2006.

Because this business is so out-of-the-door-on-a-moments-notice unpredictable, I thought nothing of phoning Michelle and rescheduling when faced with a breaking story and a stressed editor.

So I phoned with my proposed *new* date, July 19, for the interview.

Michelle graciously agreed. And as far as I knew then, it was just another day with a couple of open hours in the morning when we could talk about her son: the boy she so-longed to hold, the remarkable man he had become, and the insurgent bomb blast that killed him.

But as Michelle would tell me near the close of that interview on July 19, it was nine months to the day after the death of her son, 21-year-old U.S. Army Reserve Specialist Kendell K. Frederick.

"Nine months," I thought. The period of time – give or take a few days or a couple of weeks – Michelle had carried the gift of Kendell inside her body. Now it had been exactly nine months that she had carried the indescribable ache of his loss within her soul.

But we talked, and I learned much about the man who had shared so much love with his family – including a father, stepfather, two sisters, a little brother, a broad extended family – and many friends; given so much to his "chosen" country; and continues to give to scores of immigrants who have yet to earn their American citizenship, though they volunteer to shoulder a rifle or *man* a battle-station in America's defense.

Kendell was one such soldier.

An Army mechanic who worked on power generators, Kendell was driving down a highway in Tikrit, the provincial capital of Salah ad Din, north of Baghdad, when a roadside bomb was detonated and he was killed.

But what makes his death so poignant is that the young soldier was on a mission, not to hunt down the hidden insurgents who snatched his life away, but to achieve what the rest of us so-often take for granted. Kendell was trying to become an American.

A native of Trinidad, he was on the road returning from a visit to a U.S. Immigration branch office in Iraq, where he had been fingerprinted for his citizenship application documents. It was October 19, 2005 – just two weeks after having seen his family in Randallstown, Maryland for the last time.

The day he died, Michelle says she experienced what she believes to this day might have been a terrible omen."My husband and I were going out to dinner that evening when a car suddenly pulled out in front of us," Michelle recalls. "The car's license tag was 817, Kendell's birthday. We drove another block and I saw another tag with the same numbers reversed. I remember commenting to my husband about it. That was unnerving to me."

The next morning, two Army officers were at her doorstep.

"I knew something was wrong," she says. "But I didn't think he was dead until they asked me to sit down. Then I knew [Michelle begins crying]. I think I just started screaming."

As a boy, Kendell lived with his grandparents in Trinidad. Michelle had come to America for work. When Kendell was 15 his grandfather passed away, and Kendell too left for America.

Kendell was a unique right-brain-left-brain child with both a strong artistic and technical bent. "He was quite a talented artist," says Michelle. "He loved to draw cartoon characters, flowers, really anything." He also loved rap music. "He and his friends called it making beats," says Michelle, who fondly remembers Kendell "making beats" on his own electronic keyboard. Though art and music were his passions, Kendell wanted to be a soldier. He became involved in Randallstown High School's JROTC (Junior Reserve Officer Training Corps) program. "His room was always a mess," Michelle says, laughing. "But his ROTC uniform was *always* clean and pressed. He took such pride in that."

When he was 17, Kendell joined the Army Reserve: Because of his young age, Michelle had to sign the enlistment papers for him. He turned 18 while still in basic training, and it was after the terrorist attacks of September 11, 2001.

"I was scared to death," Michelle recalls. "I said, 'Do you understand what this means? That this is war?' But he seemed to have no fear. He saw military service as something of an adventure."

Once deployed to Iraq, Kendell was constantly talking with his family through email and instant-messaging. At one point, he phoned, almost "hysterical" Michelle would say in an interview for the *Trinidad & Tobago Express*. "Kendell called me and he couldn't stop crying. He had killed someone for the first time and he just couldn't handle it," she said. He loved being a soldier, but he hated war.

Kendell planned to come home for the holidays. He wanted to buy a car, and he had post-Army dreams of beginning a career in business, perhaps even getting his real estate license.

Kendell was also a spiritual soul. Among his personal possessions was his Bible, which he always kept on him. He also prayed, often, and his family prayed with – and for – him.

Kendell's two younger sisters, Kennisha, 15, and Kendra, 11 were naturally devastated upon learning of the loss of their big brother. Kendell's little brother, Kwesi, was only three-years-old at the time. Today, only four, he still has a difficult time accepting that Kendell will never return home.

"Kendell and Kwesi adored one another," Michelle says. "They were almost inseparable when Kendell was home on leave. On those rare times that Kendell did venture off without his brother, little Kwesi would stand at the door and cry."

Today Kwesi asks alternately, "When is Kendell coming home?" and "Why is he not?" Michelle explains to him, Kendell's in Heaven.

"He's with the angels now, and in that way, he'll always be with us."

Like all parents of children killed in war, Michelle has been asked by outsiders how she can go on after such a loss.

"I don't question God," she says. "Yes, I love my son, and would do anything to have him back. But I do believe that everything happens for a reason. And perhaps my son was killed for the other 40,000 immigrants who are serving in the military right now. That – among other things – might have been his purpose. That's something I hold on to, and in that I am blessed."The "purpose" Michelle speaks of is a bill, which – as of this writing – is before Congress.

The Kendell Frederick Citizenship Assistance Act was introduced in the House on December 14, 2005 – less than two months after Kendell was killed – and would in summary "assist members of the Armed Forces in obtaining United States citizenship, and for other purposes," including waiving fingerprinting requirements for members of the U.S. armed forces not yet American citizens.

His body interred at Arlington National Cemetery, Kendell Frederick was posthumously promoted to sergeant and awarded his life's dream: He is officially now – and will forever be – an American.

— W. Thomas Smith, Jr.
Author, national columnist, former U.S. Marine
uswriter.com

Sgt. 1st Class Daniel Henry Petithory
June 30, 1969 — December 5, 2001

Dan Petithory grew up in Cheshire, MA with big brother Michael and little sister Nicole. His parents, Barbara and Lou, affectionately acknowledge Dan's trouble-making tendencies, admitting they had been called by teachers on more than one occasion; but that's only a glimpse of Dan. He was also one of the most sensitive people you'd ever meet.

"When I was upset, Danny was the type of kid who would walk in and say 'What's wrong, mom?' even before seeing my face," said Barbara.

All through high school, Dan made a point of sitting on the bus with a fellow student who was frail and an easy target for bullies. Dan was protecting him.

As a teenager, Dan got a kick out of dressing as a ninja and climbing on rooftops for Halloween and scaring his mom by doing aerial back flips in front of her. He also loved paintball.

Dan was a natural leader without soliciting a following. Kids in his neighborhood always wanted to wear what Dan was wearing, do what Dan was doing. It never went to his head.

Dan focused on becoming a soldier, learning Farsi and training hard to master the skills of a warrior. During his 14 years of service, he participated in many military exercises and operations in places like Kuwait, Haiti, the African continent and across Southwest Asia.

His brother Michael told a reporter shortly after Dan's death that Dan was "born to be an Army man." Dan's sister Nicole added, "He died doing a job he loved, for the country he loved."

— *RP*

The Morale Builder

On Sept. 11, 2001, Dan Petithory learned of the attacks on the World Trade Center and the Pentagon while on a mission in Central Asia. The Special Forces soldier was part of a team helping to train the Kazakhstan army. He was a communications sergeant working out of the embassy in Almaty.

Dan was the one to break the news to his team.

"He was almost crying," explained former CW3 Lloyd Allard. "We had a little television we could get some BBC on…the picture was grainy but we saw the second plane hit, live."

Dan was seething. "He wanted revenge," recalled Lloyd. The group was able to complete its task in Kazakhstan, then return to the U.S. to prepare for the new missions they knew were inevitable.

Shortly after returning to the states, Dan deployed to Afghanistan to help fight the war on terror. Near Kandahar, an aberrant U.S. bomb claimed his life. He and two other Special Forces soldiers — "Green Berets" — were killed in the friendly fire incident. Sgt. 1st Class Petithory was 32-years-old.

Dan had wanted to go into the military for as long as his family can remember. "I carried all the latest G.I. Joes around in my pocket book when he was a kid," said his mother, Barbara Petithory. "As a matter of fact, to this day I have one of his G.I. Joe guns in my wallet," she laughed.

Dan played football growing up, but he was more interested in honing his ninja skills than playing team sports. "He'd be in the tallest pine tree and nobody could ever find him," Barbara reminisced, speaking of her son's games with his siblings and the neighbor kids. The Petithory's place was always a popular hangout — in large part because Dan was just a fun person to be around.

One of his regular antics in high school was to hang a deflated basketball on the outstretched hand of a President McKinley statue in a rival school's town following big games. He never got "busted." Dan would no doubt have been touched to know some of his old buddies duplicated the prank in his memory after he died.

Dan's Special Forces friends were also regularly treated to his carefree sense of humor. "He had [plastic] hillbilly teeth, and he would put those in and have a perfectly normal conversation with you," chuckled CW2 Tim Wojciehowski, who roomed with Dan for two years. "He'd even wear them going out, and he'd start talking to beautiful girls at the bars and he never cracked a smile. He would have done that to the top group commander."

Dan, Tim and a third roommate, also a Green Beret, were known for hosting parties that guests probably still talk about to this day. On one particular occasion, the guys decided to throw a luau. Dan greeted party-goers in a coconut bra and grass skirt. "It was a hilarious time — what a great bash that was," Tim laughed.

One of the best parts about Dan was his ability to make fun of himself. "Every time we did PT he was always the slowest runner," said Tim. "We knew he was sucking and he knew he was sucking, so he'd make his arm go limp like he'd been wounded and he'd start humming this really corny 1960's Captain Kirk fight music. We were supposed to be studly men…Green Berets…but he didn't take himself that seriously."

What he did take very seriously was his job as a communications sergeant. Dan's comrades always knew they could count on him. "He was renowned as the best communications sergeant in the company," said Tim.

"I could practically hand him a straw and a couple of paper clips and he could probably make a telephone call. He could figure out anything, and he was always fixing things for us."

And friends say he never rested until a job was done.

Dan's father has heard many tales of his son's unrelenting spirit, but one stands out in his mind. Several years before 9/11, Dan was among a group of Green Berets who parachuted into Pakistan's Indus River Valley out of a C-130, each of them carrying 120-lb. packs. "Danny's first team captain — Capt. John Fenzel [now a lieutenant colonel] — said they were trudging up a mountain in two columns when he heard a distinct cracking sound," said Dan's father, Lou.

Dan had apparently fallen down a ravine carrying a heavy load of radio equipment.

"His knee was badly hurt and they wanted to evacuate him, but Capt. Fenzel said Dan just told him 'Sir, you've gotta play hurt,' and he continued on." Lou added proudly, "He told that story in a speech defining what a hero is."

At 6'4", Dan could be an intimidating figure. There was no arguing he was tough. But it never took long for people to realize he was also soft. "He was one of the nicest people and gentlest men," said Lloyd Allard. "And still he was a Special Forces soldier and a consummate professional."

In Afghanistan, Dan worked closely with Hamid Karzai, who later became prime minister. Dan was part of the effort to train Karzai's soldiers. "He fought alongside them and befriended them," said Lt. Col. Fenzel. "Dan was truly a soldier-diplomat — an ambassador for everything that we stand for."

Dan would have done anything for a fellow soldier.

During his last visit home, his loved ones learned that his loyalty wasn't limited to his comrades on the battlefield. "He wanted to show his girlfriend all the landmarks and the history around Boston," said Barbara Petithory. "As they were coming out of a restaurant, Danny spotted a homeless man in fatigues; so he went and spoke to him for about an hour and a half." Dan, who learned the man was a veteran, opened his wallet and handed over every penny he had. That generous gift meant Dan had to cut short the trip. He returned home — out of money — without giving it a second thought. (It is a fitting tribute that all proceeds from an annual motorcycle ride in his honor go to help local homeless veterans.)

"Dan was the type of person who would give everything to you," said Tim Wojciehowski. No matter what the act of kindness, Dan never asked for anything in return. "He had a huge heart. If he knew you — his house was your house. He was that type of person. He would go way out of his way to make you feel welcome." Tim was so moved by his friendship with Dan that he named his son after him.

"You never saw him without a smile," said Lloyd, remembering his brother-in-arms and the team morale-builder. "He was one of the most fun people I'd ever been around — he found humor in everything. In our job you have to push yourself physically and mentally and he found joy in it all. It's a blessing to have had him in my life."

— Rebecca Pepin
Editorial director for Faces of Freedom
Author, news anchor for WEMT-TV in Bristol, VA/TN
rebeccapepin.com

ARMY

BUTLER
U.S. ARMY

Spc. Adrian Josiah Butler
January 31, 1977 — July 27, 2005

Adrian Butler had big plans.

He wanted to be a special agent with the FBI and he was getting ready to marry the love of his life. But on July 27, 2005, the 28-year-old Detroit native and another soldier died when a bomb detonated near their Humvee. The military policeman was out on patrol in Ashraf, Iraq, on his second tour of duty when it happened. Adrian was a quiet man, but his fellow soldiers say there was something strong in his silence.

"He kept to himself until you got to know him," said Sgt. Joseph Locurto, who served with Adrian during his first stint in Iraq. "I know this sounds weird, but he had an aura around him," Joseph said. "If you were in a bad mood, he would somehow make you forget the sadness and the hurt."

After knowing each other for only a month, Joseph asked Adrian to be his new daughter's godfather.

"He said, 'Yes' right off the bat," remembered Joseph.

The two were raised in different states and came from very different backgrounds, but they always felt they were more like brothers than friends or co-workers. Adrian took his role of godfather very seriously. "He always sent all my kids cards and presents on birthdays and holidays," said the father of three.

Joseph and Wendy Locurto are expecting a fourth child. They plan to name him Aiden Josiah — after Adrian. "He's the only person I've ever really considered a true friend," said Joseph. "He will always be my guardian angel."

— RP

To Serve and Protect

Huddled in a Detroit hospital during one of the city's merciless winters roughly three decades ago, Peggy Donaldson and Eldridge Lee Butler discussed what to name their newborn son. They settled on Adrian as his first name in honor of a paternal uncle, but for his middle name, they turned to the Bible, as they had for their other child, Eldridge Messiah. What at the time may have seemed random would later prove prophetic.

They chose Josiah, the Old Testament king who suffered a fatal wound fighting a war in the Middle East.

Twenty-eight years later on July 27, 2005, SPC Adrian Josiah Butler was killed by a roadside bomb in Iraq, roughly a thousand kilometers away from where his namesake battled the Egyptian army.

Raised on real-life crime dramas and spy movies that his mother often watched on TV when he was young, Adrian decided early on that he wanted to join the FBI. To enhance his resume, he majored in criminal justice at Michigan State University and enlisted in the U.S. Army in February 2000. He was assigned to the 411th Military Police Company, 720th MP Battalion, 89th MP Brigade, from Fort Hood, Texas.

"It was something he wanted to do," his mother said. "He wanted to improve his life. He wanted to improve his career opportunities by going through the service. I can't have any anger toward that. I have to accept his choice."

She realized something was amiss during an odd and ominous call from two military officers, checking to make sure she'd be at home when they visited. Despite the tacit recognition that injury and death loom constantly for the men and women in the military, Peggy was stunned.

The son she'd seen six months ago, the handsome young man she last spoke to five days earlier, was gone. Exacerbating the horrific grief that shrouds a mourning mother's heart was Peggy's memory of that phone call.

"I love you, Mom."

"I love you, son."

"Everything's alright. I'm safe, the normal stuff. How's everyone?"

"He never did say what was going on," Peggy continued. "He didn't talk to me about to it to keep me from being upset. I never thought it would come to this. There wasn't a war when he was sent over."

Once cluttered with mementoes of his favorite pastimes — shooting hoops, playing pool and video games, swimming, bowling and tooling around in his silver 2001 Mustang — Adrian's bedroom has morphed into a shrine. Filling it are dozens of telegrams, blankets, small statues and cards — many from complete strangers who, simply because they were Americans, felt compelled to console the mother of a healthy, young man spreading democracy abroad.

"I've done nothing to the room," she confessed. "I'm still grieving, so when I start messing with the room, I get upset, so I have to stop. "You carry your child for nine months and raise the child. This hurts so bad. It doesn't matter if it's in the army or on the street, like some kids are killed."

With the Redford High School graduate gone, people rarely mention his nicknames, "A-Wax" or "A," used by everyone except his maternal grandmother, Myrtle Peggy, who preferred "Tiny A," which she'd coined when he was a very chubby 3-month-old. Adrian's Michigan State University work-study friend, Julian Kirkland, called him Bishop Butler to tease him about the strong faith they both shared.

However, Adrian Josiah's first name has been resurrected for his niece, Adrianne Savannah Skye Butler, who was born Aug. 5, 2005, the day before his funeral.

Eldridge Butler, two years his brother's senior, said, "He was more than a brother. He was more than a friend. He was my mentor and a great role model. Even though he was younger, I always looked up to him.

"He was intelligent and always focused on bettering his life. He once told me, 'Never let anyone destroy your dreams.'"

Peggy marked her son's birthday, Jan. 31, not with a delicious cake topped with frosting flowers, but with morose wreaths that quickly withered in the Detroit cold. Peggy took the day off from her job as a shuttle bus driver to go to Woodmere Cemetery with her older son and some of Adrian's close friends.

"We said a prayer and everyone shed tears together," she remembered.

Among those who participated in the first informal ceremony was Brandon Barnett, Adrian's best friend since sixth grade and his MSU roommate for three years. Adrian had agreed to serve as his best man at his wedding several months later.

"He was very outgoing, very outspoken and friendly," Brandon said, recalling how his bowling buddy often regaled him with stories about the foreign cities he'd visited during his five years in the military. "He touched everyone's life."

Also struggling with that pain and loss was Adrian's fiancée, Ruth Olvera. During the last two and a half years he spent stateside, he fell in love with the Austin police department staffer, and they had planned on a May 12, 2006, wedding, according to Ruth.

"Even though we never got the chance/To say the words 'I Do'/ You didn't leave this world alone/Because you took my heart with you," read her poem "My Love," included in the 12-page program distributed at the Aug. 6, 2005, funeral.

As Ruth looks to a future that will never be, Sgt. Tony Wood, Adrian's squad leader, relives a past he wishes never was. The day Adrian and 22-year-old John Tollefson, of Fond du Lac, WI, were killed the temperature was a scorching 147 degrees and the air conditioning in the trio's Humvee broke. Before the three MPs left their camp, they traded the vehicle they considered their good luck charm for one they'd never driven before.

Tony remembers patrolling Ashraf with Adrian and John and then waking up the following month at the Walter Reed Army Medical Center in Washington, D.C. The 38-year-old Hawaii resident is left with major organ damage, a body full of shrapnel scars and agonizing "what-ifs."

"In our spare time, us three were always together," Tony said. "The squad was really close. We ate our meals together. We watched movies together."

He recalled the R&B fan's diplomacy skills, good-natured teasing (Adrian loved to call him "Old Man" and "Grandpa.") and love of sports, which they had resigned to enjoy with Army-issued fake beer. Yet theirs was a well-respected squad; the sergeant cited Adrian's intelligence and desire to help people.

"You don't think about it at the time," Tony commented. "When you're out of the gate, your game's on. There's no margin of error. You're 100 percent on. We knew what the job entailed. This is the job we signed up for."

Peggy finds some solace in that. In the end, her son, who'd dreamt about becoming an FBI agent, served his country another way. He sacrificed his life for the principles symbolized by the American flag insignia sewn on his right shoulder.

– Zlati Meyer
Staff Writer for the Detroit Free Press

CW3 Corey James Goodnature
February 13, 1970 – June 28, 2005

When Corey Goodnature said he was going to do something, he did it. No excuses. He fulfilled his dream of becoming a military pilot, despite many obstacles along the way. He wanted to get his undergraduate degree in engineering, so he doggedly worked on it, taking classes online between missions in Afghanistan. This is the same man who, as a high school kid, was so determined to camp by a river with friends on New Year's Eve that he did so, despite temperatures that were well below zero.

"He was smart, and he was a quick thinker," said Corey's youngest son, Brennan. "He had an answer for everything and always knew how to do things." Corey loved teaching his boys, Shea and Brennan, how to hunt and fish.

That dedication started early in grade school. Not only was Corey a gifted athlete – involved in football, wrestling and track – but he loved to learn. A voracious reader, Corey wrote for his high school newspaper and could often be found with his nose in the pages of *National Geographic* magazines.

"He was really intelligent, and he remembered everything he ever read or heard," said Deb Goodnature, Corey's mother.

"He was in the top 10 of his graduating class and made the national honor society," Corey's father, Don Goodnature, said proudly.
His sister, Amy (Goodnature) Purdy, said her big brother could always be counted on for advice.

"He became a big brother who would give me advice about everything. And he knew what he was talking about," Amy said. "Corey did his research and knew a lot."Corey Goodnature is buried in Albert Lea, 10 miles south of Clarks Grove, MN.

– RP

Send Me

Clarks Grove is a tiny town of about 740 people near Albert Lea in far southern Minnesota. Communities of that size often keep close track of what happens to natives when they venture out to far-flung parts of the world. So it's not surprising that neighbors took pride in the accomplishments of Army Warrant Officer Corey Goodnature. They also took it hard in the summer of 2005 when they learned he had been killed in a helicopter crash in Afghanistan.

Don Goodnature knew his son was flying hazardous missions in the Middle East, but Corey had returned safely from so many of those missions that Don had become accustomed to it. He never expected to hear of his son's death.
"We knew that there was danger," Don said, days after Corey's death. "But, see, this was his third tour of duty in Afghanistan. And also, he had one tour in Iraq. So, after that many times over there, we got kind of complacent because we got thinking, 'Well, he's already done this before. He's done this three other times; it's not that big a deal.' And he made us feel real comfortable by telling us that it was OK, too."

Corey had grown comfortable behind the controls of a helicopter during his 14 years in the Army. He flew with an elite unit – the 160th Special Operations Aviation Regiment (SOAR), also known as the "Night Stalkers."
Don says his son was driven by the goal of becoming a military pilot. He was so driven that he changed his plans more than once to realize that ambition. After graduating from Albert Lea High School, Corey enrolled in the University of Minnesota and its ROTC program. But this was in the late 1980s. The Cold War was ending and the U.S. military was shrinking rather than expanding.
"He was in Air Force ROTC with a pilot's slot," Don says. "And then he lost that because of the cuts. Then he got into the Marines and had a pilot's slot with them in ROTC. Then that got cut."

But Corey's parents knew he wouldn't give up.

"I remember when he was in the ninth grade, he looked at me and said 'Mother, you're just going to have to accept it. I want to be a pilot and I want to be in the military,'" recalled Deb Goodnature.

"He was so clear about it and that's how he went through his whole military life. When he set his mind to it, he would go forward and succeed."

"He just enlisted in the Army and worked his way up, took all the necessary tests, went through warrant officer school, and accomplished what he'd planned on doing," added Don. Along the way, Corey started a family. He and his first wife, Mari, had two sons, Shea and Brennan, before divorcing. Despite the hectic

military life, Corey was able to help raise the boys. He saw them for frequent visits, including two, month-long stints during many summers.

"We spent a lot of time at the ocean and we loved going hunting together," said 14-year-old Brennan Goodnature. "I was actually with him when I shot my first deer." Brennan says his dad was a "good wrestler" and he enjoyed playing pranks. "He was kind of mischievous," smiled Brennan.

After moving to Savannah, GA, where the Night Stalkers are based, Corey met his second wife, Lori. She was immediately attracted to his "strong body frame, his captivating eyes and cheeks that would blush when he laughed." Lori also found it impressive that Corey had the skill and knowledge to fly the large helicopters with two rotor blades she'd seen flying around Savannah. A short six months later, the two soul mates became engaged. Lori didn't think life could get better. Then she learned Corey could sew (thanks to a previous job as a parachute rigger), and he loved to cook. "I've been told stories by men he was deployed with that he could win any contest when it came to his tolerance of hot and spicy food," said Lori.

While at Savannah's Hunter Army Airfield, Corey's military career blossomed. His father says in his last years, it was clear that Corey had become one of the lead pilots in the 160th.

"We could tell, the longer he was a pilot and the longer he was in the 160th, he just got more confident all the time," Don said. "I mean, they were the best at what they do. We always heard it was the best pilots in the world that were in the 160th."

On June 28, 2005, four U.S. Navy SEALs found themselves cornered and under attack in a mountainous region of eastern Afghanistan's Kunar Province. A crew of 16 special operations forces — eight SEALs and eight Night Stalkers — answered their call for help in a Chinook helicopter co-piloted by Corey. As it approached the valley, the Chinook was apparently struck by a rocket-propelled grenade and crashed into a mountainside, killing everyone on board.

The treacherous flying conditions in Afghanistan occasionally produce helicopter crashes, but military officials say it's very rare for a chopper to be hit by ground fire.

"Indications are that it was an RPG [rocket propelled grenade], which is a pretty lucky shot, honestly, against a moving helicopter," Marine Corps Lt. Gen. James Conway told the journal Rotor & Wing. Other helicopter gunships were later able to make their way into the valley, where one of the four SEALs had survived the ambush and was rescued.

Corey and his compatriots were killed more than a year after U.S. troops had ousted the Taliban regime in Afghanistan. At the time, Don said Afghanistan seemed to have faded from public consciousness as the country focused its attention on events in Iraq.

"Afghanistan's really on the back burner," he said. "People don't realize what's going on there. We just don't hear about it and I think it's very important. It really brings it home when something like this happens."

In early July of 2005, friends and family members of those killed in the Kunar Province attack gathered in Savannah, where the Night Stalkers paid tribute to their comrades. Don says the closeness of the unit and the support its members show for one another helped the Goodnature family through Corey's loss.
It is also comforting to see the words Corey had written to his church while still in Afghanistan. They'd asked him to share something to be read at their September 11, 2001, anniversary ceremony.

"As I sit and write this letter on a dark and dusty night I would like to say I am proud of what we have done, I would not have wanted to be anywhere else, and I hope I can contribute more to this fight in the future," Corey wrote. "I do this for all those who were taken from us two years ago on September 11, I do it for everyone back home, and I will continue to serve for the future of our country."
On June 27, 2005, the day before Corey died, Lori received one last shipment of flowers — a beautiful bouquet of roses. The note read "You are the sunshine in my life. I love you with all my heart and soul. You are my true soul mate."
Lori says Corey was more than the love of her life. "He was a true hero."
She shares this Bible verse as something that embodied all that Corey was:

*"Then I heard the voice of the Lord saying, 'Whom shall I send? And who will go for us?'
And I said, 'Here I am. Send me.'"
Isaiah 6:8 (NIV)*

*— William Wilcoxen
Reporter for Minnesota Public Radio*

Spc. Larry Kenyatta Brown
December 11, 1980 – April 5, 2003

Army Spc. Larry Kenyetta Brown was called to serve in Iraq while recovering from knee surgery. He'd been injured on base while serving stateside. Larry was a gifted athlete who didn't let much slow him down. When playing pickup basketball in Kuwait, before the war in Iraq began, everyone wanted 6'2" Larry on their team. "He always kicked everybody's ass," laughed former Spc. Dustin McCarley.

"He was the kind of guy you were a better person for knowing," said Dustin. "He was quiet, but when he spoke, you listened. He chose his words wisely and they were always significant."

Larry was part of the Jessica Lynch rescue mission – one of the infantrymen providing ground support for the special operations units involved. Four days later, while taking part in another mission, he was killed.

"We were fighting street to street, house to house in Karbala," recalled Dustin. "We were sent in to take out insurgents who were shooting at our helicopters and to get control of the city."

They were successful in their mission. Those on the ground that day say Larry's platoon "paved the way for the escape and evasion" of about 200 of their fellow soldiers.

In the process, an enemy fighter shot Larry in the stomach as he and his team made their way along a dusty city street. He died from internal bleeding while being airlifted to a hospital. Larry's bright future was cut short.

"He was really smart," said Dustin, who said he thought for sure Larry would end up in law school. "He was always reading, either studying law books or his Bible. He loved God and he loved his mama. He was a good Southern boy."

— RP

A Rose in the Concrete

Rosemary Watkins Brown falls asleep after tossing and turning for what seems like hours. As the first rays of sunlight stream through her window, bringing a touch of warmth to her face, a feeling of joy washes over her as she plans to spend the day with her family. Yet, all too soon – like a shot through her heart – reality sets in and her joy is shattered, as she remembers the shot in Iraq that took the life of her oldest son.

On April 5, 2003, Larry Kenyatta Brown, 22, was one of the first U.S. soldiers killed in Operation Iraqi Freedom. He died in the Battle of Karbala during the first month of war with Iraq. Rosemary remembers the last time she saw her son, whom she called "Ken."

"One day he called and said they were sending him back over there, this time for real, and for us to come get all of his things off the base in Kansas," Rosemary said. "He had just been in Iraq for six months training before the war began, and I didn't understand why they were sending him again."

The family had a pleasant visit. But as Rosemary drove off, she remembers something not feeling right as she looked back from the car to see her son waving goodbye.

Her last conversation with Ken, this time by phone, also felt odd. "It was about a week before he got killed," Rosemary said. "He called and said, 'Mom, I probably won't talk to you again, because the war's about to start and we're getting ready to go into the field.'" Rosemary said Ken would often say he'd probably get killed over there. "I told him to not ever say that. But, sometimes I wonder if he had that feeling it was coming," she said.

Best friend Ahmad Dennie knew Larry Kenyatta Brown as "Larry," but he also called him "a rose in the concrete." Ahmad, a student at Jackson State University and firefighter with the Jackson Fire Department, was a friend of Larry's for almost 10 years.

"It's like he was something you saw one time and probably would never see again. He was that special. He was a great encourager to me," Ahmad said.

"I hated going to the gym, but he said we should go. One day, he put on a lot more weight than I could handle and I dropped it. The weights rolled all over the floor. It was so funny. We laughed about that a lot. I've got other friends, but I'll never have another friend like Larry."

At her Jackson, MS, home, Rosemary proudly flies the American flag. Inside,

she points out a curio cabinet full of memorabilia: trophies, plaques and photos of her son with his battalion; the crystal cross given in his honor by a local church; the flag that had been draped over his casket, now in a shadow-box; a certificate and photo of his fellow soldiers pointing out a landing strip they named in his honor; his Purple Heart; the Bronze Star for meritorious service; an honorable service certificate; and an Army commendation medal for outstanding patriotism and positive attitude from the 3rd Brigade Combat Team.

Rosemary finds some peace knowing her son was a Christian and is now safe in God's hands. "You've got to have some God in you or you just can't make it," she said, reaching to hold the dog tag that keeps his photo and name hanging close to her heart.

Members of the 3rd Brigade Combat Team told Rosemary about her son's last moments, dying amid the desert sands of Iraq:"When they had him in the Black Hawk helicopter, he said, 'I'm not going to make it. Tell my mama I love her.' Then he asked for water, but they couldn't give it to him because of something having to do with the morphine they gave him. My poor baby was hurting and had been out in that hot desert and just needed something cool to drink, and they couldn't give it to him. That hurts me so bad that he had to die thirsty."

Larry's brother, Nick, was 20 when his older brother died. He's lonely without his brother, and now nothing seems right to him. "He was my hero even before he joined the Army and my best friend, too," said Nick, a senior at Tougaloo College. "Pretty much everything he did, I did. He played basketball; I played basketball. He joined the Army; I joined the Air National Guard. Now I have to make my own path. When he got killed, I saw the effect it put on Mom and didn't want her to have to go through that again. I told them my situation, and they gave me a discharge. I still go out to his grave. I miss him a lot. I don't think I'll ever get over it."

Larry was also honored by Bailey Magnet School, where he graduated in 1999. As a student, he ran track, received the Sixth Man Award in basketball and the Senior Award for his excellence and dedication.

Larry's coach, Charles Rosser, knew him as a student for four years. "Out of all people, why did it have to be Larry that God had to take?" Charles asked. "He was a hard-working, dedicated, team player. There wasn't too much we could ask that he wouldn't try to do. He was an overall nice person and well-liked individual. He would always go out of his way to help others."

The young man was a team player at home, too, says mother Rosemary. "We didn't have a lot, and we had to be careful with our money," she said. "I usually couldn't get the kids new things, like school clothes, at the same time. Ken would always be the one to say 'Mom, give it to LaKeidra [his little sister] and I'll wait until the next time.' When he got a job, he brought home his first paycheck and said, 'Mom I just need one pair of shoes, and you can have the rest."

After graduation, Larry attended Hinds Community College where he studied criminal justice while working for UPS at night. But his dreams were bigger than Mississippi could hold. "He came home one day and said he felt like a bum," Rosemary said. "He said, 'I'm not doing enough. I want to go into the military. How do you feel about that?'"

Rosemary didn't want him to go, but she kept quiet, trying not to interfere with her son's dreams. "There were so many days I wondered why I didn't try, but I know I made the right decision to let him make his own decision. He got a chance to see places I could never take him," she said.

Now her only daughter, LaKeidra, wants to follow her brother's footsteps into the military, possibly into battle.

To those who knew him best, Larry Kenyatta Brown was an athlete, a brother, a best friend and a son. To the rest of us, he was an American hero who volunteered to help protect his country. And for that, Mississippi and America thank him.

— Gloria Butler Baldwin
Independent writer, reporter, author
http://web.mac.com/gloriabutler

"From this day to the ending of the world, But we in it shall be remember'd; We few, we happy few, we band of brothers. For he who today that sheds his blood with me shall be my brother..."

— William Shakespeare (Henry V)

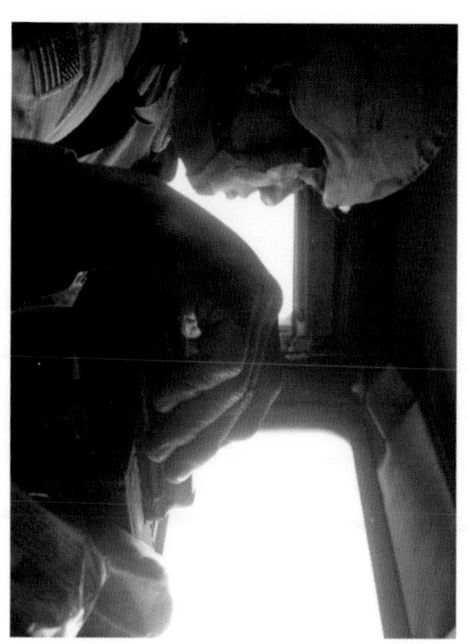

Sgt. 1st Class Michael Fuga
May 25, 1959 — September 9, 2006

Army Sgt. 1st Class Michael Fuga was killed by small arms fire in Kandahar, Afghanistan on September 9, 2006. He had been in the military for nearly three decades.

An American Samoan, Michael had lived in all parts of the United States, but Independence, MO became his home after joining the Missouri National Guard in December of 1995.

"He was a good soldier and a good infantry tactician," said fellow guardsman Sgt. Maj. James Schulte, who served in Afghanistan with Michael. But Michael also left a big impression on James in another way.

"I always tell people I'm not sure if he could run a hundred yards, but I bet he could carry a refrigerator on his back all day long. He was just a big, strong guy who was willing to tackle whatever he was given," said James. "He was just like a big likeable teddy bear who really cared about people." James says he'll never forget Michael's upbeat attitude and his ever-present smile.

Michael's family remembers him with love — *"Alofa"* in Samoan. "He always wanted a hug before I left for school and when he came home from work. Even if he got home late sometimes, I would get out of bed and give him a hug," remembered his 12-year-old daughter, Salome.

"He spoiled me a lot," she giggled. "I always went to him if I ever wanted something, or if I wanted to do something I would ask him first." Salome missed her father when he left for deployments, but she is proud of his service.

"He was a hero and he loved serving his country," she said.

— *RP*

A Soldier's Deeds

Michael T. Fuga loved to go to Seattle to visit his brother, Futi. But something else lured the Army sergeant to the city.

It was a little dog named Koco.

Michael's wife of 13 years, Justina, says he gave the purebred chow to his brother. "He had the dog when he was stationed in Ft. Riley, Kansas," Justina recalled. "His brother, Futi, had just retired in 1992, and he was on his way home to Seattle from Tennessee."

Stopping in Ft. Riley to see Michael, Futi fell in love with Koco. Futi asked to take Koco to Seattle to give to his son, Anthony. Justina says it was hard for Michael to part with his favorite dog.

"But he soon realized it was the best thing for Koco," said Justina.

His friends say there are many more stories like that about Michael. It's the kind of character he had.

"You become his friend … he'll die for you," said one friend.

Michael Fuga called Independence, MO home. He was born, though, in Oceanside, CA, on May 25, 1959. He then moved to Nuuli, American Samoa, attending Marist Catholic High School. While Michael's father served in the military, his mother stayed in her home community, caring for Michael and his 13 brothers and sisters.

Michael, himself, became a military man and served in the United States Army. After a successful career, he went to work for Southwest Airlines and joined the Missouri National Guard. With about 28 years of military service, he was carrying on a proud family tradition.

"His father was a Marine," Justina said. "Four of his brothers serve in the military. His youngest brother, Jesse, just joined the Marines." Michael didn't join the military just to follow in his father's footsteps. Justina said Michael joined the Army "to have a great career and see the world." She says they met when he was on active duty, stationed in Ft. Riley, KS.

"My husband has been my inspiration from the time we got married in 1994," she said. Their daughter, Salome, was born when they were stationed in Alaska. "We enjoyed military life," Justina recalled. "We got to meet different people." When there was time, Michael enjoyed playing rugby and golf.

Salome has fond memories of going golfing with her father during trips to Seattle.

"The only reason I went was to drive the cart," laughed Salome as she remembered how her dad teased her about her driving. "He said the way I drive was not made for little cars," Salome said. "He told me when I get a license I should get a truck!"

When it came to education, Michael always made sure Salome put school first. "He always told me no boys until after school is over," said Salome. She describes her father as someone who always put others first.

Justina says her husband and daughter were very close. "Salome is the spitting image of her father, along with the courage he had."

Michael's last assignment was one that would take a lot of courage. He was deployed to Afghanistan where he served as an embedded trainer with the Afghanistan National Army, charged with advising and mentoring troops. He lived with the soldiers, and was involved in training, planning and executing their missions.

On September 9, 2006, a battle broke out in Kandahar, a major trade center, and one of Afghanistan's largest cities. Commodities like wool, cotton, grain and fruit fill the marketplace. It is a principal city for the Pashto people. The Taliban once established a headquarters there.

As small-arms fire erupted, Michael bravely confronted the enemy. He was killed in the battle. He was 47 years old. He died fighting alongside the men and women he'd trained and lived with – people he considered his comrades and his friends.

"I felt like my life was taken away from me when I heard of his tragic death," Justina says. "But I still have my beautiful 12-year-old daughter to take care of. I know that my husband's mission is over, but I still have a mission left in this world, to raise my daughter with the values that her father wanted to instill in her."

Psychologist and philosopher William James once said, "The greatest use of life is to spend it for something that will outlast it." Sgt. 1st Class Michael T. Fuga, generous of spirit and courage, gave a legacy not only to his family but to the world, in both the way he lived and in the way he died. He demonstrated bravery and commitment. His obituary in the *Kansas City Star* carries a list of the numerous medals he earned: Bronze star, Purple Heart, Meritorious Service Medal, Army Commendation Medal, Army Good Conduct Medal, Army Achievement Medal, Expert Infantry Badge, Combat Infantry Badge and others.

Employees of Southwest Airlines left messages in his guestbook, reflecting their appreciation for a man who worked at the airlines for 10 years.
"He was an awesome worker and friend," one woman wrote, adding, "and may his daughter never doubt his love, for she was her daddy's little girl."
Justina was touched by the outpouring of love the community showed her husband at the memorial service.

"The whole community came," Justina said, "and there was a tremendous outpouring of kindness from all directions in the Samoan community."
Several four-star generals, state representatives and members of Congress all gathered with family and friends on a crisp autumn day in Independence to show their appreciation for a man who made the ultimate sacrifice.
Several weeks after the funeral, National Public Radio aired a heartfelt tribute to the decorated soldier.

"I never knew how many people he touched," Justina mused. "I want anyone and everyone to know how great a husband, father and soldier he was. He was my world. Now he is my heaven."

— Kay B. Day
Author, national columnist, poet
kayday.com

"The wave of the future is not the conquest of the world by a single dogmatic creed but the liberation of the diverse energies of free nations and free men."

— John F. Kennedy

Lance Cpl. Andrew Dennis Bedard
May 21, 1986 — October 4, 2005

Michelle and Denny Bedard raised their only child in big-sky country Missoula, MT — though he never really seemed like a child.

"Mature beyond his years," his father told reporters. "He was calm in chaos. He was very reliable. A very, very intelligent kid."

His father, a radio host, recalled that his son showed an interest in music at an early age and even joined his school's choir. Denny doesn't remember Andrew ever singing a solo. "He just never wanted to be the center of attention," said Denny.

In high school, though, Andrew blossomed into a social butterfly.

"He was so good at keeping in touch with people. It's like he knew how important those relationships were. He found a way to write and even call, all the way from Iraq, the whole time asking how we were," said Andrew's friend, Adrienne McKelvey.

Andrew's mother is sure he was homesick in Iraq, even though he never said so. "He took the movie *A River Runs Through It* with him because it took place in Missoula. He called home every chance he got. At all hours, he e-mailed and he wrote letters," said Michelle.

When his parents now think of their only child, they can't help but recall how wise he was in his early years.

One particularly fond memory they have is of 4-year-old Andrew in the bath. Denny said, "Out of nowhere he said, 'You know, Mom, I just really love life."

— *RP*

Chasing the Challenge

Semper fidelis — "always faithful" — was a principle Andrew Bedard lived by long before he enlisted in the U.S. Marine Corps.

As an only child growing up in Montana, he was somewhat of a loner, but Andrew would do anything for the friends with whom he eventually became close. Andrew had a selfless attitude and a gentle way about him.

"He always showed more interest in others rather than talking about himself," said Andrew's father and popular Missoula radio personality, Denny Bedard. "He'd make you feel at ease. He was an easy person to get to know."

Andrew's mother, Michelle Bedard, says her son took the time to talk with former teachers when it wasn't "cool" to show you like the people there to make you work and learn.

"He would call his grandmother in Minnesota every chance he got and chat with her," added Michelle. He had a deep respect for others, and not just his elders. "Andrew would smile at and try to include the kids who were left out," she said. Denny remembers how early in life Andrew learned to use "please" and "thank you." "And he carried that every time we went out to a restaurant or public place. Waitresses and servers would comment on how polite he was," Denny reminisced. "When we would go to parent-teacher conferences, his teachers were always impressed and very appreciative of his level of participation, his grades and his spirit of cooperation. At a very young age, he already had the kind of discipline that served him well in the military."

As Andrew got older, he and his dad golfed together one or two weekend nights every summer, leaving town for a golf course 70 miles north of Missoula. They became more like brothers than father and son.

"Afterward, we would have dinner or lunch together. We'd spend time in the car, on the golf course and at the restaurant. Those times meant a lot," said Denny. Andrew also loved traveling with his mom, who was a travel agent. They experienced the silence at sunset in the notorious Nazi Dachau concentration camp in Germany, they watched whales swim under a boat off Maui, HI, and they stood solemnly at Ground Zero in New York City. Andrew and his mother globe trotted the world together, seeing how others lived, enjoying different cultures and trying foreign foods.

She looks back and sees Andrew as intensely goal-driven. He was not so much competitive as much as he was self-challenged, needing to prove only to himself that he could succeed. And, along the way, he tried to make every demanding situation fun. In an English paper his senior year, Andrew talked about what motivates him in life by relating his experience as a cross country runner. "I run every race with the attitude that I can complete a challenge when it is looking me straight in the eye," he wrote. "It is easy to complete anything if you just put your mind to it. Never have doubt about anything."

During his senior year at Hellgate High School in Missoula, he jolted everyone with his decision to join the Marines after quietly researching all the armed forces. As close as he was to his friends at age 17, they didn't even realize Andrew was formulating this plan for his life. Did he come from a strongly traditional military family? No. But to his parents, it made sense. He had talked with them about the U.S. Air Force Academy when he was little. He was in Boy Scouts and the Civil Air Patrol and he liked war movies. In his high school freshman year, he put together a future class schedule of what he was going to take each semester through his senior year. And he stayed pretty close to the original plan — a four-year plan, just like his four-year enlistment with the Marines.

He chose the Marine Corps because, as Andrew put it, "They are the toughest. I want the challenge." In the beginning, with his high test scores, he was told he could take a computer job and work stateside. He said "I'm not doing this to sit behind a desk somewhere!" Andrew thought joining the Marines was the perfect choice for him because it would not only allow him the chance to serve his country, but it was also a way to help pay for college and an opportunity to travel more.

Andrew spent his last day in Missoula with his mother. "He took me to the Saturday morning farmers' market to buy me some sunflowers," Michelle recalled. "A mother couldn't have been more proud of her son than I was of him. I beamed as we walked around together. At every opportunity I would stop to say 'hi' to friends or introduce him to acquaintances, making sure they knew he was a Marine who was leaving for Iraq."

Andrew was a Marine for one year. He served in Iraq for 30 days, taking part in more than 30 combat missions. His final mission was in Ramadi. Lt. Matthew Hendricks, who was seriously wounded in the explosion that killed Andrew, wrote a letter to the Bedards about what happened that day.

He explained that insurgents were "holed up" in the southern regions of the city. "Intelligence believed that the insurgents, once they had gathered strength and weapons, would begin to move north, into the center of the city, from stronghold to stronghold. The strongholds would give them the ability to launch well-organized and deadly attacks on Marines and soldiers. Once they were deep within the city and well fortified in the strongholds, they would be difficult to flush out. Battalion believed the best way to crush these snakes was to hit them first, destroy their weapons caches and disrupt any ability of theirs to organize and coordinate well-planned attacks on any American forces. The information that was analyzed and distributed quickly provided us with a small window of opportunity to launch an effective first strike," wrote Hendricks.

He wrote that they left their base, a former Iraqi army fort, and headed off to find a location to set up a Center of Command (COC). The goal was to utilize a more strategic vantage point. Shortly after the convoy entered the streets of Ramadi, an improvised explosive device (IED) detonated under Andrew's vehicle. Andrew's Navy and Marine Corp Achievement Medal certificate reads:

"Lance Corporal Andrew D. Bedard [19-years-old] performed his duties in combat in a highly professional manner. He vigorously prepared and maintained his vehicle, working long hours to ensure that his vehicle was always combat ready. On 4 October 05, while driving the lead vehicle in a 21-vehicle convoy, Lance Corporal Bedard unselfishly maneuvered his vehicle in a manner which exposed himself to the greatest danger from a possible buried improvised explosive device. His heroic act ultimately saved the lives of three Marines and one navy corpsman. Lance Corporal Bedard's initiative, courage, and devotion to duty reflected credit upon himself and upheld the highest traditions of the Marine Corps and the United States Naval Service."

"Pfc. Bedard [posthumously promoted to lance corporal] was my driver in Iraq. I was his machine gunner. We had a special bond together that nobody else had. Bedard was a great friend, a great man and a great Marine."
— LCpl Shawn Seeley 3/7 Lima Co Weapons Platoon (survived the explosion that claimed Andrew Bedard's life).

— Monte Turner
Host for KECI-TV in Missoula, MT, U.S. Air Force veteran

KGVO
1290

Sgt. 1st Class Linda Ann Tarango-Griess
April 14, 1971 – July 11, 2004

Linda Tarango-Griess might have been thinking of fly balls and sliding safely into home plate the day she was killed in Iraq. The 33-year-old, dark-haired beauty was known for playing a mean third base.

On July 11, 2004, Linda was scheduled to play a game of softball with other members of the Nebraska Army National Guard in Iraq. She never made it.

She was killed when a roadside bomb exploded near her convoy.

"She was the type of person who her soldiers could knock on her door anytime, day or night, and she would get up with a good attitude to see what they needed and see that they were taken care of," fellow soldier Lt. Leslie Durr told Lincoln's *Journal Star*.

Linda may have always been the girl with the long, dark hair, big eyes and beautiful smile; but friends and loved ones say she was truly radiant on the inside as well. She was known for helping others.

The 14-year military veteran was not just a full-time soldier with the Guard's 276th Ordnance Company, but also a volunteer firefighter.

"She's the bravest person I know. I admire her and I've admired her since we were young," Linda's cousin, Linda Hernandez, told the Associated Press. "She was successful at everything she did."

Linda leaves behind a husband, Staff Sgt. Doug Griess, who is also a member of the Nebraska Army National Guard.

— RP

Sergeant T

"Hello Scotty, So, today is your big day? Wow! It seems like just yesterday that I was making you peanut butter and jelly sandwiches and Malt-o-Meal. You couldn't have picked a more wonderful person than Rachel. I'm sorry I can't be there to share in your day, but here (in Iraq) I am in hopes that one day, these people will have the chance to be as happy as you. Just know that I AM with you, just close your eyes, place your hands on your heart, and you will feel me there."

The e-mail written to her cousin, Scott Nehls, on his wedding day was signed *"Lots of love, Linda."*

Just two months later, Sgt. 1st Class Linda Tarango-Griess died when a make-shift bomb exploded next to her convoy near Samarra, Iraq.

Family and friends say the e-mail was vintage Linda, full of humor and heart. She had an infectious grin that could lift the spirits of her fellow soldiers, who affectionately dubbed her, "Sergeant T." Linda was a tiny fireball of energy who left an impression on many lives.

There was that long-ago summer when a young Linda and her sister, Vicky, drove the family to distraction singing Bette Midler's "The Rose" over and over again.

"She loved God, family, friends and life," says her aunt, Maria "Terry" Medrano-Nehls.

Assigned to the 267th Ordnance Company, the 33-year-old Sutton resident was the first woman in the Nebraska National Guard ever killed in combat. That day, the mission began as routine, delivering vehicle repair parts and other supplies to Camp Anaconda near Balad, Iraq. It was Linda's first time riding in a convoy. On the way back, the bomb ripped through the Humvee, killing Linda and another soldier.

It was up to Capt. Chris Weskamp to tell members of the 267th that Linda and 26-year-old Jeremy Fischer of Lincoln were dead.

"It was the toughest thing I ever did." Chris said. "Those closest to Linda and Jeremy had a more difficult time with the news. It hit home that it could have happened to any one of them."

By some accounts, Linda Tarango's childhood was difficult. She hung out with the wrong crowd and got into trouble. After she ran away from home at age 11,

her parents sent her to live about 100 miles away with her mother's sister, Terry, and her family.

At first, Linda was terrified. But her Aunt Terry recalled the sixth-grader quickly discovered she was a fast learner, who excelled academically and was a gifted athlete.

"She wanted to make something of her life," said Terry. "She would set goals, work on them so hard, and complete them. It was amazing."

One day, Terry recalled, Linda came home from school and announced she wanted to play the saxophone. Within two months of daily practice, the plucky seventh grader not only made the band, but was selected as first chair.

Determined to get a degree at the University of Nebraska at Kearney, Linda joined the National Guard at 19. She not only found a way to pay her tuition, but met the love of her life, Staff Sgt. Doug Griess, now with the 1075th Transportation Company.

"The first thing I noticed about Linda was her outgoing personality," said Doug. "She had a big smile, a fabulous smile."

The couple married in 1994 and settled in Sutton, a town of almost 2,000 residents, where Linda worked as a volunteer firefighter. In the fall of 2003, her guard unit was called up for an 18-month deployment to Iraq. Linda, who was "passionate about the Guard," took the news as a challenge, said her husband.

"She said, 'I would die for my country if I have to,'" Doug recalled.

In February of 2004, Linda arrived with the 267th at a base four hours north of Baghdad. Working as a supply sergeant, she would joke that she was in charge of "beans, bullets and boots."

Linda not only thrived with her fellow soldiers, but also became a big hit with their families back home. That included her pen pal, 9-year-old Dean Lewis, the son of Sgt. Darrell Lewis who served under Linda in Iraq.

"Dean was so excited to get her letters, and couldn't wait to read them," said Darrell's wife, Diane. "She would write about what Dean's dad was doing, and what the unit did for fun."

"In one letter Linda said she was sending Dean a surprise," said Diane. "Before the surprise package could arrive she was killed."

Word of her death devastated the fourth-grader, who cried and was silent for days.

The package eventually arrived. In it was a floppy boonie-style desert hat with Dean's name embroidered on it. It's now one of the boy's most prized possessions, kept in a glass case in the family's living room, a reminder of his beloved pen pal.

For Linda's husband Doug, news of her death was beyond belief.

He knew she was nervous about the escalating violence by insurgents against American convoys. Doug advised Linda not to leave the camp if it wasn't necessary.

Just hours before she died, Doug learned he, too, was headed to Iraq, and he called and talked to her about trying to see each other.

After her funeral, the Army told Doug he could stay home instead of deploying with his unit.

"I really didn't have to go, but I talked to the chaplain," said Doug. "I wanted to experience what she was going through. I wanted to fight for my country like she did."

Doug spent a year in Iraq. In his wallet, he carried a reminder of Linda — the St. Christopher medal she was wearing the day she was killed. He also carried a question that haunted him since her death. "I wanted to find out why she rode the convoy the day she died, why she had to leave camp," he said.
The answer came to him gradually.

"One time she sent a fellow soldier out to visit an Iraqi school to deliver pens and pencils," Doug remembered. "The convoy was ambushed. It was really terrible, but they escaped."

Doug reasoned that Linda felt so guilty about having put other soldiers in harm's way while she waited back at camp that she decided to experience for herself what her troops were going through.

That meant climbing into the passenger side of a Humvee on that July day. It was a brave move that cost Linda her life.

"Linda would never ask her soldiers to do something she wouldn't do," Doug said.

— Jane Watrel
NBC freelance correspondent, Washington, D.C.

"If you are able, save for them a place inside of you and save one backward glance when you are leaving for the places they can no longer go.

Be not ashamed to say you loved them, though you may or may not have always. Take what they have taught you with their dying and keep it with your own.

And in that time when men decide and feel safe to call the war insane, take one moment to embrace those gentle heroes you left behind."

— Major Michael Davis O'Donnell
January 1, 1970
Dak To, Vietnam

Pfc. John Lukac
April 20, 1985 – October 30, 2004

As a toddler, John Lukac's parents read fairytales to him in Hungarian and English. He was fluent in both and couldn't get enough books in any language. By the time he was 2 years old, John could identify makes of cars from a distance: Ford, Mercedes, Cadillac — it didn't matter, he knew it. He practiced walking in parking lots with his mother, Helena, making her get close to the vehicle to check if he was right. He always was.

He wasn't just a bright child, but a perceptive one.

At age 3, he came to the rescue of his extremely ill mother after she had a miscarriage. As she lay on the floor nearly unconscious, he brought her water to drink and wiped her face with a wet towel. Helena explains that John even had a phone in his little hand as his father, Jan, walked in from work early and took over.

That same year, the family was returning from buying their Christmas tree when John stepped in again. As their car headed into the garage, John yelled "Stop!" Jan slammed on the breaks, not realizing what was wrong. Little John had just saved them from crashing into the garage with the tree tied on top of the vehicle.

John had a thirst for knowledge and a deep desire to serve his country, even before he became a Marine. When he was a teenager, he volunteered with environmental groups and at a youth center. His goal was to some day become an FBI or CIA agent.

He just wanted to make a difference.

— RP

He wanted to make a difference

Fifteen-year-old Peter Lukac dropped a handful of shell casings from the 21-gun salute onto his brother's oak casket after it was lowered into a grave at the Southern Nevada Veterans Memorial Cemetery in Boulder City.
He kept one for himself.

It was a fitting farewell to his 19-year-old brother, Marine Pfc. John Lukac of Las Vegas, who was buried on the 229th birthday of the Marine Corps.
The older Lukac was the first Nevada casualty to be buried locally, out of 11 from the state who have died in the nation's war on terror.

He was killed Oct. 30, 2004, in a car bomb attack near Fallujah, Iraq, at the onset of what Pentagon officials were calling Operation al-Fajr, or "New Dawn." The 10,000-troop assault was aimed at ridding the city of terrorists like the one who rammed an explosive-laden Chevy Suburban into a truckload of Marines on Oct. 30 killing Lukac and seven others.

With his father, Jan, and mother, Helena, weeping at his side in the arms of white-gloved Marines, Peter stood composed with a blank stare, still stunned by the death of his only brother.

"He only picked on me when he was around his friends," Peter said before the burial. "When he was around me, he was the cool big brother."

"Johnny," as he was known, had been Peter's childhood playmate and at age 12 became infatuated with the Marines from watching movies and reading books.
John Lukac was born in Los Angeles on April 20, 1985. Two years before, Jan and Helena had immigrated to the United States after escaping to Austria from Czechoslovakia, where they had lived under communist rule during the Cold War, separated from their native Hungary.

The family moved to Las Vegas in 2001 so Helena, who had been a stay-at-home mom for 16 years, could work her dream job at the MGM Grand. Jan commuted to West Hollywood, CA, to maintain his business roofing and refurbishing homes.
It was the newfound freedom that his parents were so fond of that inspired their son to become a patriot, they said. "We had a dream to come to the free states," Jan, 52, said at the mortuary, while Marines stood guard over the closed, flag-draped casket. "He said, 'I'm so glad to be born here.' He was willing to die for this country."

Like many others who joined the Marines, John Lukac was further motivated by the Sept. 11, 2001, terrorist attacks on the World Trade Center and the Pentagon.
He urged his parents to sign him up at 17, fresh out of Durango High School

where he was a member of the Class of 2003. If they didn't, he told them, he would join regardless when he turned 18.

"He wanted to protect the country. He wanted to make a difference no matter what it took," said Helena, 51, gazing at a collage of childhood pictures displayed at the funeral home.

Growing up, the boys were well-behaved, she said. They never argued while playing with Matchbox cars. And they enjoyed swimming, basketball, camping, and fishing for striped bass and hiking in the forests while on vacation. They went to Disneyland and played with boogie boards on the beach.
Jan said John had a thirst for knowledge that began at young age. He could say the alphabet as a 2-year-old and recited multiplication tables as a toddler. Once, when John was not quite 6, he used a toy tape recorder and microphone to launch a make-believe TV talk show. He played Johnny Carson and Peter was Jay Leno. They fashioned tickets out of pieces of paper and sold them to Jan and Helena. John did most of the talking, his dad recalled.
His intelligence blossomed as a student in a California middle school, where he received a citation in 1999 from President Bill Clinton for scholarly achievement.

He matched the feat as a senior at Durango, where he made the national honor roll and received a certificate from President George W. Bush for "outstanding academic excellence.""He liked science very much," Helena said.
Durango teachers Tia Price and Gina Toth remembered him as a shy, quiet, soft-spoken, model student who didn't flaunt his brilliance. "He did very well, but didn't boast about it," said Price, who taught him statistics for advanced placement college credit. "I was shocked about three weeks before he graduated when he told me he wanted to join the Marines," she said. "He could have gone to any college in the country ... but his face lit up when he talked about the Marines." Once on leave, he came to visit her "in uniform with his butch hair cut," Price said. "He was impressive."

Toth, who taught him psychology, said John was intrigued by learning about phobias and the reasons for mental illness. "He enjoyed learning about different parts of the brain and what they do," she said, adding that his desire to join the Marines "seemed to fit him." "If I were to guess, I would say that was just how he figured he could make a difference. That's the reputation Marines have."Toth said she was shocked when she learned he had been killed in Iraq.
"I thought, 'Wow, he was one of my students.' He wasn't just taking up space in a classroom. He was a smart kid. You have the feeling, 'Why that one?'"
One of John Lukac's best friends, Alex Larson, 20, said he was "lost for words" to talk about his buddy. There were three who hung out often and would go to the shooting range together.

"Things aren't going to be the same without him," Larson said.
In one of his last letters home, Lukac wrote his mother asking her to send books and more stamps. The book wish list, which he signed, "Love, Johnny," included titles such as "Dissolution," by Richard Lee Byers; "Condemnation," by Richard Baker; and "Extinction" by Lisa Smedman. "He was extremely smart," said Cpl. Joshua Egolf, 20, of Blue Grass, Iowa, who went through boot camp and infantry school with him and is a member of their Hawaii-based unit.
"He loved getting into discussions with everybody. He was an outstanding Marine and was a good man. He got me out of trouble a couple times," Egolf said.
On Wednesday (Nov. 10, 2004) at the First Presbyterian Church of Las Vegas, the Rev. Jim Juhan offered guidance for healing to the 80 mourners, including two dozen Marines.

"Have courage for the great sorrows of life and patience for the small ones," he said, quoting 19th century writer Victor Hugo.

"So John is gone from us, but leaves so many memories. Each time we think of him and remember him, he lives within us," Juhan said.

With that, a procession led by Las Vegas motorcycle police and trailed by former Lt. Gov. Lonnie Hammargren's mobile Mid-East Memorial Wall, which bears names of U.S. military personnel killed in Iraq and Afghanistan, headed to the veterans cemetery. There, four stunt planes trailing plumes of smoke performed a missing man formation.

Telling the Lukacs last week that John had been killed "was the hardest thing I had to do in my 24 years in the Marine Corps," 1st Sgt. Joe Kapala said to mourners gathered at the cemetery chapel.

"As long as we live, he, too, will live for he is part of us," Kapala said. "Rest in peace, dear Marine. Semper Fi. We will never forget."

— Keith Rogers
Military writer for the Las Vegas Review-Journal
(Re-print of November 11, 2004 article; permission granted by Las Vegas Review-Journal)

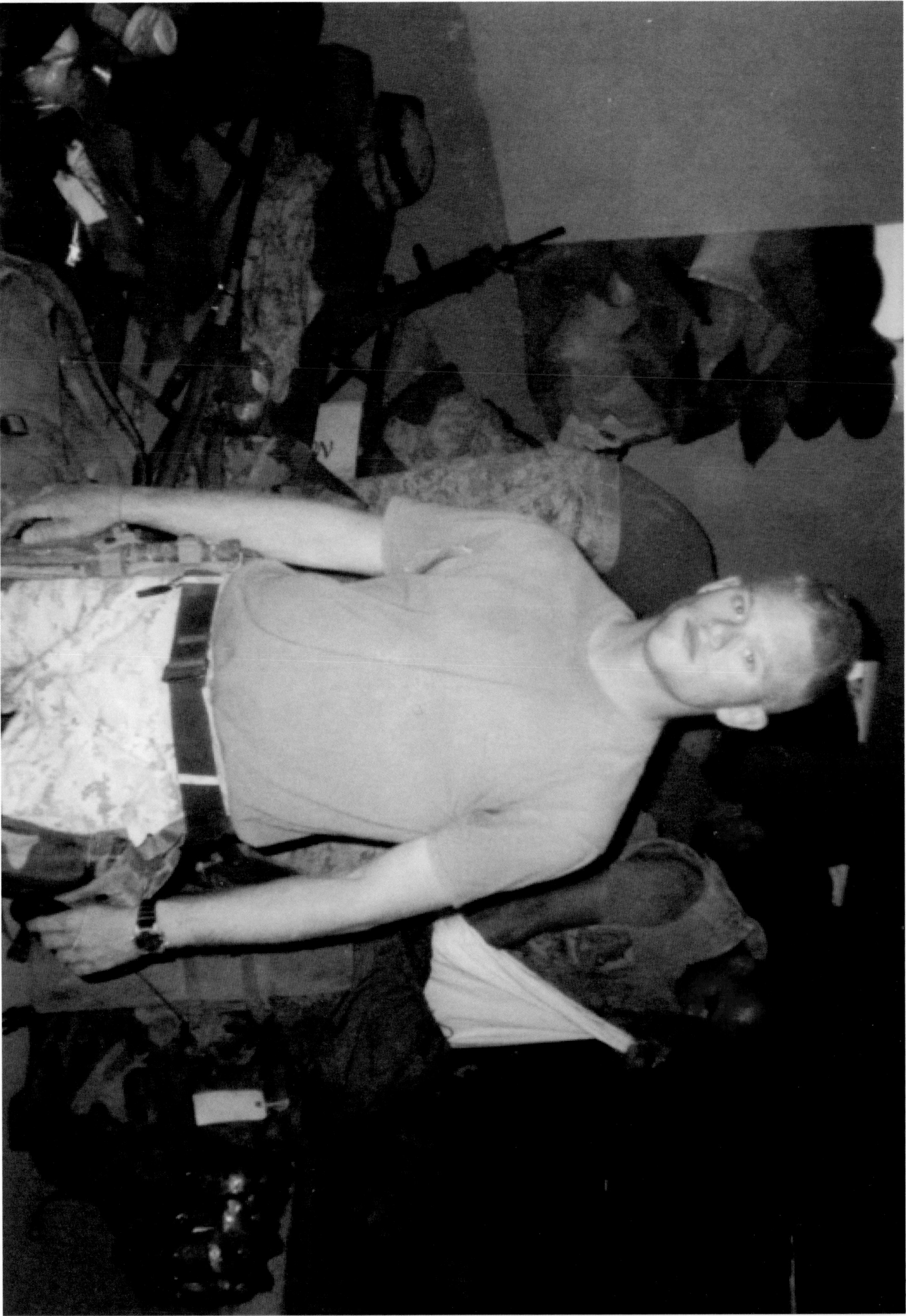

Cpl. Timothy Mark Gibson
July 24, 1981 — January 26, 2005

Known as "The Gip," Tim Gibson almost always had a smile on his face. His best friend, Cpl. Jake Ziliani, described him as the quintessential, all-American boy. Tim was the middle child of three sons who grew up in Merrimack, NH. Jake and Tim met while stationed in Hawaii. It was there Jake learned that Tim loved the beach, sappy movies and McDonald's. Tim, an excellent athlete, was also very competitive in sports.

"I remember the time he came to visit me in upstate New York while we were home on leave. We played wiffle ball until like five a.m. because that's how long it took me to win. But he didn't mind being out there, as long as I was happy," said Jake. Tim was always looking out for others.

"He was the definition of a perfect person," Jake said. "All he wanted to do was defend his country for his family and friends — his brothers. He tried to take his brother's place in Iraq so his brother could get out. That's how awesome he was." And though that effort did not succeed, when it was Tim's turn to serve in Iraq, he volunteered for all the worst assignments so his brothers-in-arms wouldn't have to take them. That included being the point man, the first person into houses while searching for insurgents.

In the end, it was a helicopter crash that claimed his life. Jake says Tim would rather it was his life than someone else's.

"When stuff happened to others, it hurt him just as much as it was hurting the other guy," Jake said. "He had such a huge heart."

— RP

Honor, Courage, Commitment

"I saw the car pull up and all I remember is a black, shiny shoe. It stepped right into the slush. I can remember the splash. I knew what he was there for. I thought, 'Tim's not coming home.'"

It wasn't the frosty, January weather that sent a shiver up her spine that day. It was the government-issued shoe that plopped itself right into the snowy mixture she had been mindlessly heaving from her Merrimack, NH, driveway.
Elaine Gibson had dreaded this scene for years. Two of her three boys were Marines and "Timmy," a 23-year-old athlete with blonde hair and striking, blue eyes was deployed to Iraq just days after his little brother, Patrick, returned from his second tour in Operation Iraqi Freedom. Despite the many sleepless nights, the Gibson family was hopeful, faithful and proud. An American flag in the front yard trumpeted their patriotism and loyalty; two spotlights flanked Old Glory to keep the Gibsons' spirits high in the darkest of times.

Tim was scheduled to leave Iraq in 18 days when those lights ominously dimmed and the Gibsons' home was shrouded in darkness. The next afternoon, bereavement officers Capt. Kevin Garbe and Gunnery Sgt. Anthony Logie pulled into the driveway where the young Marine's mother was shoveling the burdensome, New Hampshire snow.

Cpl. Timothy M. Gibson, a valiant, baby-faced Marine, was killed in a helicopter crash on Jan. 26, 2005. He was laughing and joking all the way to his last mission, according to his best friend Cpl. Jake Ziliani. Shortly after, Tim and 30 other Marines boarded a fated CH-53E helicopter that was scheduled to patrol the Iraqi borders and safeguard the upcoming elections.

The 400-page report later released by the military said the crash, which occurred near Ar Rutbah in western Iraq, close to the borders of Syria and Jordan, killed everyone on board immediately. A mixture of moisture and dust in the atmosphere — a concoction referred to as "goo" — had created conditions similar to that of a sandstorm. Elaine, who read the report in its entirety, said the pilot had 2.9 seconds to react before the helicopter, which was flying at between 150 and 170 knots, slammed into the ground.

That night, still believing their son would soon be safe at home, Elaine and Tom noticed that both spotlights in their front yard had gone out, and their flag had disappeared into the shadows of the night. They awoke the next morning and began a routine workday. Their eldest son, named after his father, did the same; Patrick was again stationed at Camp Pendleton, CA.

Nearly a week later, Tim came home in a motorcade led by his high school football coach, State Trooper Steve Tarr. He was buried in the Last Rest Cemetery

"A true leader has the confidence to stand alone, the courage to make tough decisions, and the compassion to listen to the needs of others. He does not set out to be a leader, but becomes one by the equality of his actions and the integrity of his intent."

— Gen. Douglas MacArthur

in Merrimack with more than 1,300 of his fellow Marines, former schoolmates, friends and family members in attendance. About 30 Marines were in Tim's honor detail, sitting front and center at the funeral that day. His favorite song, Lee Greenwood's "God Bless the USA," erupted from the speakers. When it comes to recalling the day of Tim's death, his father, donning an "Operation Iraqi Freedom" T-shirt with the image of a black helicopter on it, choked back tears as he leafed through a photo album. His wife devotedly clenches one of her son's dog tags and a single, bent chevron, which were recovered from the crash.

Despite the pain, the Gibsons are quick to share Timmy's stories. They reminisce about the April Fools' pranks he played, the school essay in which he wrote about how difficult it was to be Tommy Gibson's little brother and the time he helped save the life of a young woman who was trying to commit suicide. They know that their Timmy died honorably and they are at peace knowing that he did so while helping others, because although he didn't always know it, that is what Tim did best.

In a letter written to Elaine and Tom on Oct. 13, 2004, Tim, full of pride, told his parents that his platoon was preparing to embark on the Battle of Fallujah. He wrote, "By the time you read this I'll be in the middle of Fallujah somewhere, I'm not sure where, but somewhere there. I think we're going to make history on this one, so watch CNN a little more closely."
The former Merrimack High School star quarterback, who had dreams of becoming a state trooper, found his work to be extremely rewarding and meaningful. His big heart was a perfect fit for the Marines, said Patrick, who insisted his brother embodied the Marine Corp's core values: "Honor, Courage, Commitment."

"He was always looking out for the other guy," his father added, stating he later learned that when those in Tim's platoon were asked who they would want to lead them into battle, their answer was his son. In a letter written on Oct. 16, 2004, Tim wrote of that camaraderie: "I still can't believe we are here right now. It's all right though, we are gonna do what we came here to do and we are gonna be home. It might be a little longer than I thought but not much more, I guess only time will tell. I'm just glad Pat isn't the only one who got to come over here. It's kind of nerve-racking being so close to the city, but I have a bunch of good guys in my platoon to watch my back like I watch their's."

Watching out for others was nothing new to Tim, according to his family. Even at a young age, Tom and Elaine said their son was quick to stand up to bullies in school. As he grew older, Tim blossomed into a humble, gentle man. He was a friend to people from many different backgrounds, interests and beliefs. At his funeral, Elaine said a young man whom she did not know approached her. He told her, with tears in his eyes, that Tim was the only person who was nice to him in high school.

"Tim was a Marine before he was a Marine. He had a gift with people," said Elaine. "He just did what had to be done — not to be a hero — he just saw things that had to be done."

In fact, when Tim learned that his little brother was being deployed to Iraq, he asked his commanding officers if he could volunteer to go in Pat's stead. Though noble, the attempt was not successful. The last time Patrick saw his brother was at Christmas, 2003.

His father continued with the courageous tales. He said Tim heroically rescued Lance Cpl. Matt Morton when the Marine became trapped under a building during the Battle of Fallujah. Tim did all this, Patrick added, while under fire. A *New York Times* story revealed one more spirited tale. Cpl. Dan Elwyard told a newspaper reporter that Tim was first at the scene when he was shot during a firefight. He remembered Tim at his side, saying, "I'm not telling you that you are dying, but if you go, I am there for your family."

Now, Timmy's years of devotion are being repaid. The Gibsons credit their wonderful friends, neighbors and family members for helping them through Timmy's tragic death. They say that they have embraced Jake and Captain Garbe, as well as the entire Marine family, as their own and that they could not be prouder of Timmy and the sacrifices he has made. His father said that when the Iraqi elections were deemed a success, Tim's family and friends celebrated his role and that of all the other men and women who have made the ultimate sacrifice in that victory.

On Jan. 26, 2006, the one-year anniversary of Tim's death, Jake Ziliani ventured from his New York state home to spend some time with the Gibson family, which has grown to encompass all those who were touched by Tim's life. That same day, for the first time since the morning of Tim's death, the spotlights in the front yard dimmed and the Gibsons' cherished American flag eerily went dark once again.

— Marci J. Hait
Publicist, former newspaper editor
bissonbarcelona.com

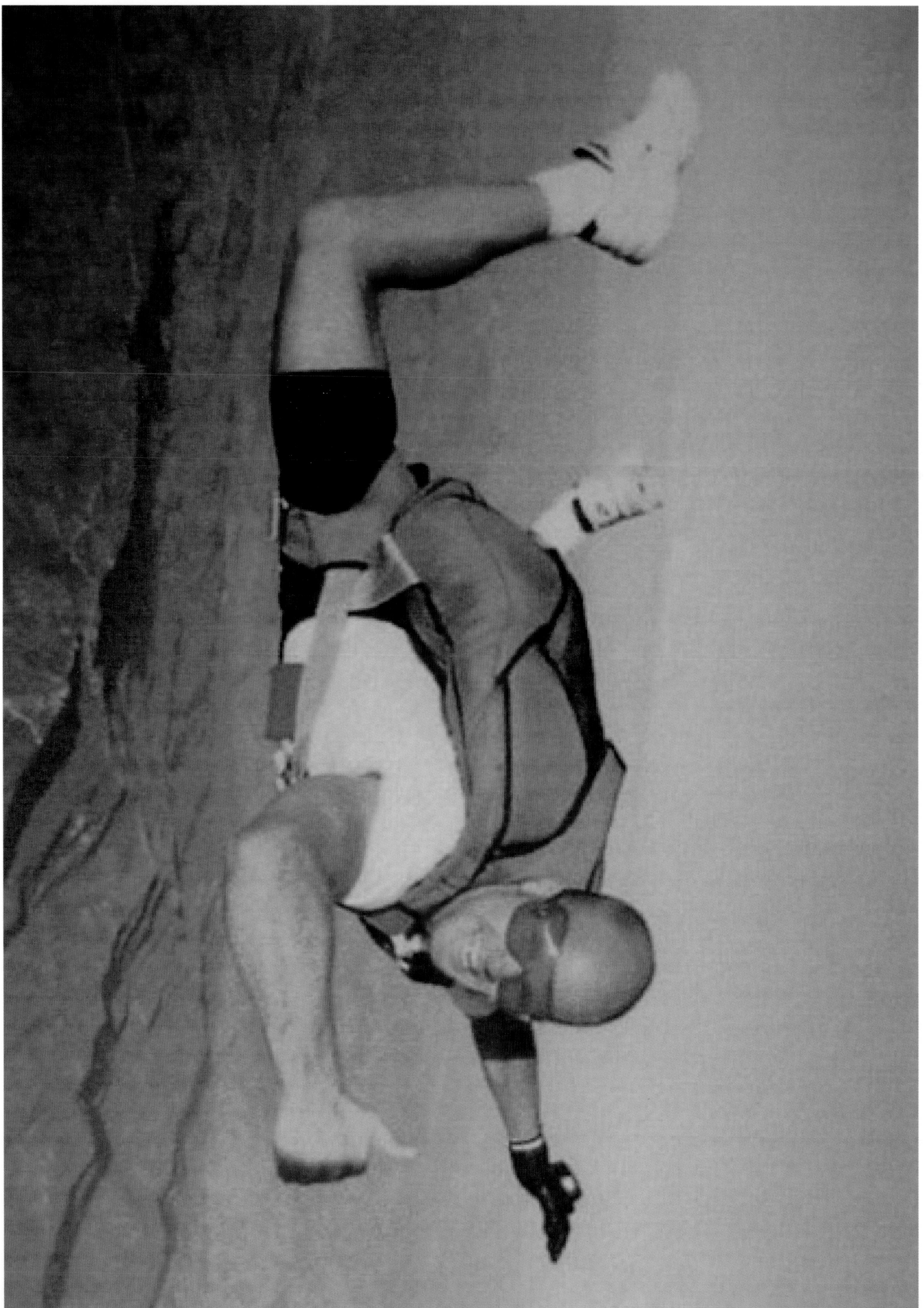

Petty Officer 1st Class David Martin Tapper
August 16, 1971 – August 20, 2003

David Tapper of Atco, NJ had been in the Navy for 13 years. Most of that time, he was a Navy SEAL (SEa, Air and Land commando), trained in special/unconventional warfare.

Senior Chief M.C. (full name withheld for security reasons) knew David for nearly a decade. "He was great with his four kids — very attentive, very focused … he looked at each one of them as an individual," said M.C. "Sometimes we'd share a ride when we had to catch a plane early in the morning, and he'd always run back in to kiss his kids goodbye, even though they were asleep."

M.C. says David also had a very self-deprecating sense of humor. "We sometimes called him Costanza — like Seinfeld's George Costanza — because of his Type-A personality; and he was a good looking guy, but he was balding a little," he said. "He rolled with it! He had a great sense of humor."

What you saw was what you got with David. His buddies remember him as a competitive, positive person, and a "straight-up-guy." "He was about 5'7", but even if he was in a situation where he was the runt of the litter he'd make sure he was on top of the heap. He was just a ball of energy," said M.C.

David spoke Spanish and was also an excellent photographer — two things he learned in the Navy. "He was very good at his job," added M.C. "He loved being a Navy SEAL. I don't think there was anything he would have wanted to do more."

David, 32, was killed by small arms fire while conducting combat operations near the Pakistani border. He was shot in the back during an ambush in Paktika Province, Afghanistan.

— RP

A Mother's Love

For Judi Tapper, the memories are crystal clear. She remembers swimming and adventures, and walking down the beach with a little boy who loved the ocean. His name was David Tapper, and he was Judi's sixth child and only son. The two shared an unbreakable bond.

"We were so close. He was my baby," Judi said. "At night, he'd always come to my room and give me a kiss and say, 'I love you, Mom.'"

Summers at the family beach retreat in Townsend's Inlet in New Jersey sparked David's interest in the Navy. He signed up right after graduating from Edgewood Regional High School in 1989, in his hometown of Atco, NJ.

"When the Navy picked him up that morning, I still remember him with tears in his eyes saying, 'Mom, don't ever sell this house because it's the only one I want to come home to,'" Judi said.

Judi remembers the respect and love her son showed her.

"He didn't care who he was in front of. He'd always kiss me. At boot camp, I can still see him running across the lawn," she said.

David's family knew he would be successful because he was good at everything. A true athlete, he was a wrestler, skydiver, swimmer and scuba diver. David qualified for the elite Navy SEAL training in Coronado, CA. Out of the 135 people who started, David was one of only 23 to graduate.

"They take a pledge that, if necessary, they'll sacrifice their life for their country," Judi said. That worried the loving mother. "I said, 'Don't say that, David. You're my only son,'" said Judi.

During SEAL training, David met and married his wife, Tracy. Their relationship began because of his persistence.

"He just never gave up," laughed Tracy, looking back on what it was about David that drew her to him. "In the end, it was the qualities he had until the day he died." Tracy describes her husband as someone who would do "anything for anybody – no matter what." She admired the way David treated other people. He was also fun to be around, and his positive and jovial outlook was contagious. David and Tracy had four beautiful children: Raimen, Vanessa, Talia and Jared.

David's military career took him around the world. He was in Kuwait at the end of the Gulf War. He also went to Australia, Taiwan, Jordan and Israel.

During early deployments, he instructed foreign nationals in diving. He also helped train his special operations brothers.

In 1997, David passed the difficult and demanding seven-month training program with the Naval Special Warfare Development Group.

Between four- to six-month deployments, David did "double time" with his children, devoting all of his time to them. "He lived for those kids," said Tracy. "When he was home he wanted to be the one to take them to soccer and go to their events. He wanted to make up for the time he'd been gone … even changing diapers by the fourth child."

The Tapper family was last stationed at Virginia Beach, VA. One of David's favorite places to spend time with the kids was at the beach.

"He loved to take him there after dinner. They would go body surfing, run around, take the dog. He wanted them all to be there," said Tracy.

Then came Sept. 11, 2001.

Judi said, "I went to church that night. I was devastated and depressed. I knew this was going to be the beginning of him having to be in a war. And I was scared. I never wanted him to say goodbye." David told her not to worry because they were well-protected, but Judi knew she wouldn't stop worrying about her only son.

In the Middle East, David's work ethic and attitude led to the success of numerous missions in hostile environments, for which he earned a Bronze Star for valor.

"He believed in what he was doing. It was something he said he had to do," Judi said.

David also earned a second Bronze Star, the Defense Meritorious Service Medal, Joint Service Commendation Medal, Joint Service Achievement Medal, two Navy and Marine Corps Achievement Medals, two Combat Action Ribbons and numerous other awards.

David's father, Ken Tapper, said he is proud of his son's accomplishments

"He was dedicated to helping resolve the problems we have today, he was very good at what he did and his team members looked up to him," said Ken, a Navy veteran himself. "He made a lot of sacrifices." Ken said David had four uncles who are Navy veterans as well, along with another who was in the Air Force.

His mother said, "David loved his job. He loved the men he worked with. He was proud to be a Navy Seal."

On August 20, 2003, four days after his 32nd birthday, David was killed in an Al-Qaeda ambush in Afghanistan.

Judi says she's still devastated and that she misses her son everyday. "There is no greater pain in life," she said. But she is also proud of her son and what his life meant.

"I am most proud of what he stood for and how much he honored his country. He fought for freedom," Judi said. "My prayers have always been that more people would be aware of how much these soldiers give, and how many give the supreme sacrifice."

She continues to keep his memory alive. "I have a scrapbook," she said. "I sit down and look at it over and over again." She also tells David's children stories about their father.

Today, there is a monument honoring David at the Waterford Township War Memorial in David's hometown of Atco, New Jersey.

Judi wrote a letter about David to the people who supported the building of the memorial. In it, she said, "David was a courageous protector, first of his family and friends, then of our country. In the end, he gave the ultimate sacrifice to stand up for what he loved and believed in. His life shall be honored with loving memories of a special man who was a son, a brother, a husband, a father and a warrior."

— Jennifer Wilson
News reporter for WIS-TV in Columbia, SC

G J3
G J3

Lance Cpl. Christopher Adlesperger
October 24, 1984 — December 9, 2004

On Nov. 10, 2004, in 30 minutes of close combat, Marine Pfc. Christopher Adlesperger (posthumously promoted to lance corporal and awarded the Navy Cross), a soft-spoken, religious young man who loved poetry and art, attacked an enemy stronghold in Fallujah, Iraq. He killed at least 11 insurgents with his M-16 and his grenade launcher.

The enemy fighters were heavily armed and probably high on drugs — and they had just killed his close friend, Lance Cpl. Erick Hodges. Christopher protected two wounded squad members from attack and saved innumerable Marines.

When it was over, Christopher's face had been bloodied by shrapnel and he had bullet holes in the sleeve and collar of his uniform. He refused to be evacuated until Erick's body was recovered.

"It was a tremendous bit of fighting," said Col. Patrick Malay, the battalion commander. "He was a quiet kid, but he was remarkable. He was one tough bastard."

For his bravery, Christopher was nominated for the Medal of Honor in Iraq. He was also promoted meritoriously to lance corporal. His mother, Annette Griego, remembers "Chris" calling home to tell her about the promotion, saying "How cool is that?"

A month after his heroic efforts in that firefight, Christopher was killed. On Dec. 9, 2004 he led Marines in storming another building where insurgents were hiding. He was shot in the heart and died instantly.

— Tony Perry

Marine hero knew only one way: straight ahead

Only after his death did family members learn of Christopher Adlesperger's bravery. At first they were shocked -- this was the same person who had once cringed at the thought of shooting birds on a hunting trip. Then they recognized in the details of the firefight the determined youth they knew and loved.

"That was Chris. Whatever he did, he always went in with the idea that nobody was going to beat him, nobody," said Dennis Adlesperger, 53, his uncle.
Centuries of warfare have not entirely answered the question of why some fighters, in times of maximum chaos and danger, act in a heroic fashion, putting concern for their own lives in abeyance.

Much of the Marine philosophy about bravery can be found in the classic study "The Anatomy of Courage," published in 1945 by Lord Moran, a British physician who served at the front during World War I.

Dr. Moran's thesis is that men fight not just for survival or patriotism but in response to strong leadership -- and because they have grown to identify with their group so tightly that any threat to the group is seen as intolerable.

Courage, Dr. Moran suggests, is a moral quality that comes from an unwillingness to quit. Fear, he says, is a critical part of it. Without fear, he argues, there is no courage; fear provides the energy, the resolve.

In boot camp in San Diego, one of Christopher Adlesperger's drill instructors instilled the reality of combat when he scanned more than 100 recruits sitting attentively on the exercise field and picked 10 at random to stand up.

"When your company goes to Iraq, this is the number of Marines who won't be coming home alive," the DI barked.
He ordered 10 more to stand. "And this is how many more will die if you don't start listening to me."

Normally self-confident, Pfc. Aldesperger sounded shaken when he told his mother about the lecture.

"Chris said the DI scared him, but it helped him realize what Iraq was going to be like, that he was going to have to learn to protect his Marines," said Annette Griego, 41, Pfc. Aldesperger's mother.

Looking back, family members realized Pfc. Aldesperger was a nearly perfect candidate to become a Marine. He loved family and structure, even though he did not always have that. His mother and father were unmarried when he was born, and their hasty marriage soon dissolved.

Pfc. Aldesperger grew up in Albuquerque mostly with his father, Gary, a pipe fitter and recovering alcoholic with a checkered employment history. He also lived for several years with his paternal grandmother, spent some summers with his mother and finished high school at the home of his mother's parents. He accommodated all of the moves.

"He was always trying to please people; he was starved for affection," Pfc. Aldesperger's uncle Dennis said.

He was close to his aunts and uncles and cousins and particularly to his grandfather, Edwin Adlesperger, a retired oil-company sales representative. The two enjoyed camping and fishing, and Ed gave his grandson a used Ford Contour.

Ed Adlesperger died unexpectedly in August 2003 at age 73. Chris Adlesperger, who had enrolled at the University of New Mexico, quit after a few weeks. Family members believe that if his grandfather hadn't died, he would not have enlisted.

"He was grieving his grandfather, looking for something he lost, some structure," said Phillip Blackman, who had been Chris Adlesperger's tae-kwon-do coach and gave the eulogy at his funeral. Under Mr. Blackman's tutelage, Pfc. Aldesperger had become a national champion.

"He only knew one way: straight ahead," Mr. Blackman said. "There was no 'retreat' in his vocabulary."
By all accounts, Pfc. Aldesperger loved the Marine Corps. He thrived on the physical challenge and packed muscle onto his 5-foot-8, 150-pound frame. He got a tattoo, USMC, down the right side of his stomach. He formed fast friendships.

"The Marine Corps became his family, and when they went to fight, he was looking out for his brothers," said Debra McAtee, 42, whose sister is Pfc. Aldesperger's mother.

Shortly after dawn on Nov. 10, 2004, the Marines of Kilo Company in the 3rd Battalion, 5th Regiment, pushed out. The battalion had drawn one of the most dangerous sectors, the Jolan neighborhood in Fallujah's northwest corner.

Like window washers trying to clean a grime-streaked window, the Marines would sweep methodically through Fallujah, searching each house for insurgents in what they called the squeegee tactic.

For hours, they faced only minor resistance. A few more buildings and they could stop for the night.

"We had cleared buildings all day, hundreds of them, but on that 101st house, that's the one that gets you, and that's what happened," said Gunnery Sgt. Paul Starner, Pfc. Aldesperger's platoon sergeant.

Like a lot of buildings in Jolan, the structure had a wall around it. There was a courtyard in front and an outdoor stairway leading to the roof.

Pfc. Aldesperger, acting as the point man for the four-man fire team, attempted to knock down a gate. Cpl. Hodges moved forward and was immediately felled by a hail of bullets, probably from a concealed opening in the masonry wall.

As they rushed the house, Navy corpsman Alonso Rogero was hit in the stomach and Lance Cpl. Ryan Sunnerville in the leg. Grainy, shaky film of the incident shows Cpl. Sunnerville hopping on one leg, still firing his M-16. Marines and insurgents exchanged gunfire at a distance of no more than 20 feet. From inside the building, the insurgents threw grenades.

The insurgents had hoped to spring what is called a Chechen ambush. The strategy, Marines determined later, was to wound Marines attempting to enter the building. When other Marines came to help, an insurgent sniper down an alleyway was to pick off corpsmen, radio operators and officers. And when enough Marines or vehicles were gathered, the insurgents planned to fire rocket-propelled grenades.

Pfc. Aldesperger fired at the insurgent machine-gun position as he ran toward Corpsman Rogero and Cpl. Sunnerville. He helped the two up the outside stairway to the roof.

As insurgents tried to storm the stairway, Pfc. Aldesperger killed them before they could reach the roof. Shrapnel ripped into his face.

From his rooftop position, he could see insurgents peppering Cpl. Hodges' lifeless body with bullets, including two to his head. When one insurgent ran from the building to seize Cpl. Hodges' weapon, Pfc. Aldesperger killed the insurgent with a single shot.

Still, the machine-gun position inside the building had not been touched, and it was pinning down Marines gathering to assault the building from the front. With no time to consult officers, and with other Marine units engaged in firefights, Pfc. Aldesperger was left to his own initiative.

"Chris essentially took over," Col. Malay said.

Unable to penetrate the building with his M-16, Pfc. Aldesperger shifted to the grenade launcher. Standing on the roof, he blew holes in the building and then rained down gunfire on the insurgents below. They returned fire and then fled. Pfc. Aldesperger killed four insurgents who fled into the courtyard, each with a shot to the head. By Col. Malay's estimate, Pfc. Aldesperger killed a total of 11 insurgents. The actual number may be higher.

The building had been an insurgent command-and-control center. Failure to quickly subdue it, Col. Malay concluded, could have thrown off the timetable for the Fallujah assault, which depended on speed and keeping U.S. casualties to a minimum.

Marines from other rooftops joined Pfc. Aldesperger and began preparing the wounded for evacuation. Once that was done and Cpl. Hodges' body was removed, the Marines pushed in one side of the building with an amphibious assault vehicle. Pfc. Aldesperger insisted on being the first Marine to search the building to make sure all the insurgents were dead.

On Thanksgiving weekend, with the entire company watching, Pfc. Aldesperger, who had just turned 20, was promoted to lance corporal because of his actions on Nov. 10. Sgt. Starner also started talking with Pfc. Aldesperger about attending sniper school, a prized assignment.

In early December, Central Command ordered a second round of squeegee to catch insurgents who had been overlooked or who had managed to sneak back into the city.

This time, fewer troops were assigned; some battalions had been redeployed to other cities as the U.S. military tried to decrease its Fallujah "footprint" in advance of the city being reopened to residents.

This time, Pfc. Aldesperger's battalion was assigned to sweep a different neighborhood. "We moved across the Line of Departure, and 20 minutes later Chris was dead," Col. Malay said.

Pfc. Aldesperger had taken the lead in approaching a nondescript house. He was hit in his flak vest by multiple rounds. The impact spun him around, and one round struck his side, where there were no protective plates. He died instantly from a bullet to the heart.

Sgt. Starner and other Marines lifted Pfc. Aldesperger's body onto a Humvee. An air strike demolished the building, burying the living and dead in rubble.

Months later, when the deployment ended, the boot camp DI's prediction had proved eerily accurate. In Pfc. Aldesperger's Kilo Company, 11 Marines had been killed.

— Tony Perry
Writer for the Los Angeles Times

Cpl. Seamus M. Davey
October 24, 1979 – October 21, 2005

Seamus Davey grew up in a rural community in upstate New York. The natural athlete was also the son of a Marine, so it came as little surprise when he joined the Corps right out of high school.

The young Marine, who quickly showed his talents in infantry tactics, was later assigned to the elite 4th Force Reconnaissance Battalion in Reno, Nevada – a unit specializing in parachute and scuba operations.

Seamus's first stint in Iraq came not as a Marine, but as a military contractor. He spent several months working on a personal security detail in which he protected State Department officials near Tikrit. A short time later, Seamus was back in Iraq fighting for his country. Only two and a half months into the deployment, he was killed in action during combat operations. His friend and fellow Marine who survived the firefight, Sgt. Derek Lee, credits Seamus for saving his life that day.

"Seamus, my one and only Big Brother. Now you are looked upon as a hero to many...you have ALWAYS been a hero to me. You fought for what you believed in just as you had the past 25 years," wrote Brittany Davey, one of Seamus's little sisters.

Seamus, a Bronze Star recipient, is survived by his parents, Lorene and Derek Davey and three sisters: Shiloh, Brittany and Austin.

– *RP*

Selfless Actions

Cpl. Seamus Davey's story is the stuff of blockbuster movies, but his friend who lived to tell the tale wept because it is so real.

Derek Lee recalled that night when he, Seamus and a handful of Marines conducted a sweep of an Iraqi town known to be a staging area for insurgents. Derek said they were going house to house looking for terrorists, weapons and explosives. During daylight sweeps, Marines are peacefully allowed to enter a house and search with no problem.

This time things went differently.

Derek's pale blue eyes were streaked with red, his face covered in tears as he told the story. Derek made it out alive on that October day, but it seemed as if a part of him was dying as he relived what happened – the day he said Seamus Davey saved his life.

Derek said it started when he went into the backroom of a house they were searching. There, he saw blankets, four men and one AK-47 assault rifle. Each Iraqi home is allowed to have one rifle for defense, so the Marines weren't particularly alarmed. One of the men moved a little and Derek yelled in Arabic for the man to stop.

That's when the bottom fell out.

There were three more automatic weapons under the blankets, and when Derek yelled "stop," all four of the men instantly started firing. Derek was hit several times, but the body armor and the equipment hanging on his chest and belt kept the bullets from penetrating. The impact of the bullets knocked him down. Derek said Seamus Davey stood beside him and started shooting back. Seamus carried a big belt-fed automatic weapon called a SAW. He posed the biggest threat and the enemy knew it. They unloaded their weapons on him. Amazingly, Seamus stood his ground and fired back; he drew the attention off his friend so Derek could crawl out of the line of fire and out of the room. Derek made it back to home to the United States to his wife and new baby.

Seamus was killed three days shy of his 26th birthday.

"I love him, I miss him, I'm sorry we couldn't bring him back," Derek said.

All you could hear was the rumbling of the boat engine after Derek finished talking. Nearly 50 Marines had joined the Davey family for a memorial service onboard a two story cruise boat in the middle of the St. Lawrence River in upstate New York. On a boat called the *Freedom One*, Seamus was posthumously awarded the Bronze Star for the heroic actions he took that day.

As Derek knelt down to present the medal to Seamus's mother, Lorene Davey, a number of the men there fought back tears. Others cried openly. It's a scene you don't often see depicted in Hollywood: real men, fit, many with tattoos, all trained to take out the enemy if necessary, standing there fighting the pits in their stomachs, and the emptiness in their hearts. It's a natural reaction when you lose a friend — a brother. Seamus's sisters lost a brother, too. The three beautiful young ladies loved Seamus deeply and by all accounts, they were his world. They said they can't remember a time when their protective older brother wasn't looking out for them.

When Seamus was in kindergarten and the teacher assigned the class a project, he would wait until all of the other kids left before asking the teacher for two more of everything. Then he'd run home with extra crayons and worksheets to meet two sisters anxiously waiting for him on the front porch, ready to hear what Seamus had learned that day.

Seamus and his oldest sister Shiloh were born less than a year apart, but they might have well have been twins. They always had an extra special connection. On her birthday, Seamus always tried to call Shiloh first. In fact, Shiloh said that's the last time she talked to her big brother. He called from overseas on her birthday; he wasn't one to break family tradition. On Shiloh's wedding day, months after Seamus was killed, a lone seagull flew in circles over the wedding party. Everyone who saw it decided it had to be Seamus' spirit, continuing to watch over his sister.

Seamus had also been known to call his youngest sister from Iraq to wish her luck before her soccer games. The girls have made a pact. The sister who has a son first will name the boy Seamus in honor of their big brother.
On board the boat, the girls stood with their arms around their parents. Each one took a turn sprinkling their brother's ashes into the water.

Seamus' dad, also a Marine, remembered his last conversation with his son. Derek Davey said he was a manly man, too tough to tell his son that he loved him while Seamus was growing up. Derek said he's glad he finally came to his senses when Seamus was in his twenties. "I love you" was the last thing he said to his son when Seamus called by satellite phone. A few short weeks later, Seamus was dead.

Before he deployed, Seamus told his mom that if something happened to him, he wanted to be cremated and have his ashes sprinkled into the ocean. She made the pact with her only son, thinking that if she said it out loud, it would be like an insurance policy that they would never need.

When Lorene Davey asked her son which ocean, he told her she would know when the time was right. While the Davey family shared special moments on a number of beaches, Lorene said Seamus considered the St. Lawrence River, which winds its way along the Canadian border into the Atlantic, his home. Lorene said Seamus was always a good swimmer, and he will eventually find his way to the perfect spot.

As the Daveys stood side by side saying their final goodbyes, the waves lapped against the side of the boat. A stone cross sat atop a hillside on an island in the distance. From the deck above, red and white roses sprinkled into the water like rain — the flowers signifying messages, thoughts and words left unspoken. They will accompany Seamus on his journey to the Atlantic, to the place of which he and his mother spoke while he was still alive.

— Kara Gormley Meador
News anchor and reporter for WIS-TV in Columbia, SC

Sgt. Mark Phillip Adams
August 8, 1981 – October 15, 2005

Marine Sgt. Mark Adams' parents had never seen their son so driven as when he began wrestling.

Until that point, nearly everything he did was practically effortless.

Schoolwork became so unchallenging that he convinced one teacher to let him keep his head down on his desk — on the condition he made all As. And he did.

Growing up, Mark spent a lot of time trying to get out chores, often complaining his way out of them. He didn't like to break a sweat. But that was then.

When faced with being the underdog as a wrestler at Cary High School in Cary, NC, Mark rose to the challenge and conquered. What he lacked in talent, he more than made up for in tenacity and drive.

He was so dedicated that, after a stint in the United States Marine Corps, he returned to Cary High as a volunteer wrestling coach while attending college. Mark selflessly devoted his time, hoping to make a difference in the young athletes' lives. After he died, Mark's mother, René, felt proud when she heard from a student wrestler's father that Mark was a major influence in his son's life and was responsible for some truly positive changes.

It was no surprise to his family to learn he had decided he owed the Marines more. Although he had served for four years, he had not yet done a tour of duty in Iraq. At that point in his life, volunteering for combat with his brothers-in-arms was more important than obtaining a college education.

"When you're in an infantry platoon you've got to be able to count on people around you — Mark was one of those people. He was a quick decision-maker and you could always count on him to make the right decision," said former active duty Marine Sgt. Nick Werner, who served with Mark. "He wasn't the kind of leader who barked orders from the rear and expected people to follow … he lead by example. There was this charisma — people naturally followed him."

— RP

Driven

A former captain of Cary High School's powerhouse wrestling team was killed in Iraq on Saturday, October 15, 2005 while on patrol with his Marine unit. Sergeant Mark P. Adams, 24, who grew up in Morrisville, NC, died near Ramadi, west of Baghdad, after a roadside bomb exploded near his Humvee. Adams, whom the Pentagon identified on October 17, was the sixth Triangle serviceman to be killed in Iraq since the war began in 2003.

The Adams' home is tucked down a dirt road in a leftover pocket of pre-boom Wake County. Parents Phillip and René, and brothers Marshall, 28, and Mike, 25, recently sat at a table on the deck there and remembered.

They remembered a kid who said what was on his mind, who complained at such length about garden work that his father sent him inside — where he grinned ear-to-ear at dodging the steamy chore. They remembered a boy who followed his brothers in playing with G.I. Joes, in dressing in camouflage and running backyard patrols, then into the real military.

They remembered his Michael Jackson act on the dance floor at Marshall's wedding reception in full Marine dress uniform -- except for one missing white glove. "Always the life of the party," his dad said. Mostly they laughed. Sometimes they couldn't."I look right there," said Phillip Adams, going silent for a minute, able only to gesture at an empty chair between Mike and Marshall.

He got his breath again.

"There will be an empty chair at the table from now on."

They agreed that Adams' wrestling career was a turning point. His was not a tale of natural talent. That's why Cary High wrestling coach Jerry Winterton has shared it to inspire his team every year since Adams graduated. Adams signed up to wrestle as a short, pudgy and unskilled ninth-grader. As his father put it, Adams was "beaten like a wet dog" his freshman year. Winterton said he was surprised that Adams stayed to finish the season on the team, which has won 13 state titles.

Something had happened to Adams, though.

The kid who had complained about gardening was gone. Adams worked hard in the off-season, honing his body, going to wrestling camps, doing everything he could to improve. Though he didn't start his freshman year or his sophomore year or his junior year, he began to catch up to the kids who had been wrestling years longer.

Then he caught them.

Then he passed them.

For the 1998-1999 team, Winterton did something he wouldn't have thought possible three years earlier: He made Adams a captain.

"He had just outworked everybody," Winterton said. "He went from no potential in the sport, to a little, to OK, maybe, to someone we relied upon to win."It was easy to make the decision to put him out front."
That year, the team won another state championship, and Adams graduated and joined the Marines.

After the September 11 terrorist attacks, Adams wanted to get into the fight, said brother Mike. Instead, he was stuck on deployment in Okinawa, Japan. When his enlistment ran out, he left the Marines in frustration and spent about a year studying at Wake Tech, though he wasn't quite sure what he wanted to do. He came back to Cary High as a volunteer assistant to Winterton, and the team won two more titles with his help.

But Adams decided he was wasting his time in school; and in late June 2005, he went to see his former gunnery sergeant and said he wanted back in -- on the condition that the Corps sent him to Iraq.

In September 2005, when his unit was getting ready to ship out, Adams' parents went to Camp Lejeune to say goodbye. Mark wore sunglasses all day, probably because tree-stump-tough Marines aren't supposed to shed tears, his father said.

In his last call home on Thursday, October 13, 2005, he called his father and was in good spirits -- in part because he had been promoted to platoon sergeant, but also because he so strongly believed in his cause, his parents said.

"He was a Marine's Marine, and he was doing exactly what he wanted to do," his father said.

The following Sunday afternoon, Adams' parents drove home from church and his father saw a strange car at the end of their dead-end road.
When they turned in their driveway, the car came toward them. Phillip Adams saw the two men in Marine uniforms and his heart clenched.
Mark Adams, they told him, had been standing in the machine gun turret of the armored Humvee, the only position on the truck that's exposed. A piece of shrapnel from a bomb blast struck him just under the back of his Kevlar helmet. No one else in the Humvee was hurt.

It's unusual for a platoon sergeant, with 30 Marines under him, to take the turret. But before Mark had left for Iraq, Mike Adams said, he mentioned another sergeant who had said he'd never get up in the turret. "Mark said he wouldn't ask his Marines to do something he wouldn't do himself."
"That was Mark," said Marshall Adams.

— Jay Price
Military Writer
Reprinted with permission of The News & Observer of Raleigh, NC
Original Title: War Claims Wake Native

Spc. Jon Paul Fettig
January 3, 1973 — July 22, 2003

Army Spc. Jon Fettig didn't have to go to Iraq. He volunteered. The 11-year veteran of Dickinson's 164th Engineer Battalion switched to a National Guard unit that was in need of more soldiers so he could help out. Jon's wife, Cody, said her husband told her he was willing to give his life for his country.

The deployment meant the couple would have to put their plans of starting a family on hold, but that didn't stop Jon from being a devoted husband. He called home whenever he could.

Family was important to Jon. He spoke to his parents, Larry and Shirley Fettig, often while in Iraq. He even checked in from time to time with his younger brother and sister, Craig and Tenille. The day before he died, Jon called his grandmother to wish her a happy birthday.

Jon was killed when his unit was ambushed outside Ar Ramadi while traveling to the Euphrates River. He was with a convoy that was delivering supplies and dropping off soldiers to relieve others with the 957th who were on river patrol. That included Jon's brother-in-law, Donny Ladwig. The two were great friends.

It's hard for Jon's family to accept that they will never again pick up the phone to find him on the other line. But they are comforted by the memories. Because of the way he lived his life, there was never a question about how much he loved them. Jon was 30 years old.

— RP

Our Rock

Jon Fettig had a knack for fixing things, and computers were his specialty.
"He could hit one or two keys," said his father, Larry Fettig, with a chuckle of admiration, "and he wouldn't tell you what the hell he did, but it was fixed."
The North Dakota Army National Guard specialist was also an avid reader, escaping into the magical world of Harry Potter. He loved computerized video games based on Dungeons & Dragons, where mystical heroes set out to conquer evil empires, battling monsters and collecting magic items along the way. Family members say the high-tech games stirred the imagination and creativity of the soft-spoken Dickinson man.

"Jon and my brother, Craig, connected their computers together in a room and they would never have any lights on," said Jon's sister, Tenille Ehrmantraut, smiling at the memory of the all-night video games her brothers and their close buddies would frequently play, creating "their own computer dungeon."
The games were intense. At one point, Craig Fettig said, a Dungeons & Dragon marathon with his brother lasted almost four months.

Jon's passion for computers and video games was so encompassing that he almost missed out on the love of his life. It took his sharp-eyed sister, playing matchmaker, to bring Jon and his future wife, Cody, together.
"He met Cody while working at Happy Joe's," said Tenille. "One night, Cody told me she thought Jon was cute." After checking with her shy brother, she discovered the feeling was mutual. "I said to him 'Well, this is silly. Ask her out.'"
He did, and the couple married in 1999.

Thirty-year-old Jon joined the National Guard in Dickinson to help pay for college and was working on a degree as a computer programmer when he volunteered to go to Iraq to fill a vacancy in another unit, the 957th Multi-Role Bridge Company out of Bismarck. Sitting in the screened front porch of the Fettig family home on a warm July afternoon, parents Larry and Shirley, along with Tenille, talked about Jon's decision to go to Iraq in early 2003.

"I said to him: 'This is not a war game. This is live bullets. You may not return. Are you sure you are ready to do this?'" recalled his father. "Jon replied 'I trained for this for 12 years. I want to go.'"

While in Iraq, Jon made sure to call Cody as often as possible. After speaking with her as long as he could, he would turn right around and get back in line to use the phone after hanging up.

On July 22, 2003, 18 soldiers from the 957th set out in five vehicles for a supply run west of Baghdad. Jon was at the wheel of a large cargo truck when the convoy was ambushed by attackers using rocket propelled grenades (RPGs) and automatic weapons. He was the first North Dakota Army National Guard soldier killed in battle since the Korean War.

"Jon's death took a toll on the unit as the loss of any member does," said Command Sgt. Maj. Kevin Remington, Jon's former mission commander. "The impact of his death was perhaps magnified by the fact that he was the first soldier from our unit and our state that was seriously wounded, much less killed. Until that day, we had only a couple of soldiers who had received shrapnel wounds. In addition to Jon's death, Spc. Brandon Erickson was severely injured and ended up having his right arm amputated as a result of the ambush. All of this together hit the unit hard. Most of the unit was young and only a handful had ever been in a combat zone before."
Remington also spoke of Jon's character.

"Jon, like many others, was an absolute team player," he said. "He was not concerned with how a tasking would affect him personally, but rather with how his piece of the puzzle fit into the bigger picture. He understood very well that all have a role to play in a team effort and Jon gave his best in whatever role he was assigned ... I cannot remember Jon ever creating a leadership challenge, even in the smallest way. He was just one of those guys that took his job seriously and accepted what he was tasked with and did the best he could to meet whatever intent he was given."

For the Fettig family, the void left by Jon's death was almost unbearable. The son who spent hours setting up model trains with his father, cooked pancakes with his mother, shared books with his brother, teased his sister and worshiped his wife of four years was gone.

"He was our rock," said his mother.

Then the mail came.

Condolence cards and letters started arriving in the Fettigs' mailbox, many from relatives and friends, but hundreds more from strangers across the United States and Canada. The family says the heartfelt personal messages of thanks found in each card helped them cope with their loss.
In all, they estimate they received more than a thousand pieces of mail in the weeks following Jon's death — enough to fill four apple crates.

"We read every card, every word, every verse," said Shirley. "Many of the cards would trigger a memory about Jon and we would talk about him. They say memories heal. Well, we have a lot of memories."

To the Fettigs' surprise, many of the cards contained money. Five-, 10- and 20-dollar bills to honor the fallen soldier, along with two very large donations, were sent mostly by strangers. After it all came in, the family realized there was enough money to help establish a scholarship fund in Jon's name at nearby Dickinson State University. The Fettigs decided the money would help aspiring computer students with connections to the local or state National Guard. So far, the Fettigs have chosen three individuals to receive the annual scholarships. Jon's parents say the scholarship is a fitting legacy for a soldier who dreamed of working on computers while devoting his days to his friends, family and the National Guard, and who gave his life for his country.

— Jane Watrel
NBC freelance correspondent, Washington, D.C.

"The ultimate measure of a man is not where he stands in moments of comfort and convenience, but where he stands at times of challenge and controversy."

— Martin Luther King, Jr.

Lance Cpl. Brian Paul Montgomery
June 8, 1979 — August 1, 2005

Marine Lance Cpl. Brian Paul Montgomery of Willoughby, Ohio served as a sniper in Iraq. He and five other Marines were killed by enemy small-arms fire while conducting dismounted operations outside Haditha. Brian was 26 years old with a wife and baby boy.

"Alex and his wife Pam were his life," said Eric Montgomery, Brian's younger brother by four years. The pair served together in Iraq. Brian had a deep conviction that he wanted to defend this country against terrorism.

"He wanted to make the world a little safer for [his son] Alex to grow up in and it didn't matter if he was killed. That's the type of guy he was," said Eric who remembers how his brother's courage and mental strength helped others around him endure the mission.

Brian's sense of humor also played a big role in getting his comrades through the day- to-day operations.

"He'd light up the room when he was around," remembered Eric. "He was the type of guy who always wanted to entertain people and make sure everyone around him was laughing."

Anyone who knew Brian also knew he loved to debate. He would argue about anything, from politics to cartoons.

"You could be totally agreeing on the subject and he'd still argue with you. He'd violently agree!" laughed Eric.

Now, the Montgomery family is beginning to see a lot of Brian's traits in his toddler son. Young Alex does not yet comprehend his loss. But his family hopes he grows up to understand his father's sacrifice and that he died a hero.

— RP

My Brother's Keeper

Growing up, Lance Cpl. Brian Montgomery and Lance Cpl. Eric Montgomery were as different as night and day, but the best of friends. Big brother Brian liked to create video games, Eric liked to play them. Brian was focused and patient, Eric was active and athletic. Whenever Eric needed help, Brian was there to protect him. But on August 1st, 2005 the boyhood roles reversed. Eric became his brother's keeper when he escorted Brian's body home to Willoughby, Ohio.

"It wasn't real; I couldn't believe it," said Eric. "It was utter devastation. Right away I thought, 'What am I going to say to my mom and dad?'"

Ask anyone about Lance Cpl. Brian Montgomery, and you'll get the same answer: he was the Marine with the contagious smile. It was his trademark and now his everlasting legacy.

"He was a very fun-loving person," remembers his proud father, Paul Montgomery. "I don't think I have a picture of him that he doesn't have a smile on his face."

Since he was a young child, Brian had deep convictions: help when you can, and defend those who cannot defend themselves. His calling became even stronger after the September 11 attacks. Brian chose to put college and his job on hold to join the Marine Corps Reserves. He scored so highly on his aptitude tests that he could have chosen a job away from the front lines, but his father says that wasn't Brian.

"He said, 'No. Real Marines are grunts. They're the boots on the ground, they carry a rifle, and they're at the front lines and that's where I want to be because that's where you make a difference.'"

It was that loyalty and charming smile that swept Brian's wife, Pamela, off her feet. The two had been friends since they were teenagers. Brian graduated from Willoughby South High School. Pamela graduated from neighboring Mentor High School. They didn't start dating until a few years later when Brian was a customer at the bar where Pamela was working. They talked all night long.

"I just looked at him, and I said this is the man I'm going to marry." Pamela remembered. "I just knew it."

The two bought a video rental store and later opened a video gaming center. On August 3, 2004, the couple had their first child, Alexander Michael. A few months later, Brian and Eric's unit, 3rd Battalion, 25th Marines, Marine Forces Reserve, out of Brook Park, Ohio, was deployed. Even though Pamela was concerned about her husband's safety and understood the risk of becoming a widow with a small child and two businesses to run, she says they both believed strongly in the mission.

"I had a really good feeling. It never happens to you. It happens to everybody else, but not you," Pamela said.

Brian's Father was a little more concerned. "I said, 'With a newborn, you shouldn't be going.' And Brian said, 'That's irrelevant. The bottom line is somebody needs to do this, and I'm as able as anyone else.'"

In January, 2005, the unit left Akron, Ohio for additional training before heading to Iraq. Paul hugged both his boys goodbye. He was worried and had a feeling that he couldn't shake. He sensed that Eric would be all right, but with Brian there was more of a concern.

"I told him jokingly, 'If you don't come back I'll never speak to you again.' He kinda chuckled about that and he gave me a great big hug and he said, 'Dad, don't worry, I'll be back, nothing is going to happen.'"

Brian and Eric were both stationed at the Haditha Dam for most of their deployment in Iraq. Brian was a sniper, and Eric was a field radio operator who also served in a mobile assault platoon. Despite fighting a war, Eric says serving together was the best experience of his life. "We had good times getting to hang out with each other every day."

But the camaraderie and brotherly bond soon turned to grief.

On August 1st, Eric heard that two sniper teams had been ambushed. Five Marines were killed and one was missing. Eric feared the worst when officers told him that Brian was among them, but they couldn't confirm if Brian was still alive. Eric paced the room for an hour before he learned that the attack killed all six Marines, Cpl. Jeffrey Boskovitch, Lance Cpl. Roger Castleberry Jr., Sgt. David Coullard, Lance Cpl. Daniel Deyarmin Jr., Sgt. Nathaniel Rock, and Lance Cpl. Brian Montgomery. During that same week another fourteen Marines were killed from the 3/25. The Marine in Eric wanted his platoon to go out and help in anyway he could, but his officers convinced him to cut his tour of duty short and take care of his family.

Back in Ohio, Paul remembers the sinking feeling when he got that heart-stopping knock on the door. In a split second, he figured that if Brian had been killed the Marines would notify Pam. With tears already rolling down his face, he opened the door and said, "Eric?"

They said, "No Eric is fine."

For a moment, he felt relief, thinking both his sons were safe. But then it hit him "As quickly as I got happy," said Paul, "it dawned on me that they're here because of Brian."

As Eric was escorting Brian's body home, he thought about a promise he made to his brother.

"He said to me, 'If I go down you make sure my son gets my tags, and you make sure you take care of Alexander and look after him,'" Eric remembered. "And I said, 'Absolutely.'"

Even though Brian is gone, his spirit and that contagious smile live on in his son.

"He is so much like his father it's just amazing," said Paul. "He looks like Brian did when he was young. He's always smiling and he has the same kind of disposition. He's just a very lovable, little guy. I'm so thankful we have him."

Paul still has a message that Brian left on the family's answering machine. He hopes to play it someday for Alexander so he can hear his father's voice. He wants to tell Alexander what a hero his dad was and how he loved his country so much he was willing to die for it.

For Eric, he sees Brian's death as a gift of life. It was Brian's way of continuing to be his brother's keeper, like he had done since childhood. From the day the two found out they were going to Iraq, to the moment they touched down on Iraqi soil, Brian wanted to protect Eric no matter what the cost.

"I feel like he just wanted to make sure I got home, and he brought me home early. I think that's all that really mattered to him," Eric said. "I feel like he was still looking out for me."

— Kristin Anderson
News reporter for WKYC-TV in Cleveland, OH

HENDRIX
U.S. ARMY

COCKS.
Sports Illustrated

Staff Sgt. Jason Hendrix
October 26, 1976 – February 16, 2005

If you ever asked 28-year-old Army Staff Sgt. Jason Hendrix what was most important to him, he would say finding true love, fighting for his country and protecting his family.

Jason's sister, Amanda Patterson, knows how protective her older brother could be. "I'll never forget a particular movie date. Jason showed up at the theater, shook the guy's hand, pulled him close and warned him not to treat me wrong."

Jason was also a typical big brother. "We would get into so much trouble together," said Jason's younger brother Justin. "One day we played tennis in my dad's shop with bats and basketballs. We broke everything! Dad was not happy. Jason thought it was hysterical but also took the blame for me."

Looking after Amanda and Justin helped shape Jason's personality. That maturity made him a leader in the military. Former Army specialist Anthony Koller, who served with Jason in Korea and Iraq, said, "He was into body building. He knew strength could give him an edge if any of us got into trouble. Sgt. Hendrix was always the first to step up and help, the first to risk his life for us."

Jason put his life on the line every day, but he also put his heart on the line, falling in love with Nuha Susey, an interpreter for his unit. "He would gush over her and say she was 'the one,'" Amanda said. "They were two peas in a pod. I'm just thankful that he knew true love before he died. Some people never find it."

Jason Hendrix of Claremore, OK died February 16, 2005. He was awarded 16 service coins and 15 decorations, including the Purple Heart, Bronze Star, Meritorious Service Medal and the Combat Infantryman's Badge.

— Chera Kimiko
News anchor for KOKI Fox 23 in Tulsa, OK

Anything for His Kids

Army Staff Sgt. Jason Hendrix loved his kids. His father, Russ Hendrix would know. "He'd call with a list of things they needed, and we'd go pick it all up and ship it for them," said Russ. "Anything from batteries for laser sights, to boots, or toys and candy for them to give out. Jason spent a lot of his own money." Jason's "kids" were the soldiers serving under him in Iraq, and the most important thing to him was making sure they all made it home. Danna Malone, a close family friend, mentions the first time Jason lost one of his soldiers. "He called home and was just devastated, because he was holding Tyler when he died," Danna recalled.

"Jason was a soldier's soldier," Danna said. "He cared about his men more than himself."

It had always been this way. Jason put others first.

Born on October 26, 1976, Jason was the oldest of three children. His parents divorced when he was young, and in 1989, Russ Hendrix was given full custody. As a teenager, Jason moved from California to Oklahoma to live with his father. He attended Claremore Sequoyah High School, where he was an avid bodybuilder and football player who found time to spend with family as well.

"He loved babysitting his cousins," Danna said, "and I remember hearing them ask Jason to bring out the 'old music' from the 60's, and he would teach them to dance. I don't even know if he thought of himself as a role model, but that's what he was."

As dedicated as Jason was to his family, he loved his country just as much. When he was 17, he joined the Oklahoma National Guard and served until he graduated, deciding then to enlist in the active duty Army. Jason was sworn in a few days before the Oklahoma City bombing in 1995. "He was born for the Army," said Danna. "Everything was black and white for Jason. There was no gray." His father agrees. "He was very dedicated – very caring. He wouldn't back down from anything he believed in," and Jason believed his place was in Iraq, defending his country. Danna explains why Jason had to go.

"After 9/11, he made a promise that whoever we went to war against; he was going to be there. Jason always kept his word. He stood up for our country, and he made sure that he was a part of that war, because he felt that his country had been attacked."

Keeping his word wouldn't be easy as just asking the Army to be sent to Iraq. Jason ended up having to change units several times before finding one that was on its way out. He deployed to Iraq as an infantry first responder, and his personality spilled over into his leadership style and relationships with the soldiers under him.

"He would call them his kids," Russ Hendrix remembers. "He'd say 'those are my boys.' But after the Battle of Fallujah, he didn't call them his boys anymore. He called them his men."

In December of 2004, Jason had an opportunity to come back to the States on leave and see his family. Instead, he gave his leave to one of his soldiers who had just become a father. Jason wanted him to go home and hold his new baby.

A month and a half later, on February 16, 2005, Jason's unit was returning from a mission in Ramadi when the front vehicle was hit by an IED. Jason ran to the burning armored vehicle, pulling one of his wounded men out and getting him to safety. Even though they were taking heavy fire, Jason stayed to make sure all of his men were accounted for. He was the last person to walk away from the wreckage, and as he made his way through the gunfire back to the relative safety of his vehicle, terrorists detonated a second bomb. Jason died there in Ramadi.

Danna remembers the day when the world collapsed.

"[The Army] went to Jason's mother's house on February 17th, the day after he was killed. She called his father, and he went and got Jason's brother, and they all went to Jason's grandmother's house. Russ called me then, and I was actually just backing into a parking space when the phone rang…I literally lost control in the parking lot. I collapsed on the ground and someone was there, thankfully, to pull me together after a while," recalled Danna. "That was probably the worst day of my life. I had mailed him a package the day before, filled with a lot of things that he liked. That was a hard thing to realize, knowing that he wasn't going to get that." She said Russ didn't take the news well at all.

"We sat on the phone for 4 or 5 hours and just cried together. The Army showed up and talked to him for a few minutes, and afterward we just talked on the phone again for hours." Russ says Jason's brother took it the hardest. The men Jason had led, counseled, befriended and tried to protect were crushed by his loss. Sgt. Jose Soliz, the soldier that Jason saved that day, tried to explain in a message to Jason's family how he felt about the man who gave his own life to save a fellow soldier.

"While we were engaged in battle your son gave orders to soldiers like a true leader. Not once did he flinch under fire. I remember him telling me, 'Don't worry Soliz, you're going to be okay.' Then he went on to tell the lieutenant that 'We must make a move now before it's too late and we get ambushed again,'" wrote Jose. "SSG Hendrix was not in the best position to come to the rescue, but he made his way through hell to get to us. He came to get us even though he knew what it could mean for him and his men but he did it anyway...I can't tell you that I don't get tears in my eyes when I think about what he has done for me...Jason, you gave your life so that I could live mine. I have no words that could ever thank you...I am only here because God made men like you. I hope that I can live my life in a manner that honors you, Jason. I look at my wife and thank God that you were there for me. My scars from the blast have faded away since that day, but you are forever in my heart."

The family decided to honor Jason's life and memory instead of drowning in their grief, so they started an organization that would have made Jason proud. "One of the things that Jason wanted to do after retiring from the Army was work at Thunderbird Youth Academy in Pryor, Oklahoma," explained Danna. "They take at-risk youth — mostly kids that have dropped out of high school — and they really just help them turn their lives around. It's a military style of life, and they give these kids the ability to make good decisions for themselves. Jason had planned on working there."

Jason's Peace, the organization that Danna and Russ founded, administers the Staff Sgt. Jason R. Hendrix Memorial Scholarship. The scholarship is offered to Thunderbird Youth Academy cadets who graduate from the program and wish to go on to college. In December of 2006, the first scholarship in Jason's name was awarded to a cadet entering Northeastern State University in Oklahoma.

When asked what people should remember about Jason, his father Russ waited a moment before answering.

"He really had a loyalty for his kids and his country."

— Kit Lange
Talk radio host, military writer, U.S. Air Force veteran
Euphoricreality.com

Lance Cpl. James Huston
September 14, 1981 – July 2, 2004

Marine Lance Cpl. James Huston was awarded the Navy and Marine Corps Achievement Medal for his actions on March 21, 2003. His parents have been told that what he did that day saved the life of at least one Iraqi child. James' citation reads, in part:

> Upon engaging the enemy, several non-combatants were caught in the crossfire and company corpsmen were sent in to render first aid. With little regard for his personal safety, Lance Corporal Huston dismounted his vehicle and took up a defensive position in the vicinity of the Corpsmen to provide local security as they administered first aid. His actions in aiding with the medical treatment of non-combatants went above and beyond his normal duties. Lance Cpl. Huston's initiative, perseverance, and total dedication to duty reflected credit upon himself and were in keeping with the highest traditions of the Marine Corps and the United States Naval Service.

James barely mentioned the award to his family. They found out the details only after he died in a Humvee accident more than a year later. They now have the award proudly framed and displayed above their mantel. James' fellow Marines are not surprised he kept the accolade to himself.

"He was a very humble person," said Nick Long, who served with James in Iraq. The two also roomed together their first year and a half in the Corps. Nick called James a talented artist who was quiet until you got to know him. James opened up to Nick about his passion for hunting and love for his family.

"He enjoyed sharing stories of things they'd done together, and he'd show pictures," Nick said.

In a letter home to his parents, James told them not to worry about him. "Think of all of the married Marines with kids," he wrote. "Not some punk like me."

— RP

From Golden Fields to Desert Sands

James B. Huston Jr. grew up in a town edged by fields of sweet striped melons, golden dry grasses, fluffy white cottonwoods and the rolling Columbia River.

In Huston's hometown of Hermiston, Oregon, a fellow can leave his keys in the tractor's ignition or leave the front door unlocked without worry. In Hermiston, the banker knew his mama and daddy by their first names. He even knew James and his younger brother Matt by name.

The UPS driver didn't know the boys by name, but he knew they lived in a yellow house on property bordering the canal. He'd seen them outside many times chasing after the lambs or each other. It was the UPS man who carried James home from his first misadventure.

"James wasn't but two or three years old," his mother, Shirley, remembered. "I was in my office, but I thought I knew where Matt and James were and what they were doing. I thought they were playing here in the living room.

"Somebody knocked on the front door. It was the UPS man. He'd found James by the canal. One of the lambs was missing and James had snuck out the back door and followed the lamb to a nearby field just beyond the bridge."

With his blonde hair and humor-glinted eyes as blue as robin eggs, James looked like his mother. Shirley Huston laughs at the recollections of her son and his first misadventure, but that memory chills her still.

"It scared me to death," she said. "We're so close to the canal on this county road. I became a lot more watchful after that."

Strangely, a canal on the other side of the world would prove to be the most dangerous to the 22-year-old Marine. James died in Fallujah after his Humvee rolled down a canal embankment, flipped over and pinned him. The rifleman and his unit were on their way to secure the site of an improvised explosive device (IED) in Anbar province when the accident happened on July 2, 2004.

The military's casualty assistance team drove out the same road that the UPS man had all those earlier years, bringing word to Jim and Shirley Huston of their son's last misadventure.

James hadn't enlisted for lack of other career options. He could've stayed home and worked in the family business alongside his father or for any one of the hundreds of local farm outfits. Instead, he enlisted in June 2001 as a diesel mechanic, before anyone had ever heard of 9/11 or a war on terror. Marine recruiters had

come out to the house to visit with Matt, but James overheard the conversation and decided he would join the Marines because he liked the tough-guy image.

"James didn't want to be just anybody," his mother said. "He always wanted to be somebody."

His parents didn't learn until after 9/11 that he had requested to be part of the infantry."He knew there was going to be action and he wanted to be where things were happening," Shirley said. "He kept it a secret until right before he headed out to boot camp."

The brothers, just 16 months apart, competed with each other. A month after James enlisted in the Marines, Matt enlisted in the Navy.

Around his family, James was the reflective soul, always quiet. He was a lot like his father that way. James Huston Sr. putters around the house and shop while Shirley talks about their beloved son, but even though James Sr. doesn't share his memories, evidence of the unspoken is all around. There are the senior pictures — Matt's on one side, James' on the other. There are framed snapshots of James and his father kneeling by an elk. The biggest bull of all, the five-point he got right before he shipped out to boot camp, hangs above the rocker where Jim sits.

"If anyone was going to get an elk, it was James," Shirley said. "Hunting was a major part of his life. He and his dad were close because hunting was something they could do together. James was his late-in-life child. They didn't have problems. They understood each other."

Shirley was 31 years old when she had James. Her husband, who had been married before, had an older son and daughter.

"I had waited so long to have him that he was very, very special from that first day," Shirley said.

He also had special talents, including an artistic one.

Even on the battlefield in Iraq, James carried a drawing pad and pencil with him, waiting for downtime to sketch something. As a boy, James honed his pencil-drawing by sketching out wildlife — mostly elk or deer. But in Fallujah, his drawings reflected more of the chaos around him.

There was a brief time, right after her son died, that Shirley thought about taking down family photos that had James in them. It was hard to see his smile and not feel like her heart was breaking all over again. Family and friends who visited had a hard time seeing his sly grin, those softly-lidded eyes reflected back at them. But now Shirley says photos no longer represent pain. They are a reflection of a life she never wants to forget – that of her oldest son.

"That's our past," she said, nodding toward a photo of her son and his father. "And this is our present." Shirley nods to the photos of James with buddies in Iraq.

After James died those buddies wrote, called and visited. Shirley refers to them as "our Marines." A few still call to check in to see how family is doing and to say they are thinking of her on Mother's Day, and at Christmas.

"When your child dies, you lose a whole circle of friends," she said. "All those kids who were always around the house all those years."
Future generations lose out, too. While playing around their grandpa's feet recently, Emile, 5, and Saira, 2, came across a flag lapel pin. Emile handed it to her sister. Saira turned it over in her hands, studying it for a moment, then declared, "Uncle James!"

"I thought that was really telling," Shirley said, "that's what a two-year-old, who never knew James, associates as her uncle — an American flag."
James' Marine buddies and his childhood friends will never forget the friend they've lost. To his Marine friends, James was a man of quiet confidence. He knew the outdoors. He was always the older-brother figure and they looked up to him.

It's the brother thing that bothers Shirley most. As long as Matt is away, she can trick herself into believing that James isn't dead. But it's when Matt is home on leave that Shirley realizes James will never again come home.
"My memory of James always gets tuned in around Matt," Shirley said. "I don't know why it triggers it as much as it does. I'm careful to make sure Matt gets fully recognized. I think it would be very hard to be the little brother of a hero."

There is often talk of widows, children, or parents left behind when a soldier dies, but the siblings of the fallen are rarely mentioned. Their grief; however, is no less real. There isn't a day that will go by for the rest of his life that Matt won't miss James.

Who will be around for Matt to share the memories of growing up in a town edged by fields of sweet striped melons, golden dry grasses, fluffy white cottonwoods, and the rolling Columbia River, now that James is gone?

— Karen Spears Zacharias
Author, journalist
heromama.org

"Of all the properties which belong to honorable men, not one is so highly prized as that of character."

— Henry Clay

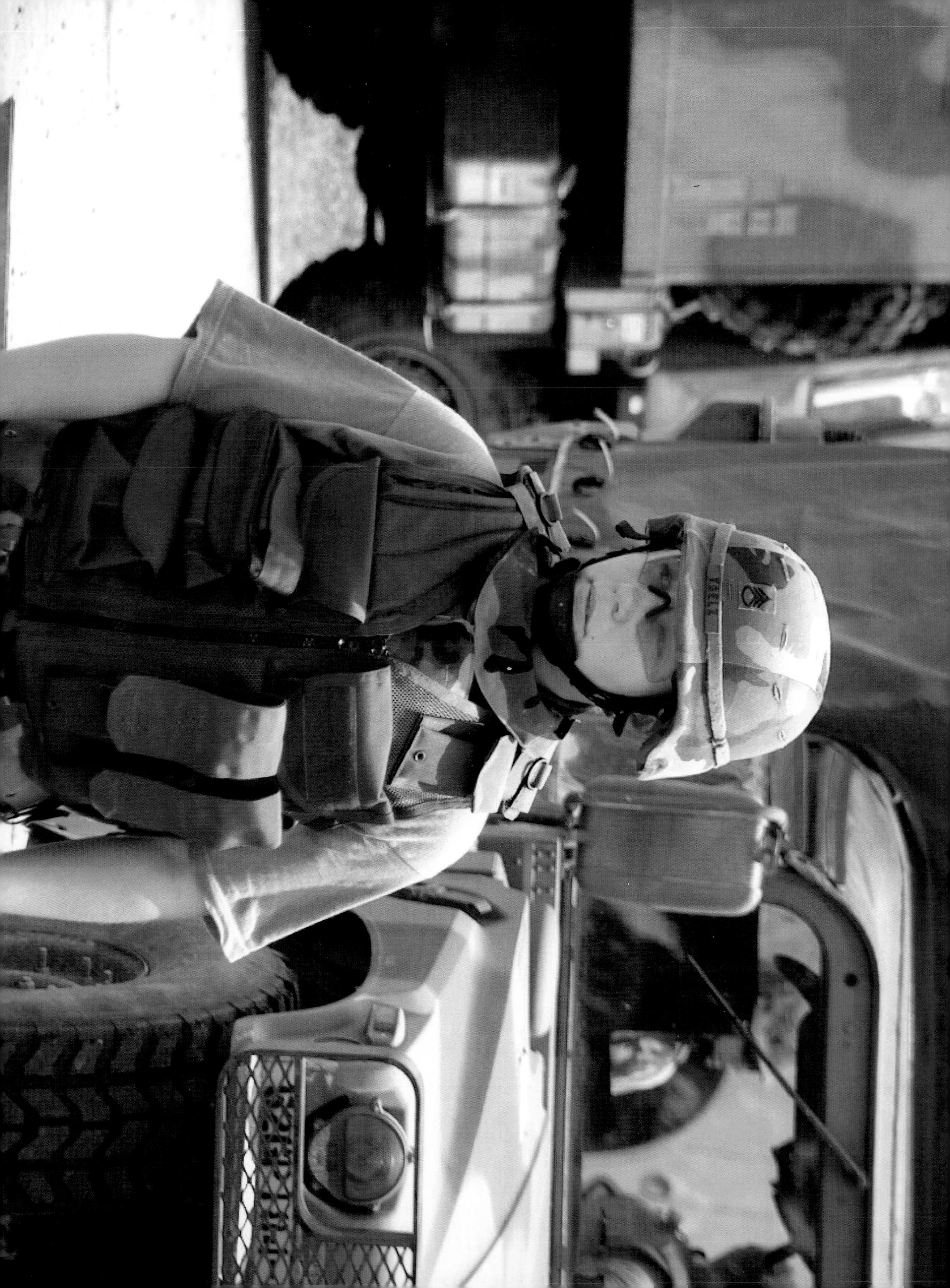

Staff Sgt. Kimberly Fahnestock Voelz
August 24, 1976 — December 14, 2003

It wasn't enough for Kimberly Fahnestock Voelz to enlist in the Army. She picked a job requiring nerves of steel.

Kimberly was a member of the Army's Explosive Ordnance Unit or, as some call it, the bomb squad. It's a specially-trained group of soldiers — mostly men — who explore battlefields for hidden explosives.

Kim was very good at her dangerous job. Many considered her to be the best.

"She was looked up to in her unit because she would go above and beyond. She always pulled her weight...nobody ever cut her any slack, and she didn't want them to," said Kim's mother, Carol Fahnestock.

Kim grew up riding horses and playing baseball in rural Pennsylvania with her older brother Mark, and younger sister and brother, Kelly and Chad. Although she was a tomboy, she took lots of pride in her carefully decorated room, where the primary color was pink.

Kim was also known for her wild streak and sense of humor. She loved to play practical jokes on friends. Once, she scrounged up "open house" signs and placed them around her neighbor's lovely home. Kim got a kick out of watching all the people turn out hoping to have a tour.

Carol said though she misses horseback riding on the trails with her daughter, she would not change Kim's path in life. Her advice to other parents is to let their children go after their dreams, and they will live life to its fullest.

"Even though Kim's life ended early...she still did a wonderful and heroic thing," said her mother.

— RP

Far from Ordinary

On December 14, 2003, Staff Sergeant Kimberly (Fahnestock) Voelz died in her husband's arms. They were in a hospital in Baghdad. She had been about to defuse an improvised explosive device when it went off. Kim was 27-years-old.

Kim had always been independent. Her mom, Carol, laughs when she talks about the day "Kimmy" and her brother skipped school to go to Philadelphia, two hours away from their small rural town. Carol had no idea until a month later when a man the pair had met called to check on them. Apparently, they had gotten lost.

"When she had her mind set to something, she always did it," Carol said.

Floyd and Carol Fahnestock raised their four children on a farm in Central Pennsylvania. Kim was part of the 4-H Club and loved showing and training horses. For a long time, her mom thought she would be a veterinarian.

But, Carol knew her daughter wanted to experience more than country living. "She didn't want to be stuck in a small town. She wanted to do exciting things with her life," Carol said. So, days before her twentieth birthday, she informed her parents she'd enlisted in the army. They weren't all that surprised.

"We were behind her 100 percent. We never really worried because we knew God has a whole life plan," said Carol. "We wanted her to be happy with whatever she chose."

And what Kim chose wasn't easy. She decided she wanted to defuse bombs. After basic training, she trained to be an ammunition specialist before heading to Explosive Ordnance Disposal School. That's where she met Max Voelz, the man who would eventually become her husband.

"She was level-headed, smart and tough," Max said.

It is an ultra-competitive field where only the best survive. Only five of the original 35 soldiers made it through the tough course on the first try. Kim and Max were two of them.

For a while, Carol had worried her opinionated and strong-willed daughter might never find a husband. But when Max went home with Kim to Pennsylvania, Carol knew she was in love.

Bless those who have been set apart

By hazardous duty, give support to

Those families and loved ones

Who with high hope and prayer

Must wait each tense call.

Receive into eternal rest those

Who have given their lives,

And bring healing to those who mourn.

— Excerpt from prayer for explosive ordnance disposal (EOD) professionals

"She needed someone smart, strong and courageous," she said. "I didn't think she'd ever find a man to suit her."

Then, Carol peeked out the window at the new couple as they said their goodbyes. "She threw her arms around him and gave him a kiss," Carol remembered. "She wouldn't do that to anyone."

The two were married in June 1999 in Mechanicsburg, PA. The Army stationed them together at Fort Knox. In that time, Kim worked special details with the Secret Service. She conducted bomb sweeps in advance of the President and of the Pope when he visited St. Louis in 1999. She also worked the Salt Lake City Olympics in 2002.

In their business, you can't afford to make mistakes. Her husband says Kim never did and that she was well-respected and promoted quickly. In a field made up of 99 percent men, it was tough. Max says, "She thrived in that kind of environment. She was one of the guys."

Max and Kim were called up to Iraq in September of 2003. Each led separate bomb-disposal teams. Her mother says she wasn't nervous about it; Kim told her she trusted God would take care of them.

As often as she could, Kim would call home. The first question out of her mouth, "Hey, Mom. What's up? It's just me. Did you find anything?"

Carol was looking for land for Kim to buy nearby. Kim thought she and Max would eventually settle down and start a family. Rarely did she talk about what was going on overseas, except to ask for canned peas or flea collars to put around her ankles.

Over three months, Kim and Max defused more than 70 improvised explosive devices in Iraq. The night of December 13, she was headed toward a power line tower that had three timed IEDs loosely strapped to it. As she approached, one of the devices suddenly fell and hit the concrete. She was within 15 feet when it detonated.

Kim was conscious, but in shock and her left leg was badly injured. A member of the security element with whom she was working put a tourniquet on her leg. Max says she would have bled to death without it.

He was in Fallujah at the time, checking his email, when his captain came into the room."I knew something was wrong," Max says when the captain told everyone to "take off." He told him Kim had been injured.

Max tried to get to Baghdad right away, but the one-hour helicopter trip was delayed because of cloud cover. He finally made it to the hospital eight hours later. There, he found Kim sedated with a breathing tube in a drug-induced coma. Doctors wanted to remove fragments near her lungs and spine.

He couldn't talk with her, but he called her parents to tell them what happened. Back in Carlisle, the phone ran at 1:30 Sunday morning. Max told Floyd that Kim was hurt, but that doctors were operating and were optimistic she'd pull through. There was even talk of flying her to Walter Reed Army hospital in Washington D.C. The Fahnestocks stayed awake all night praying.

But a few hours later, she took a turn for the worse. There was trauma to her lungs from the blast. The ballistic plate in her vest did little to help her. In fact, Max says it made her injuries worse because it magnified the effects of the explosion.

At 5:45 EST that morning, Kim died. Max was holding her. He took a few moments before calling Carol and Floyd. "I needed to tell them. I didn't want some stranger knocking on their door," he said. "It was the most horrible thing I've ever had to do."

Carol said, "I gave her to God."

A few months after Kim's death, a letter addressed to Carol came in the mail. It was from the man who had helped Kim with her leg when the bomb exploded. He apologized for waiting so long. He'd wanted to write for some time but it had been too hard to talk about the incident. He wrote, "I tried to help her and she took my hand and thanked me. I just wanted you to know how beautiful and courageous your daughter was."

For the Fahnestocks, the loss is still hard. And it's not easy for Max either. He still thinks of Kim every day, but says time helps heal.

"When you let those feelings out, it never hurts less. It just comes less often," he said. He still works as a bomb specialist at the Aberdeen Proving Grounds in Maryland and expects to stay in the Army for another three years. Before Kim died, they had both re-enlisted.

In Pennsylvania, Kim is still in many hearts. "She died a hero. How great is that?" asks Carol, who loves to talk about her daughter, the 453rd soldier to die in Iraq. Carol often laughs after delivering a good Kim story, but still, there are times she cries. "I still miss her," Carol said. "I'm going to suffer forever because we're separated."

She visits Kim's grave every day -- sometimes twice -- and often finds letters or gifts in plastic bags from strangers. One person's message: "Thank you for the person you are and for dying as a sacrifice for our country."

— Heather Brown
Reporter for WCCO-TV in Minneapolis, MN

Petty Officer 3rd Class Fernando Mendez-Aceves
March 6, 1977 — April 6, 2004

Fernando "Doc" Mendez-Aceves was a Navy Corpsman in Iraq.

Navy Corpsmen* are the angels who serve alongside Marines in combat. They are there to patch up the wounded, and often do so while under fire. Although Navy Corpsmen are officially considered non-combatants, many have lost their lives in battle.

Fernando was known for his skills and his level head. "He was really knowledgeable about trauma, and he gave me advice on the different kinds of injuries I would see in Iraq," said fellow Corpsman Victor Urena about his mentor. Victor describes Fernando as a "really funny guy" who always had a smile on his face. He knew how to lighten the mood, and he knew when to get serious. He took the uncertain Victor under his wing, instilling confidence in a dangerous and volatile environment.

Fernando was in Iraq for about two months when he was killed in an ambush in the city of Ramadi. The last time he was seen alive he was helping wounded Marines. Victor said he will never forget the lessons Fernando taught him. "I miss him very much. I love him to death. He is the most inspirational person in my life. It is because of him that I am the man I am today."

**Of the six American warriors raising the flag atop Mount Suribachi on Iwo Jima in 1945, five of them were U.S. Marines. One was a U.S. sailor, a Navy Corpsman (also known as a hospital corpsman or a medical corpsman). The battlefield relationship between Navy Corpsmen and Marines is a longstanding tradition of the Navy/Marine Corps team, reflecting the 230-year union between the two naval services.*

— RP

Echo Company

The day he left for Iraq, they took pictures - one after another of him in his fatigues, cap shading his eyes from the sunlight, with medic's insignia pinned to his collar.

To the mother of Navy Petty Officer 3rd Class Fernando Mendez-Aceves, the pictures capture the way things used to be: her beaming with pride, head leaning on his right shoulder, his younger brother at his left shoulder, Fernando's muscular arms encircling them both.

Friends teased him, but Fernando was never embarrassed to show his devotion to his family. "The thing is, he was a very unusual son," said his mother, Sandra. "Very unusual for American standards, or even Mexican standards, because he actually liked hanging out with me and my mother."

"They would say, 'Oh, mama's boy,' but he didn't care," said his younger brother, Kenneth, who's 15. "He was proud of us."

Fernando knew the importance of family from his birth, 27 years ago in Mexico City. He was the third boy his mother had in as many years, for years the youngest member of a home shared by four generations.

Fernando was smaller than his brothers, a gentle boy who brought home wounded birds. "He was always extremely sensitive. His heart was always hurting for someone," his mother said.

When she slept, he would line his GI Joe dolls alongside her bed, to protect her. Fernando was 11 when Kenneth was born. Jealous at first, Fernando soon fell in love with his younger brother, helping to change his diapers, playing with him, caring for him to allow a rest for his mother, who had malaria.
"I would be taking care of Kenneth in the middle of the night having fever and crying and Fernando would be right there, and he would calm him down," she remembers. "I have pictures of Fernando exhausted and Kenneth like a little teddy bear on top of him, both asleep."

"He's a little like my son," Fernando once told a friend.

The boys grew up all over the world. Sandra's second husband worked in research, and the family moved from Mexico to Ghana, West Africa, then to Thailand.

Fernando became a U.S. citizen, but he embraced his Mexican heritage, wearing a custom-tailored Charro suit to graduate from high school in Ponce, Puerto Rico.

Another family tradition was respect for military service, instilled in the boys since infancy, when their great-grandmother would rock them to sleep humming soldier's marches. No one was surprised when Fernando's older brother Enrique joined the Air Force. A year later, at 21, Fernando signed up for the Navy, choosing a career as a combat medic.

He'd been a scrawny kid. Boot camp changed that.

Fernando outran everyone, won top marks on every fitness test. His biceps grew so thick he needed to wear oversize shirts. He began training as a Navy SEAL, but was forced to quit after suffering from hypothermia. When Fernando was assigned to Southern California, he brought his mother and Kenneth along and rented a small apartment for the three of them.
He took Kenneth everywhere. Girlfriends used to joke that his younger brother came along as a chaperone. "You wanted to see him furious? Touch me. Touch his brothers," his mother said.

He could intimidate anyone with the mean, cold stare he developed. "If he looked at you, you would feel his eyes on you," Kenneth said. "You would feel a very heavy look."

Fernando lifted weights at work, then again in the afternoon with his brother. They hung a pull-up bar in the bathroom.

At the Naval Medical Center in San Diego, friends nicknamed him for his bulk, calling him Rocky, the Muscle Man or simply Hulk. His job was preparing troops for Iraq, but he volunteered to go himself, not wanting to waste his combat training. Fernando left on Feb. 16.

"You have no idea how much I miss you," he wrote two days later. "I hope these seven months pass very soon so we can see each other again." Snapshots taken in Iraq showed that Doc Mendez - as he was known to the Marines of Echo Company - hadn't lost his goofy grin.

"He kind of struck me as different because you don't see a lot of smiling people around the base," his platoon leader wrote in a letter to Sandra after

Fernando was killed on April 6. "He never complained at all, even if he went on missions that lasted day and night. ...

"I could tell he was a good man, and whoever raised him did a good job."

When his convoy was ambushed in Iraq, Fernando was seen dragging people to safety before he was killed. His mother said she knew that he must have been afraid. "He would have been a fool not to, and my son was no fool."
A candle burns continuously on the memorial altar they've built, where Fernando watches over them from a half-dozen photographs. There's a bottle of Corona, his favorite beer; a not-quite-complete deck of playing cards; a last letter from a female friend, still sealed because Fernando never had the chance to open it. Inside a plain navy blue sack is the box that contains Fernando's remains.

His mother returns, again and again, to one comforting thought: Fernando believed that all things happen for a reason, and it's not our place to question God's plan.

Kenneth honors his brother in his own way, continuing his running and weightlifting, as Fernando would have wanted. He wears the T-shirt his brother used to wear to the gym, worn from many washings, along with a baseball cap darkened by a ring of his brother's sweat.

"I loved him so much," he said, voice not wavering. "I'm so proud of him. I'm really proud of him."

— Sara Steffens
Writer for the Contra Costa Times
Reprinted with permission from Contra Costa Times, CA

"It wasn't a matter of living or dying or fighting. It was a matter of helping your friends."

— Corpsman Robert Degeus

Lance Cpl. Holly Ann Charette
September 27, 1983 — June 23, 2005

When Cpl. Sarah Flores first laid eyes on fellow Marine Holly Charette, she was blown away. "She looked sharp. Her hair was just so perfect, and I remember being surprised at how beautiful she was. She was squared away and salty. I was so intimidated by her," said Sarah.

The two became roommates while stationed at Camp Lejuene in North Carolina, and Sarah got to know the lighter side of Holly. "She could be off the wall. Her smile, her laughter and her craziness were contagious. You just couldn't help but laugh when you were around her. She became one of my best friends."

Cpl. Shannon Oehlschlager and Holly began their Marine Corps careers together in March of 2002. Shannon says Holly was a great motivator who could encourage friends to do things they never thought they could. She credits Holly for helping her get through boot camp. "She could get you smiling while you were suffering and things were getting tough. We couldn't make jokes, of course, but she had these looks," said Shannon. She says Holly became like a sister to her. "She had this way about her. Every time she talked to you, she made you feel like you were the most important person in the world and you had her undivided attention. She was all-around awesome."

Lance Cpl. Holly Charette shared her Marine boot camp experiences with her Army dad, whom she greatly admired. A loving big sister to her three brothers and a best friend to her mother, her death left a void in many lives.

— RP

A Marine's Dream Realized

The loss of a loved one leaves a scar on the soul that never completely heals, but the family and friends of Lance Cpl. Holly Charette, a Marine from Cranston, RI, can find some comfort knowing one of her dreams has been realized.

Holly was one of those American high school students inspired to join the ranks of the military after watching the horrors of 9/11. After graduating, she took a job at a movie theater and began classes at a local community college. But the memory lingered. As she observed the events in Afghanistan and Iraq, the popular blond field hockey player and cheerleader, known for her patriotism and her desire to make a difference in people's lives, decided she wanted to contribute to the effort in some way. Holly left her job to join the U.S. Marine Corps in 2002.

Family and friends were uneasy about the decision and told her so. "When she told me what she was going to do, I cried. I was scared," recalled Holly's best friend, Danielle Gilbert. Holly and Danielle had done everything together since the 10th grade, from cheerleading in high school to classes at the community college. When Holly graduated from boot camp, Danielle went with Holly's family to Parris Island, SC. Holly's mother, Regina Roberts, remembers that when Holly smiled, she glowed, so when they saw Holly's famous smile at the graduation ceremony, they could tell that she was proud to be a Marine. Once a shy teenager, Holly had changed. She was more confident and self-assured. "She grew fast into a Marine," agreed her grandfather Cy Wheetman.

Shortly after boot camp, Danielle drove with Holly on the trip to Camp Lejeune, NC. To pass the time, the two friends laughed and sang during the road trip. "It was a long ride, but Holly and I made it fun. We would put on Jessica Simpson and sing at the top of our lungs, 'til our throats hurt," said Danielle. Holly was about to be deployed to Iraq and they had no idea that this would be their last adventure together.

The day Holly left for Iraq, Danielle was a nervous wreck. She began watching the news every day. They continued to stay in close touch, talking by phone often and sending text messages across the thousands of miles separating them. Holly told Danielle that her experience in Iraq made her realize how lucky we are in the United States, and not to take anything for granted.

Holly was assigned a support role, delivering the mail to fellow Marines, which is no easy task in a war zone like Iraq. A typical load of mail might be 70 bags, each weighing upwards of 60 pounds. The hundreds of pieces of mail had to be delivered to fellow Marines quickly and efficiently. She had thought about the post

office as a career, but did not seriously consider it until she saw how much the mail messages and packages she delivered meant to those in Iraq. She loved seeing the looks of joy and appreciation on the faces of fellow Marines. Those who served with Holly recall seeing her walking down the dusty dirt roads of the camp with a yellow mailbag slung over her shoulder. No matter how heavy the mailbag or how much grit she had in her teeth, Holly always had a ready smile for her fellow Marines. She was nicknamed "Chompers" by her fellow Marines. Like her classmates back home, they remember her sunny personality and her ability to make others laugh and feel good Holly saw her role as a critical link, often the only one, between those serving in Iraq and their loved ones back home. As someone who was deeply missing her own family, especially her parents, Regina and Ed Roberts, the job took on a special significance.

Military mail delivery gave Holly a new mission in life. She went out of her way to get mail to fellow Marines, frequently tracking them down in chow halls and barracks to hand-deliver a piece of mail that she thought might be important or expected. She took great pride and joy in her contribution. Her dedication to duty and exemplary sense of mission were recognized in a *Marine Corps Times* article, published in May 2005. She said the job had a lot of stresses, but knowing the importance of her service made all her efforts worthwhile.

With one year left on her enlistment contract, Holly told the *Times* that she intended to apply for a job as a mail carrier at the Cranston, RI U.S. Post Office when she got out of the Marines. She wanted to continue delivering the mail, a job she saw as a life's mission.

That dream came to a tragic end on June 23, 2005, when a suicide bomber attacked Holly's convoy as they were returning to base after working an entry control point in the city of Fallujah. She was temporarily assigned to search Iraqi women and female children in an effort to protect the area from weapons threats. The blast killed four Marines and one sailor and wounded 13 others, 11 of them women. Al Qaeda claimed responsibility for the ambush. Posthumously promoted, Corporal Holly Charette became the first U.S. Marine woman killed in Iraq.

"She only had a week left in Fallujah," said her mother. "Then, she would return to Camp Blue Diamond, which was safer." Holly had a fiancé, who was also a Marine in Iraq at the same time. Being on the front lines, the family worried about him more than Holly, who they felt was in a safer situation.

Holly had waited for him through three tours to the Mideast, and they planned to marry when they both finished their tours of duty.

The day the bad news arrived, Danielle felt like her life, too, had come to a halt. "I thought I was in a bad dream, and that I was going to wake up … but I didn't," she said. Her many friends, schoolmates and family in her hometown of Cranston were struck by the loss of Holly. A memorial plaque was placed on a tree planted in front of the high school where she and Danielle met and became friends for life. The memorial gained attention, and U.S. Senator Jack Reed from Rhode Island took one more step to honor Holly's special sense of mission. He introduced a bill in November 2005 to rename her hometown post office. On October 15, 2006, the Post Office in Cranston was officially named the "Holly Charette Cranston Post Office." Though Holly's mission ended prematurely, a dream inspired by her dedicated work was realized. Her name will be a permanent reminder of her ultimate sacrifice to her country, and she will always be associated with the post office where she dreamed of working.

"Her memory will live on as generations ask, 'who is Holly Charette?' and her story can be told," said Danielle. "She was a postwoman in the Marine Corps and was sent to Iraq to honor and defend our country."

Holly's grandfather summed it up this way: "She is our hero."

— Gene Retske
Independent writer
solvox.com & prepaid-press.com

Capt. Kimberly Nicole Hampton
August 18, 1976 — January 2, 2004

Kimberly Nicole Hampton's parents thought of her as their miracle baby.

They'd been married for 12 years, gone through surgery, and done lots of praying when, finally, the happy news came.

"There was not a day that went by that I did not think about that miracle and thank God for giving her to us. What a gift! We only had her with us for 27 years, not nearly long enough, but we have a lifetime of memories," shared Ann Hampton, Kimberly's mother.

That baby would grow up to be a beautiful, charismatic brunette who excelled at anything she tried. The super-achiever graduated with honors from Presbyterian College in Clinton, SC, where she was also a tennis ace. In fact, she never lost a game in three years of singles.

She was also dedicated to ROTC. The honors English graduate went to Presbyterian on a full-ride ROTC scholarship.

Kimberly fulfilled a childhood dream when she became a pilot in the United States Army. Those who served with her knew her as a skilled aviatrix with a positive attitude. Friends and family agree Kimberly was truly doing what she loved.

As commander of Delta Troop of the 1st Squadron, 17th Cavalry Regiment, 82nd Airborne Division, Kimberly's call sign was "Dark Horse Six." Her comrades say she was doing everything right on Jan. 2, 2004, when enemy ground fire struck her OH-58 Kiowa. She was killed when the crippled chopper crashed into a wall.

She was the first woman in the 82nd to die from hostile fire and the division's first company commander killed in the War on Terrorism.

Dale and Ann Hampton's only child was also the first female from South Carolina to make the ultimate sacrifice in Iraq.

— RP

Kimberly's Flight

In a third grade essay, Kimberly Hampton wrote, "I want to fly like a bird."

Such comments might seem like nothing more than a young girl's fanciful musings. For Kimberly, however, it was less wish and more prophecy, as she would eventually become a helicopter pilot in the U.S. Army.

Sadly, the place in which she was able to "fly like a bird" was also an unforgiving battlespace that cut short her life. On January 2, 2004, Kimberly was killed when her Kiowa helicopter was shot down over the Iraqi city of Fallujah.

Becoming a military helicopter pilot — traditionally an all-male combatant role — was (and is) not easy. For Kimberly, like all other pilot candidates, the selection process was intense; the training demanding; the elimination rate, high. But Kimberly's drive, ambition, and competitive spirit led to her winning the silver wings of an Army aviator on August 26, 1999.

Kimberly's determination to excel was recognized at an early age. In fact, in elementary school, a teacher made the comment that Kimberly actually needed to be a bit less serious about her schoolwork!

At Easley High School in South Carolina, where she served as student body president, she was considered "outstanding" in the classroom and a standout on the tennis court. She was the first cadet battalion commander in the school's Navy Junior Reserve Officer Training Corps (NJROTC) program. And though nominated and appointed to West Point, she chose to attend Presbyterian College (PC) in the nearby town of Clinton.

At PC, Kimberly was named the Female Athlete of the Year in tennis for the South Atlantic Conference while posting an undefeated record in singles conference play. She earned Dean's list honors for her work in the classroom and received the Wysor Saber award as her ROTC battalion's top graduate.

Kimberly was commissioned in the U.S. Army and continued her quest to fly, becoming honor graduate of her flight school class. She served in Korea and Afghanistan before commanding Delta Troop – eight OH-58D Kiowa Warrior Helicopters – of the 1st Squadron, 17th Cavalry in Iraq.

On the day Kimberly's helicopter was downed, her parents, Ann and Dale, began to feel a sense of foreboding before receiving word of her death.

"I can remember having an uneasy feeling that morning when I woke up," Dale says. "Ann had been reading on the Internet that morning about a helicopter being downed in Fallujah. She had a look in her eyes, and I could tell she was really disturbed about it."

As it turned out, the Army was trying to locate the Hamptons, who had recently moved to a new home. A co-worker of Dale's had bought the old Hampton house and called, saying the Army had been there looking for them.

"At that point I knew it was Kimberly," Dale says. "I walked out in the yard, unable to believe what was happening. As I turned and saw the Army's van pull into my driveway, I began shaking and dropped to my knees." As Ann would say,

"Our world became complete when she was born, and it shattered when she died."

Kimberly's fiancé, Major Will Braman (a captain at the time) was in Baghdad the day Kimberly's helicopter was shot down. He had spoken briefly with her the night before, and she informed him the next day's mission would be the most dangerous by far. It was the last time he would hear her voice.

Kimberly's fellow officers remember her as a compassionate leader. In the early stages of war in Iraq, there was limited availability of phone usage. Since most of her unit consisted of men with families, Kimberly sacrificed her own phone time to allow them the chance to talk with their wives and children.

"Kimberly's exceptional proficiency gained the immediate respect of her peers," said her commander, Lt. Col. Terry Morgan. "However, what separated her most was her air of confidence and the bright smile she displayed even in the face of great challenges."

Kimberly earnestly tried to calm the worries of her parents while stationed in Iraq. On one occasion she wrote:

"If there is anything I can do to ease your mind…If anything ever happens to me, you can be certain that I am doing the things I love. I wouldn't trade this life for anything — I truly love it! So, you can be sure that your only child is living a full, exciting life. Thank you for always supporting me. I love you."

Kimberly was a selfless child, recalls Ann. "Just a good person," she says. "She made everybody feel loved, everyone feel important."

Kimberly herself once said, "It's not how you die that matters but how you live that counts."

On days Dale seeks comfort, he reflects on fun times shared with Kimberly. He remembers a camping trip to Wyoming and Colorado just the two of them made when she was 12. He remembers the day he took Kimberly to college — how incredibly proud he was of her, yet how difficult it was to return home without her.

"We never ended a conversation without saying 'I love you'," Ann says. "I so wanted her to experience the incredible joy that I felt for twenty-seven years. I miss her beautiful smile; I miss her unconditional love. Most of all, I miss my best friend."

Through their faith in God and the love and support from friends, they persevere. "Sometimes the emotions spill over when our hearts become so full," says Dale. "We have wounds that will never fully heal, but prayer gives solace to our souls." Knowing that Kimberly's spirit lives on in others also soothes their sadness. "We never quite knew the extent of the lives she touched until after she died. So many people have told us that she enhanced their day-to-day lives. She touched so many people."

The sacrifices of a soldier are many, and likewise for the family. Though soldiers leave the safety of home and loved ones behind to protect their country, families are left anxiously waiting, never really knowing, always clinging to thoughts and memories for comfort until their soldier returns. For the Hamptons, memories are all that remain: memories of a precocious five-year-old sitting at the top of the stairs on Christmas morning; of a small, outstretched hand feeding cows through the back-yard fence; of a soft voice whispering "Hi, Mom" from a dorm room phone; and an email from a brave, young daughter half-way across the world.

— *Chuck Walsh*
Independent writer

MARINE CORPS

Cpl. Brett Lee Lundstrom
June 12, 1983 — January 7, 2006

Brett Lundstrom is the one who came up with the idea to carry a 230 lb., sleeping comrade to the flight line at Bagram Airbase in Iraq. They left the poor sap snoring away on his cot with helicopters buzzing all around. Former Marine sergeant, Tony Rizzo, a friend of Brett's who was in on the amusing plan, says Brett was quite the prankster.

Brett was also quick at coming up with nicknames for his friends. He even had his own — "Lundy" — tattooed on his arm. He got it during a trip to Stafford, VA from Camp Lejeune one weekend. His uncle, who also served in the Army, had the same tattoo.

But when it came to his job as a United States Marine, Brett was focused and disciplined, and a quick learner. If someone showed him how to do something once, it would only take one try for Brett to have it down, perfectly.

"The younger guys looked up to him, and the older guys knew they could trust him," said Tony. The South Dakotan was serving his second tour of duty in the Middle East when he was killed during combat operations in Fallujah, Iraq. Brett's father, Ed Lundstrom, was a career Marine. Brett's younger brother, Ed Jr., refused to accept an early discharge from the Army after his brother's death.

His mother, Doyla Lundstrom, said he was the kind of son who never forgot a birthday or Mother's Day. "He was just an awesome kid — just sweet and fun-loving."

— RP

The Warrior

The two bands of warriors met each other near the rolling brown grass of the Badlands, and nodded to each other. Three tribal chiefs in feathered headdresses waited on horseback off to the side of the road, along with a dozen other riders and a small empty wooden wagon.

A group of Marines stood at attention in spotless dress blue uniforms and white gloves. They lifted the flag-draped casket from the new Cadillac hearse, transferred it to the old wagon, and fell in line, issuing clipped commands under their breath. They walked together, the Marines marching in crisp formation behind the chiefs. The last horse in the procession -- an old paint -- ambled along behind them all. In a funeral tradition that goes back generations, its saddle was empty.

The procession was quiet, other than occasional war whoops and horse whinnies, until it reached the gym at Little Wound High School on the Pine Ridge IndianReservation. Then the drumbeat began.

Inside the gymnasium -- "Home of the Mustangs" -- a 30-foot-tall tepee dominated one end of the hardwood floor.The Marines brought the flag-draped casket to the front of the tepee, and two of them took their post at each end, beginning a shift that would last without interruption for the next two days.

Several rows of elderly men moved forward slowly, some supported by gnarled canes. Many had pulled their hair into dark gray ponytails, framing faces that looked like the landscape.

Many of them wore old caps and uniforms emblazoned with distinctive patches: Airborne, Special Forces and the revered combat infantry badge, along with dozens of gleaming medals. On the back of their caps, some also wore a single eagle feather.At the front of the tepee, a funeral director opened the casket, revealing the body of the first Lakota Sioux service member killed in the war in Iraq.

The 42-hour wake for Cpl. Brett Lee Lundstrom had begun.

He grew up in the path of warriors.Among Brett Lundstrom's distant relations was Dewey Beard, also known as Iron Hail, who survived the 1890 massacre at nearby Wounded Knee. A grandfather on his father's side was Red Cloud, one of the great Lakota leaders of the 1800s.

More recently, his great-uncle, Charlie Underbaggage, was killed at the Battle of the Bulge during World War II. He has relatives at Pine Ridge who served in Vietnam and Desert Storm. His father, Ed, was a career Marine, and retired recently as a major. At the time of Brett's death, his brother Eddy was serving in the Army, stationed in the Iraqi hot spot of Tikrit.

Lundstrom's parents grew up on and around reservations -- his father at nearby Rosebud, his mother at Pine Ridge -- but Ed's Marine career forced the family to

move around the country, spending most of their time in Virginia. Though the family returned to the reservation only periodically, Brett retained an interest in Indian tradition, and in January 2003 he enlisted in the Marines as an infantryman.

"I always told him he volunteered twice. Not only did he volunteer as a Marine, he volunteered to be infantry," Ed Lundstrom said. "I tried to talk him out of it. He had so many other options besides enlisting. But he knew what he was getting into. He went into it eyes wide open."

Brett served three months in Afghanistan in 2004. In September 2005, he headed to Iraq with the 2nd Battalion, 6th Marines, 2nd Marine Division based at Camp Lejeune, N.C.

Cpl. Lundstrom was killed by small-arms fire January 7, 2006 in Fallujah. He was 22. Next to the casket in the Pine Ridge gym stood a tall staff crested with buffalo hair and lined with eagle feathers to represent local members of the tribe stationed in Iraq. The middle of the staff was pinned with photos of their faces. Upon their return from Iraq, tribe members receive the highest honor for bravery: an eagle feather. If they are injured in combat, the feather may be stained red with blood.

Before the first night's ceremony began, a 65-year-old Vietnam veteran named John Around Him looked at Brett Lundstrom's flag-draped casket. "He earns the American flag from his government," he said. "He earns the eagle feather from his people." Near 11 on Saturday night, the gymnasium fell silent. "This evening, I want to take a few minutes of your time to name my grandson," said Birgil Kills Straight, Cpl. Lundstrom's great-uncle. "Before he enters the spirit world, it's important for him to have an Indian name, because that's how the ancestors will know him," he said."His name is *Wanbli Iɔnala,*" Kills Straight said, and then translated: "Lone Eagle."

With that, he took the eagle feather, walked to the open casket, and placed it on the Marine's chest.

By the time the wake entered its 30th hour, eyes had begun to sag, clothes had rumpled and stubble covered the faces of many male mourners. But their energy level never waned.

While most tribe members left each night to return home, some slept near family members on the floor of the gym, or under the bleachers, refusing to leave the man few of them had ever met.

All the while, a group of 12 young Marines from Colorado -- most of whom had never visited an Indian reservation -- continued to post watch in 30-minute shifts. They stood without flinching, listening to relatives cry over the open casket, and as friends and family members placed letters, a rose and sports jerseys alongside his body.

As the ceremony progressed, many of the mourners brought handmade gifts, including elaborate dream catchers, miniature illuminated tepees and traditional star quilts. By Sunday night, more than 50 elaborate and painstakingly-crafted quilts — which can take weeks to make and can sell for between $300 and $600 each — lined an entire wall of the gymnasium.

Then, as is customary, the family gave them all away.

"Value doesn't mean nothing to the family. Earthly property, it doesn't mean nothing right now. It's life that has worth," said 82-year-old Sylvester Bad Cob, a World War II and Korean War veteran. "They give it out now, but they'll get it back someday."

One by one, the family called up everyone who had helped organize the ceremony, and presented them with one of the elaborate star quilts. They began with the Marines."I had a picture of this in my mind, but to actually see it. It's just overwhelming," said Capt. Chris Sutherland, shortly after Doyla and Ed Lundstrom wrapped him in one of the quilts, and as they did with each of his Marines, sealed their gift with a hug.

"If you think about it, in our culture, we give thank-you notes," Sutherland said, shaking his head. "Just thank-you notes."

Once the gifting ceremony was over; however, the Lundstroms found out that Sutherland also had something to return. As the gym once again quieted, Sutherland took out a small red velvet bag, and walked toward the Marine's parents.

He dropped to one knee and tilted the bag. He then pulled out a watch - the same one that the corporal was wearing when he was killed. He handed it to Ed Lundstrom, who hadn't slept for the past 36 hours, while remaining near his son's casket. The former Marine major held tight to the watch, then crumbled in tears.

Sutherland tipped the bag again, and softly folded the remaining contents into the hands of Brett Lundstrom's mother: Her son's dog tags.

As night fell at the reservation, more than a hundred men and women lined up from all services, ages 19 to 90. Some hobbled in walkers, others stood in desert camouflage, and some wore the same clothes they had for the past two days. As Sunday stretched into Monday, they came to attention.

As the Lakota warrior songs began, John Around Him took the microphone once more. He looked over at the groups of young and old and thought of all the wars in between.

"To all the veterans who are here tonight, welcome home," he said.
Then, he looked over at the open casket at the man with the feather on his chest, and said it again, "Welcome home."

— Jim Sheeler

Reporter for the Rocky Mountain News

The entire story, published on Jan. 21, 2006, can be found at rockymountainnews.com.

Soaring Above

Daniel McClenney had cat eyes. His pupils weren't round, but oblong ovals narrowing at the top and bottom. Behind the glasses he usually wore, they probably went without notice by many of his peers growing up in Shelbyville, TN. In many ways he floated under the radar.

Daniel wasn't a football star in high school. He didn't serve on the student council and wasn't crowned Homecoming King, but real heroes aren't really defined by those titles. In fact, high school accolades become inconsequential in the remote mountains of a hostile land. There are two kinds of heroes: the everyday hero that no one hears about, and the hero that does extraordinary things. Daniel McClenney was both.

Long before Daniel enlisted in the Marines, he was an attentive grandson who loved watching NASCAR races at his grandparents' house on Sundays, a protective older brother who took care of his little sister, a hard worker who went out of his way to help co-workers, and a loyal son who loved his parents and their farm on the outskirts of town. Daniel deeply mourned the loss of his mother, Veda, who died of breast cancer when he was just 16 years old.

His grandmother, Sarah Dean, recalls that difficult time. "Daniel didn't know how to talk to her," she said. "My daughter told me once, 'Mom, he just holds me until I quit crying.' He was just 15 or 16 then. Daniel, in my eyes, has been a hero forever."

He called his grandparents MeMa and Joe and decided to live with them after his mother's death.

"When he came to live with us, it helped me with my daughter's death. With Daniel, I felt like I still had her," explained Sarah.

They were not strict with Daniel, but there were rules, Sarah remembered.
"I said, 'Daniel you're smart! During the week, you've got to get home by 10 o'clock. On the weekends, they're yours, but you can't stay out all night. And no babies, Daniel!"

Some teenagers may have taken advantage of the freedom, but Daniel preferred to split his time between family, work and preparing for his future as a Marine. He exercised to shed his baby fat during high school, working at the Bedford Farmers Co-op to earn money. His co-workers remember him as honest, hard-working and kind, bringing in breakfast for the staff on Saturday mornings. He continued the ritual when home on leave.

"He came back to see us the last time before going to Afghanistan and we talked for 45 minutes to an hour. I'm glad to have had that opportunity with him before he left," remembered his former boss, Vickey Stewart. "He was a wonderful young man. He was the kind of person if you had a son, you'd want it be like him."

Pfc. Daniel Bradley McClenney
November 10, 1984 — June 24, 2004

At just 19 years old, Marine Pfc. Daniel B. McClenney was the youngest in his squad serving in Afghanistan.

"We teased him a lot like older brothers would," said 30-year-old Marine Sgt. Pete Lindenthal. "He was serious and quiet, and kind of shy," recalled Pete, who said Daniel eventually began to come out of his shell and grow into a fine Marine.

The Tennessee son was inquisitive and eager to learn.

"He was always asking his fire team leader, Lance Cpl. Juston Thacker, questions all the time because he wanted to be brought up to speed," said Pete.

Daniel was also known for always having his gear neat and organized. Pete said , "I joked about how clean he was, especially for where we were!"

On the day Daniel died, it became clear that this quiet professional was also a hero.

"He really surprised the hell out of me that day," said Pete, recalling the insurgent ambush on his men, including Daniel, Juston (KIA), and Lance Cpl. Brian Molby (survived). Daniel was on the radios. "When he was calling back for situation and position reports, considering the circumstances, he was really calm. He wasn't freaking out or flipping out, he was just doing what he had to do. And he kept fighting until the end."

Daniel received the Silver Star for his actions that day. As it turned out, he and his comrades saved countless other lives.

"The [insurgents] they encountered were setting up an ambush for a squad that had gone up north. Daniel and the guys caught them digging holes for IEDs and setting up a gun position," said Pete. Daniel quickly radioed in what he saw before he was silenced forever.

— RP

Co-worker Dana Rodriguez was particularly close to Daniel and remembered helping him make things to put on his mother's grave and listening to him talk about his sister, Melissa, about whom he worried. Dana feared for Daniel when he told her he was being deployed, but admired his patriotism and determination to become a Marine.

"I have a letter he wrote me," she said with regret in her voice. "It was one of the last letters anybody received. In it he described how exciting it was going to be that they were going to do something. What a difference they had made."

Daniel wanted to make a difference, not just as a Marine, but as a private citizen, too. He planned to go into law enforcement after his tour.

"He would have been a police officer," said his father, Randy McClenney.

"When he set his mind to do something, he would do it."

Randy remembered his last moments with Daniel in person and on a static-filled phone line in the wee hours of the morning of June 24, 2004.

"When he came home in May, I took him out to eat. He told me, 'Whenever I go back, I have to go to Afghanistan, '" Randy said quietly. "I said 'I'd rather you go there, instead of Iraq.' That's what I told him," he said shaking his head.
"He called me about two weeks before he got killed. He called me Sunday morning at 2:30. He said, 'I'm in the mountains in Afghanistan. I can't talk long, but I want to let you know I'm OK.' That's the last time I got to talk to him, I didn't get to tell him bye or nothing."

Daniel was on a mission with two other Marines from his unit on June 24th. They'd been sent back to an observation point near Bari Khout, Afghanistan, where a pair of night vision goggles had been left behind earlier in the day. They retrieved the equipment and were on their way back to their unit when they were ambushed from two locations.

One of his comrades was shot in the chest and died instantly. The other took a bullet in the back. Daniel was shot in the abdomen, but remained conscious. He was severely wounded and in pain, but kept fighting.

"He took the radio and was calling for backup, for help," said Randy, recounting what the Marines told him. "They said before they could get to them, the enemy had come down. Daniel ran out of ammunition...he had more than 200 rounds and fired them all. They executed him from close range. They broke his arm, fought with him trying to get that radio. He fought for 30-45 minutes by himself. That's what they told me and that's why he got the Silver Star."

Randy remembered his son's funeral two weeks later. "We had the funeral at a big church and the church was packed. And all along the way, the streets were lined with people, standing outside their cars and holding flags."

Dana Rodriguez recalled the drive from the service to the cemetery.
"I remember they had put the flags out for Fourth of July in the town and all the flags were there. And it was perfect because it was like it was decorated just for him. The whole entire town stopped on the side of the road. People got out of their cars and had such reverence for him. There had just been a flood and all the people where soaking wet and they were all standing out there. I've never seen anything like that," she said, wiping away a tear. "Daniel deserved that. If he'd died any other way, he never would have gotten the respect he deserved in that way."

Daniel is buried next his mother at the Flat Creek Cemetery. That brings some comfort to his family and friends. "I feel like Daniel is exactly where he wants to be," said Dana.

The rest have found individual ways to deal with Daniel's loss. His father filled a curio cabinet displaying Daniel's picture, his Silver Star and the American flag that was given to him at the funeral. Another flag flies in the front yard. His sister finds solace remembering their weekly dinners at a local restaurant, just the two of them and always Daniel's treat. She finds it difficult to talk about Daniel, but summed up her feelings simply by saying, "He was the best brother in the world."
His grandparents, Sarah and Joe, cherish memories of those Sunday races and a poem found in Daniel's room months after he died.

To my MeMa, who tried to give me all the world,
As far as I could see.
Who always has two open arms,
And smiles just made for me.
Who always finds some special times,
That we two can share.
And never is too busy,
To show how much she cares.
There's no one else quite like her,
She's the best "win, lose, or draw,"
I'm so glad God gave me you,
I love you so, MeMa."

Daniel McClenney may have felt like he floated under the radar in life. In truth, he soared above it.

— Nicole Henrich
Professional writer/producer

5 30 '02

Pvt. Ruben Estrella-Soto
April 22, 1984 – March 23, 2003

Army Pvt. Ruben Estrella-Soto was among nine soldiers killed in action when insurgents ambushed their convoy near the Iraqi city, Nasiriyah. The son of a mechanic, he was serving with the 507th Maintenance Company out of Fort Bliss, TX. Five other soldiers with the unit were wounded, and seven were captured when the convoy made a wrong turn.

Ruben's family has been told that he and his driver shot at the enemy trying to protect what was left of the convoy before they, too, were taken down. He was awarded the Purple Heart and the Bronze Star. Like so many young soldiers, the 18- year- old was barely seven months out of boot camp when he was sent to Iraq. His father, Ruben Estrella Sr., told one newspaper reporter, "He only wanted to fight for his country, and he was proud of that. That's what gives me strength." Ruben was also looking forward to getting an education when he got out.

Ruben's loved ones say he could have been a comedian; he was always laughing and joking. And he cared about his appearance, often re-ironing clothes his mom had already pressed, telling her, "Twice is better than once." When good things happened to him at school, he would tell his family to ask him about it again so he could tell the story over and over. His loved ones miss the happiness that surrounded Ruben and his true love of life.

A peace garden has been planted in Ruben's honor in front of the family's church, San Juan Diego Roman Catholic Church in El Paso.

— RP

The Last Dance

Sometimes when Amalia Estrella-Soto was cooking dinner, her oldest son, Ruben, would come into the kitchen and make her dance with him.

Ruben was a happy boy, Amalia says. He was funny, optimistic and smart. He was the kind of boy everyone liked to be around, and the kind who could find a solution to any problem.

Amalia will never know what kind of man Ruben would have become because he was killed in Iraq just weeks before his 19th birthday.

The Estrella-Soto family speaks by telephone from El Paso on an autumn Sunday afternoon. Ruben's sister, 16-year-old Cindy, is translating for her mother and father, Ruben Estrella Sr., because neither speak English. This is a worst-case scenario for a reporter trying to know the young man who walked such a short time on Earth. But with the television on in the background ("wrestling," Cindy says with a little giggle) and everyone at home, a strong sense of both the tight-knit family they are and the enormity of the hole that Ruben's death left comes across the phone lines and the miles. I can practically smell Sunday dinner cooking and, in the voices that still seem weighted by grief three years after the loss, feel the melancholy hope that at any minute, the door will open and Ruben will return to dance with his mother and laugh with his siblings again.

The graduation photo that runs with news articles about Ruben's death shows a baby-faced young man in a mortarboard. Ruben, who was born in Ciudad Juarez, Mexico, but later became a naturalized citizen, was a good student who cared about education and encouraged his siblings to take their studies seriously.

"He was always looking after me," says 19-year-old Edgar, who confesses to not being a school kind of guy. "He would tell me to continue school, not to give up. And to do what you want."

Although Ruben was a good student, "he would get distracted because he always wanted to get attention, he was the kind of student who would make jokes in the classroom and that sometimes affected his grades," his mother says. But teachers liked him, Cindy says — she knows because she is now a student at Mountain View High School in El Paso, and many of her teachers remember her beloved big brother.

The family's memories of Ruben are filled with small and intimate joys. Ruben used to take his younger brother to parties after high school football games, Edgar says. And Cindy still giggles recalling a time she and Ruben were in a restaurant together and he decided that when Edgar arrived, they should pretend they

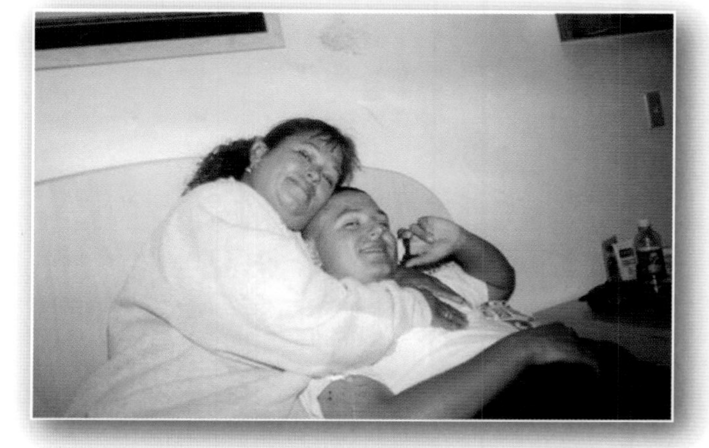

"Honor those who have served our country, especially those who made the ultimate sacrifice. Educate future generations about the price paid for the freedom we enjoy in America the beautiful."

— Freeman V. Horner
WWII Medal of Honor recipient
(Medal of Honor: Portraits of Valor Beyond the Call of Duty)

were boyfriend and girlfriend and didn't know their brother. Ruben met his real girlfriend when he was a sophomore in high school and the two planned to marry.

From the time he was a little boy, Ruben was interested in clothes. "He always wanted to be the first one to wear the new shirt or whatever," Cindy remembers. "If someone was wearing shoes he already had, he wouldn't wear them anymore. He wanted everyone to know he was one of a kind."
Ruben adored and looked up to his father, who owns an auto body shop. Today, Ruben Sr. feels his loss most keenly when he's working outside, doing the things he used to do with his firstborn.

Ruben was good at math and aspired to be a math teacher or an architect or an engineer some day. He was determined to make something of himself and lift himself out of the close-knit but ragged little border community in which he lived. "He always used to say that someday he was going to be famous," Cindy says. "He didn't know how, but he was the type of guy who was really unique."

Recruiters are frequent visitors to Mountain View High School, Cindy says, and when one also visited the family's home, Ruben decided to enlist after high school as a step toward college and his future.
His family was startled because Ruben had never mentioned the military before.

"My mother was sad," Cindy says. "She didn't want him to leave. We had never been separated from our parents. And for him to leave for months was very sad. It hurt her."

The family went to Fort Jackson, SC, when Ruben graduated boot camp and were surprised by the changes military training had wrought in their carefree boy. "Like, he would be wearing his hat outside and when we would go into a building he would take it off," Cindy recalls. "That's what they taught him to do. He was really changed. It was just weird how he was so disciplined." After boot camp, Ruben returned home for a visit and then was stationed at Fort Bliss, TX.

On March 23, 2003, a car pulled up at the Estrella-Soto home and a lieutenant and sergeant got out. Cindy saw them arrive and expected to see Ruben climb out of the car behind them. "We were all home," Cindy says. "My dad and my brother were working at the back, my mom was asleep and I was watching TV. I went to wake up my mom and I called my dad."The news, of course, was bad. Ruben, who was an automated logistics specialist for the Army Ordnance Maintenance Company, was missing in action. For the family, the shock was compounded by the fact that they didn't know Ruben was in Iraq — last they'd heard he was taking materials to Germany. Nine soldiers of the 507th Maintenance Company were separated from a supply convoy in An Nasiriyah when they stopped to repair stalled vehicles, Ruben among them. They were ambushed by Iraqi forces. In later conversations with other 507th soldiers involved in the ambush, Ruben Sr. learned that they lost track of his son in the fracas.

"It was a nightmare," Amalia says. "I never thought it would happen in the real world. I had only ever seen it in movies and now it was happening to me."
For days, the family lived in suspended animation while they waited for word on Ruben. "My mom wouldn't eat," Cindy says. "My parents wouldn't sleep. They just kept thinking all night — where was my brother?" Family and friends from both sides of the border came to the house to offer comfort. And any minute, they expected the phone to ring and to hear Ruben on the other end, calling to tell them all about his exciting experiences.
They also knew that if Ruben was found among the casualties, the lieutenant would return with a pastor. Thirteen days after her first visit, the lieutenant returned to the Estrella-Soto home — with a pastor.

Ruben was buried in April, eight days before his 19th birthday. At his funeral mass, mourners sang "Las Mananitas," the traditional Mexican birthday song. "He was a hero," Edgar says. "He fought for our country."
Three years later, the family still aches for the loss. "We don't live anymore," Amalia says. "We just survive." Each year around the time of Ruben's birth and death, masses are said for him on both sides of the border. "It's still hard to believe Ruben is gone," Cindy says. "And it's kind of harder because we never got to see the body. For three years, we've always had the thought 'What if it wasn't him?'"

The family makes sure Ruben's grave always has fresh flowers and Amalia has photos of her firstborn son in her car, in her room and in a locket around her neck. The family prefers photos of him before he entered the military because that is the Ruben they remember best. They loved the boy, but never had a chance to love the man he was becoming.

— Sophia Dembling
Author, syndicated columnist
sophiadembling.com

"Courage is reckoned the greatest of all virtues; because, unless a man has that virtue, he has no security for preserving any other."

— Samuel Johnson

0043
0043

Staff Sgt. Nino Dugue Livaudais
April 30, 1979 — April 3, 2003

"Livaudais" is pronounced "live a day."

And it couldn't be more accurate for Nino Livaudais, who truly did live each day fully, passionately and always with gusto.

It was that zeal for life that empowered the 23-year-old Army Ranger to fearlessly parachute into Afghanistan just weeks after the September 11th terror attacks. After two tours there, Nino deployed to Iraq.

On April 3, 2003, while working a coalition checkpoint northwest of Baghdad, a screaming pregnant woman begging for help caught Nino's attention. He and two of his fellow soldiers immediately rushed to her aid. Perhaps he was thinking of his own wife, who was four months pregnant back at home in Georgia. As it turned out, it was a deadly ploy.

The car exploded, killing the two people inside, the pregnant woman and three American soldiers, including Nino. A few months later, Nino's wife gave birth to their third son.Nino is also survived by four brothers, two sisters and his mother, Divina.

The country he proudly served isn't even the one in which he was born. A native of the Philippines, Nino came to the United States as a child, the proud son of a Navy veteran. The late Howard Livaudais survived the Bataan Death March during World War II, then went on to serve in Vietnam.

Nino left behind a letter for his family that reads, in part: "Please know that I died defending my family and my beliefs. I just hope that in the event of my death, that a lot more of my comrades and fellow Americans' lives will be saved."

— RP

Fallen Ranger

In December of 1978, an estimated two million people marched at Azadi Square, angrily protesting the regime of the Shah of Iran. That uprising was enough to convince Davina Livaudais, then eight-months pregnant, that she needed to flee the country for the safety of her unborn child.

Unnerved by the political climate in Iran, where her husband had been working, Davina insisted upon going to her homeland, the Philippines, to await the birth of their first child. From that moment on, political unrest played predominantly into the life of Nino D. Livaudais.

Staff Sgt. Nino Livaudais, 23, was killed in Iraq on April, 3, 2003. Livaudais served as the squad leader with A Company, 3rd Battalion, 75th Ranger Regiment. He'd already completed two combat missions in Afghanistan when he got his orders for Iraq in March of 2003.

The regimented life of a Ranger suited Nino well. His wife, Jackie, recalled, "Nino was so formal. He signed every card, every letter the same way: 'Your loving husband, Nino D. Livaudais.' I asked him once, isn't it time we moved beyond such formalities? He said, 'Nope. I'm a formal guy.'"

Nino kept his dark hair close-cropped and his gear battle-ready.

Recalling his various deployments, Jackie said, "Nino would come home and say 'Hey honey, I've got to leave.' I would always ask where to, but he would never tell me." Rangers never reveal their missions. March 2003 was no different. Nino couldn't tell Jackie where he was headed, but he did tell her he didn't have a good feeling about it.

"Sooner or later your luck runs out," he said. He told Jackie not to worry, but she said, "Every military wife worries." Knowing that Army Rangers are the first boots on the ground only heightened her concerns. "Before he left for Iraq, I kind of knew where he was headed because of the news on television," she said. She was particularly distraught when Nino deployed because she was pregnant, again. Destre, the couple's oldest boy, was 5. His brother, Carson was 3. Grant was born five months after his daddy died.

"For Grant, Daddy is always going to be a paper picture that we hold and kiss," she said. Tears rushed, then, abruptly stopped — a flash flood of muddy emotions. In typical military-spouse fashion, Jackie had a plan in case something happened to Nino. She had made a pact with a girlfriend, another military spouse, who happened to be over at Jackie's house when the Army officers arrived with news of Nino's death.

"We were all watching a movie when I saw the headlights and a vehicle pull up. I saw the officers get out of the car," she said. "I told my girlfriend, 'Take the boys to the bedroom.'"

That was the plan they had agreed upon — one would take the children to another room, while the other answered the door. Jackie knew that if they were coming to her house, it must be because they had news about Nino. Still, she hoped that he was only injured — not dead. It was a hope unrealized. House calls are reserved for a soldier's death. The families of the wounded get a phone call.

A pregnant Jackie refused to fall apart. Could grief damage her unborn child? So she sucked up the sorrow and steadied herself before she told her sons that Daddy wouldn't be coming home. He was with Jesus now. (The family wouldn't find out until the next day, while watching CNN, that it was a pregnant suicide bomber who had killed Nino.)

Five-year-old Destre pondered the news of his father's death and then told the Army officers, "Daddy is in a better place. He's in heaven. A place where there is no hate and no wars."

Nino and Jackie met as youngsters growing up in Clinton, UT. Nino loved Utah — the lakes, the mountains, the skiing. He also liked hanging with his friends, one of whom was Jackie's brother. He introduced the two.

Young and impulsive, their early relationship was marred with poor choices. When Jackie ended up pregnant, she dropped out of school. Nino asked Jackie to marry him. She refused. He begged. She turned him away, time after time. Frustrated, Nino gave up and left Utah, determined to prove himself worthy of Jackie. By the time he returned, Nino was a certified soldier. He had enlisted in the Army on one condition — that he be given the chance to become a Ranger. His career choice didn't surprise Jackie.

"I knew I'd never get Nino behind a desk for a job," Jackie said.

"He lived life on the edge, but he took it seriously and he was always cautious. Nino cared for life — not just the thrill of it — but the purpose of what he was doing."

The one thing he refused to do was to live a life undirected. "Nino always talked about going into politics one day," Jackie said. "He was dead-set on making a difference with his life. He'd never choose a job for money; he wanted his life to count."

Once he earned Ranger status, Nino returned to Utah, married Jackie and whisked her and Destre off to Fort Benning, GA. It's not just a cliché. The military made a man out of Nino. "Once he joined the Army, he became very responsible. He had a good head on his shoulders and he had a really strong faith," Jackie said.

Whenever Jackie expressed apprehension about his deployments, Nino tried to reassure her. Fear was never a deterrent for Nino. But he wasn't dismissive of her concerns. Nino spent those last weeks nesting with his family, telling Jackie that he would do his darndest to be home for the birth of their third child. "We buried ourselves in what we loved best — spending time with friends, cuddling with the boys. We dealt with our fears that way and with prayers," she said.

Prior to his last deployment, Nino discussed in detail what Jackie should do if he died. He wanted to be buried at Arlington National Cemetery, and he was. He wanted to her to buy a home and enroll the boys in a good school district. Jackie's done that, too.

The last few years have gone by in a haze for Jackie and the boys as they've tried to create a life without a husband and father. Destre, now 8, doesn't tell the other kids at school that his daddy died in Iraq. When asked why, Destre said, "It makes me sad to talk about my daddy. And besides, the other kids at school think it's cool if your daddy dies in a war, but I know it's not cool. It hurts."

Life without Nino is surreal.

"Living life without Nino is difficult. I feel like half of me is missing. I thought it was just shock — that I'd get over it one day. Now I know I'll never get over it. I feel impaired," Jackie said.

But taking a life lesson from Sergeant Livaudais, Jackie said she's determined that her children will know their father.

"The hardest part is watching the kids. It's a constant job, trying to stay on top of their grief, and trying to guide them in healthy ways. I make sure they always know that Daddy is an open topic in this house, forever. He's something we can cry about and laugh about freely."

Nino D. Livaudais wouldn't want it any other way.

— Karen Spears Zacharias
Author, journalist
heromama.org

"The stories of past courage can offer hope, they can provide inspiration. But they cannot supply courage itself. For this each man must look into his own soul."

— John F. Kennedy

Pfc. Kyle Charles Gilbert
January 16, 1983 — August 6, 2003

On August 6, 2003, Pfc. Kyle Gilbert and his unit stopped a car that was driving on the wrong side of the road past curfew in Baghdad. Kyle was operating the radio from the lead vehicle when they were ambushed by a passing vehicle. The insurgents' fire killed Kyle instantly.

In his 20 years, he left an indelible impression on all who knew him. "Being over there is obviously not the best of times, but he tried to turn it into the best," said former Army Sgt. Eric Torres. He said he can't recall an instance when he wasn't laughing in Kyle's presence.

One day, while Kyle and Eric were guarding a police station, they took off their boots to relax during a break. An angry sergeant caught them and demanded they put on their boots. Kyle sported that familiar smirk, and Eric knew he was up to something. Kyle not only put on his boots, but also his 40-pound pack, helmet, night vision goggles and body armor. He told Eric to do the same and they went to see the sergeant. Needless to say, their superior wasn't amused and the pair had to stand guard in full gear for the rest of their shift. Kyle just laughed the whole time.

Despite the antics, Kyle was a good soldier who worked hard. He was someone his friends could depend on. Eric says Kyle, an only child, spoke often about his parents. He said his mother Regina was "always there for him" and he considered his father Robert his best friend.

— RP

Don't forget me

Kyle Gilbert loved Halloween, and October 31, 1989 was no exception.

Then only six-years-old, Kyle was all set to *be* Mickey Mouse. "Mom bought me the costume," he would later write in his diary. "We [classmates] wore them parading around the classrooms. Then I went out for recess, and was running and it got ripped. I was sad."

That afternoon, Kyle's mom, Regina, raced down to J.C. Penney, bought a pattern for a pirate costume and got to work sewing. "It didn't turn out very well," she says. But little Kyle – not wanting to hurt his mom's feelings – said, "That's okay, Mom, I'll wear it anyway." He did, and without a care for what others might think.

Kyle was a unique child. Unlike many who, at that age, perceive a world revolving around themselves, Kyle saw himself revolving around the world with a lot of other people in it. It was an unusual characteristic for a child, but it blossomed inside of him as a young man and ultimately defined his soul.

"He helped people he didn't even know," says Regina. "He never asked for anything. Never had his hand out. Never complained. He was the kindest, gentlest, funniest, most honest person in my life. Not just as my son, but as a human being."

Regina well-remembers the Halloween she stitched that costume together for her excited little boy some 17-years-ago.

Fresh memories of it came rushing back in the months following Kyle's death in Iraq, August 6, 2003, while serving with the Army's vaunted 82nd Airborne Division.

Boxing up Kyle's things for her and husband Robert's move to a new house, Regina found Kyle's elementary school diary where he penned his thoughts about that earlier Halloween: "Even though it [the pirate costume] wasn't too great, I think Mom did a good job," Kyle wrote. It seems Mom making the costume was all that really mattered.

Mickey Mouse and pirates weren't the only characters Kyle dressed-up as for Halloween. Like most American kids of his generation, he loved the Teenage Mutant Ninja Turtles. "Everything from his room to his pajamas was Ninja Turtles," recalls Regina. "He even met them at the World Trade Center in New York when he was nine" during a martial arts tournament.

Kyle was a martial arts expert. He began karate training at five-years-old. Was soon rated number two in the nation in Tai Kwon Do (17-and-under category). And by the time he was 11, he had earned his black belt. "He embraced the sport," says Regina. "He trained hard every day, and was often on the road going to karate tournaments."

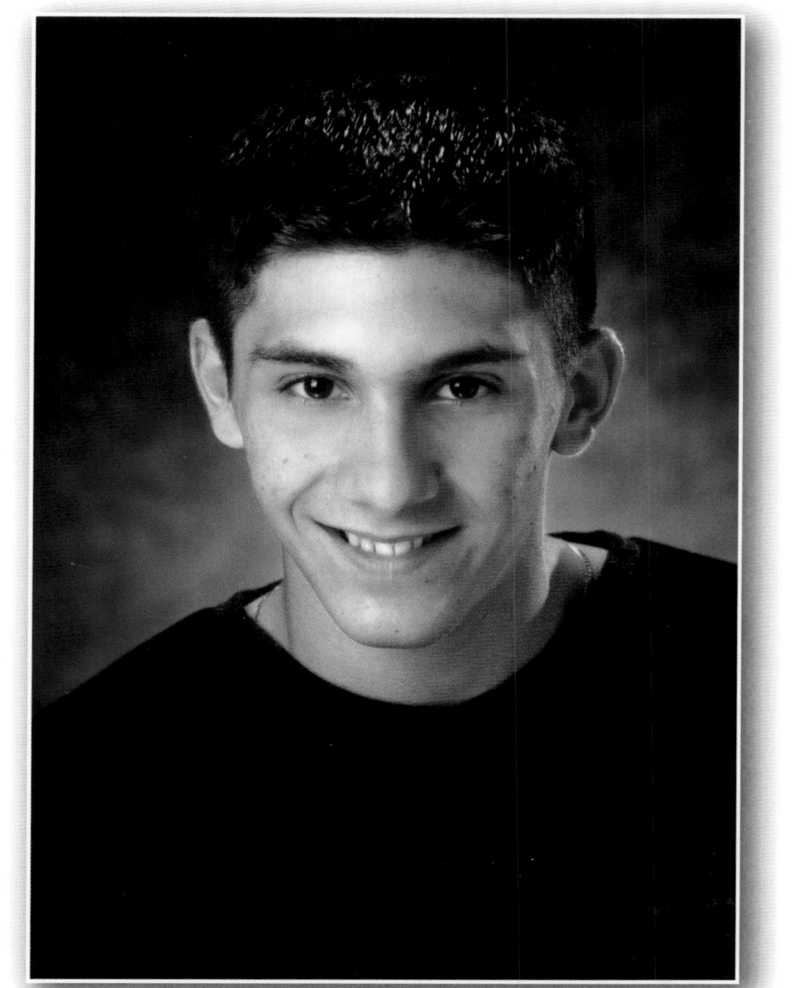

Regina and Robert traveled with Kyle – their only son – everywhere he went. Everything was together, and Kyle loved everything: finding pleasure in training for competition, learning about and tinkering with cars, going out for pizza and playing practical jokes with friends, and generally helping others wherever he saw a need.

He was also very protective of his mom. At a dinner in Boston, when Kyle was only seven, he was thrilled to be introduced to karate legend Bill "Superfoot" Wallace. But when Wallace seemed-to-Kyle to be getting overly friendly with Regina, Kyle marched up to him and stated flatly, "I'll have you know my mother is very happily married."

Life with Kyle was beyond rich for Regina and Robert. Then came that terrible day."I had this ritual when the war started," Regina says. "I would go into the cafeteria at work and get coffee and a copy of USA Today. I'd get there at 6:30 am, so I could read the paper."

On August 7, 2003, Regina picked up a paper and read where two soldiers from the 82nd had been killed in action. The name of one of the soldiers was published. The other, pending notification of the family, had not been released.Unnerved by the unknown death from Kyle's unit, Regina recalls telling her co-workers how "scary it is" to read that.

The following morning was much worse. Regina was again at work when she received a call from Robert. "He said, 'I'm coming to get you. Pick up your purse, and I'll meet you downstairs,'" she recalls."'Why?' I said." "'I'll tell you when I get there.'" "'No! I'm not moving until you tell me!'"

Robert then told her there was an Army officer who needed to speak to them together. "I knew. I just dropped the phone and ran into one of my bosses offices and locked the door. I wanted to believe that if I never went outside again, it wouldn't be true."

But it was true. Kyle, 20, was with his unit – Charlie Company, 2nd Battalion, 325th Parachute Infantry Regiment of the 82nd – when he was killed during an attack in Baghdad.
Like his father, Robert (who served in the Army's Special Forces), Kyle had wanted to jump out of airplanes. He ultimately did as an Army paratrooper, and Robert had the honor of pinning his very own silver parachute-wings on his beaming son's chest when Kyle graduated from jump school at Fort Benning, Georgia.

Following the attacks of September 11, 2001, Regina and Robert received a phone call from Kyle, who was then stationed at Fort Bragg, North Carolina. "Something's going on Mom," he said. "Tell you the truth, Mom, I'm scared. We're all scared. But we have a job to do."

After Kyle deployed to Iraq, the Gilberts received a few calls from him – every chance he had. "He really didn't talk about where he was or what he was doing," Regina says. "He just wanted to know how we were, how his friends were, and how his car, a '69 Chevelle, which he had put a lot of time into, was doing."

During one of his calls, Regina called him Bud-bud [Her nickname for Kyle]. "I could tell he loved hearing that, because I could tell from his voice he was holding back tears," she says.

Kyle's final call was received on July 18, 2003. He said he missed home, he wanted to come home, and "we're making strides." Then out of the blue – before Kyle and Regina were inadvertently cut off by the loss of the satellite signal – Kyle said, "Mom, don't forget me."

Like so many soldiers before and since, who have lost their lives in action, there was a letter found on Kyle. A portion reads: "I guess, Mom, Dad, if you got this letter, I'm not here anymore. But I'm going to be with you [again] one day, and I just want you to be happy. Don't be sad. I love you."

This past year, Regina and Robert moved to another home not far from Kyle's boyhood home in Brattleboro, Vermont. The new riverfront location is exactly where Kyle would have wanted them to be. He had always dreamed of living on the river. And Kyle is indeed still with them. The move required two extra trucks for his bedroom furniture and all of his martial arts belts and trophies, pictures, and posters. His name is also on the telephone answering-machine message with Regina's voice, saying, "Hi you've reached Robert, Kyle, and Regina's phone number… "

Regina says she knows people may wonder why. "What they don't understand is that just because he's not coming home, doesn't mean he won't forever be part of our family." How do Regina and Robert endure the pain of the loss?

"Things like the book you are doing helps," she says [crying]. "I don't want anyone to forget about him. It also helps us to be with other families who have lost children.

"There is this pain that never goes away: a hole in you that can never be refilled. But I believe God did not create us just to be born, work, and die. There is something else out there. And I believe I'll see my son again."

Regina's still finding Kyle in the small ways: Some leftover Easter candy from years ago, a few letters, some old toys, and that precious diary that continues to bare the purity of Kyle's soul as she and Robert always knew it to be.

— W. Thomas Smith, Jr.
Author, national columnist, former U.S. Marine
(uswriter.com)

1st Lt. Donald "Ryan" McGlothlin
July 12, 1979 – November 16, 2005

Ryan McGlothlin and his older brothers, Nathan and Sean, loved playing in the mountains of southwest Virginia when they were children. Ryan was proud of that heritage and he always knew exactly who he was as a person.

His coaches described him as "coachable," always learning and wanting to improve. His fourth-grade teacher called him a "wise little boy." Ryan's insight was beyond his years.

As an Eagle Scout, 14-year-old Ryan was chosen by kids two and three years older than him to lead a major camping trip. He took charge of everything from figuring out what supplies to take, to mapping out a route. Ryan rose to the challenge.

His father served in the Army; his grandfather, the Navy. From very early on, Ryan also wanted to serve this country. He immersed himself in all things military. "He looked like a Marine before he was a Marine," said his father, Don McGlothlin.

The bookshelf beside Ryan's bed remains as it was, loaded with books about Chesty Puller, the Corps and photographs from World War II.

Ryan was not only well-read, he was brilliant. He was on his way to getting a doctorate in chemistry and making a comfortable living for himself. But Ryan wanted to do more.

There was an impressive earnestness about him. Nothing he did was for show. "He was the best of all five of us melded into one," said Ruth McGlothlin of her youngest son. Ryan reminded everyone who knew him of all that was right with the world.

Ryan was killed by small arms fire in Iraq during Operation Steel Curtain.

— RP

Don't Quit

When things go wrong, as they sometimes will
When the road you're trudging seems all uphill
When the funds are low and the debts are high
And you want to smile, but you have to sigh
When care is pressing you down a bit
Rest if you must, but don't you quit.

Ryan McGlothlin's favorite poem was "Don't Quit," by Edgar Guest. He ended his class of '97 valedictory address at Lebanon High School by reading it aloud. Ryan loved to collect words of wisdom: Mark Twain, Shakespeare, even Metallica. He wrote down every quote that he found to be inspirational.

He was carrying his beloved poem in his wallet when he died. It exemplified how Ryan lived.

To call Ryan intense may be an understatement. He never procrastinated and he always did the unpleasant tasks first. While in elementary school, Ryan had a two-minute bus ride home. The perpetual master of time management, he used those precious minutes to begin his homework. He would finish at the kitchen table, then head out to play; and Ryan played as hard as he worked. He was driven to make every moment count.

Yet Ryan competed only with himself, shunning failure in all that he endeavored. It wasn't until he became part of a team that his aggressive side came out. In the football off-season during high school, Ryan ran track to stay in shape, but his only event was the relay. He preferred to be part of something bigger than himself. He never courted the spotlight.

On the gridiron, the 6'1", 165-pound athlete pushed himself to the limit as both a tight-end and defensive-end for the Lebanon Pioneers. "In his three years of playing, he never let anyone get outside of him," said Ryan's father. Both Ryan's parents, Don and Ruth McGlothlin, remember the game when that perfect record was nearly blemished.

"He almost let a guy get outside of him. The guy was much faster than Ryan and Ryan had stumbled. He somehow pulled it out of himself … he just reached and dived at the last minute and his fingers got caught like this on the guy's pants," said Don, as he demonstrated on his own belt. Ryan would not let go despite the fact he had ripped the tendons in one of his fingers. "He played the rest of the game, too," Ruth added, shaking her head and smiling.

Football was Ryan's all-time favorite sport. He played intramural football at the

College of William and Mary, and he allotted time to watch other college games on television when he set up his class and study schedules. Ryan had every minute planned out so he could be the best student possible without forgetting to take time to enjoy life. Ryan always relished a good laugh and it was difficult to catch him without that mischievous grin.

Ryan also wanted to be the best person he could be.

"His moral compass never wavered.

He always did what was right," said Ruth. In fact, while looking into colleges, he discovered that one institution required applicants to write an essay answering the question, "Is there ever an acceptable time to lie or cheat?" Ryan could not even fathom an instance where either would be appropriate. He did not apply to that school.

As a freshman at Virginia's William and Mary, he was offered a full Reserve Officers' Training Corps (ROTC) scholarship. His goal was to join the military upon graduation. That scholarship was taken away, however, after medical records revealed he had a severe respiratory problem as a child. Ryan had long since overcome the impediment, but regulations prohibited him from going forward with his dream to become a Marine. He turned all of his efforts toward his studies, but would not give up hope that he would one day serve in the Corps.

After graduating as the top chemistry student in his class, Ryan was invited to further his studies at several prestigious institutions. He chose Stanford. It was during his drive to California on September 11, 2001, that terrorists attacked this country. "He had venom in his voice when he called home," said Don. It took a lot of convincing, but Don was able to talk his son out of immediately going to a Marine recruiting station.

Ryan completed a master's degree in chemistry but left the program before finishing his doctorate. His heart was with the Marines. He was able to join with the help of a waiver for his childhood health issues. Ryan would have been a Marine much sooner had he known such a waiver existed.

As a newly commissioned officer, Ryan learned the finer points of the commanding Marines at The Basic School (TBS) in Quantico, VA. The six-month course taught numerous skills, including: leadership, map reading, infantry tactics and marksmanship. Ryan was a leader among leaders. Out of a class of 220 fellow 2nd lieutenants graduating from TBS, Ryan was number one. He was the honor graduate.

That meant a choice of assignments. Ryan considered being a pilot; his loved ones had hoped he'd take a desk job far from harm's way. Instead, he chose the infantry. He wanted to serve on the frontlines of war where fear takes a back-seat to adrenaline and ordinary men do extraordinary things. Ryan would lead troops into battle.

Second Lieutenant Ryan McGlothlin (posthumously promoted to first lieutenant) was assigned to Battalion Landing Team 2nd Battalion, 1st Marine Regiment. He was known for having one of the best-trained platoons in his battalion. His troops respected him so much that they gave more when there was nothing left to give. In Iraq, they became the assault platoon because of that "don't quit" attitude.

On November 16, 2005, two years after Ryan joined the Marines, he led his final mission. There was an intense firefight in the town of Ubaydi, Iraq, a hotbed of activity along the Syrian border. Ryan and his platoon had pushed back several insurgents and were clearing houses to make sure none remained. That's when a group of the enemy fighters, hell-bent on inflicting casualties, ambushed some of the Marines. Ryan heard gunfire coming from inside one of the homes the troops had entered. He and a few of his men secured the area and went toward the other Marines.

The insurgents had already wounded and killed some of them. Ryan fired back, instructing one of his guys to continue moving out the injured. As the Marine followed his orders, he could hear Ryan's M-16 continuing to blast the enemy. A short time later, Ryan's weapon fell silent. He was 26 years old.

The McGlothlins were touched to learn about the profound impact Ryan had on the lives of those who knew him. At his funeral, one of his buddies told the family that people always thought he was smarter and nicer than he was, simply because he was Ryan's friend. A woman they'd never met was moved by his truly "pure heart." Ryan's Marines called him their hero.

When faced with the question of how the family gets through each day without Ryan, his mom points to his favorite poem:

So stick to the fight when you're hardest hit.
It's when things seem worst that you mustn't quit.

"We do it for Ryan," said Ruth McGlothlin.

— Rebecca Pepin
Editorial director for Faces of Freedom
Author, news anchor for WEMT-TV in Bristol, VA/TN
rebeccapepin.com

EXIT-PULL

1st Lt. Jaime Lynn Campbell
June 14, 1980 — January 7, 2006

Two and a half months after Jaime Campbell was killed in a helicopter crash near Tal Afar, Iraq, her beloved husband, Capt. Sam Campbell, returned to the country. He knows Jaime would have done the same if it were he who had lost his life.

"Our sense of duty is something we had in common," Sam wrote in an e-mail from Iraq.

"It is one of the many reasons I fell in love with her. She cared more about others than herself, and she was very passionate about the things she believed in," he wrote. "She was a platoon leader and would feel it was her duty and calling to lead her soldiers."

Campbell says his wife was a confident and self-assured young woman. She had strong convictions and wouldn't hesitate to stand up for them. "Basically, she wouldn't put up with any crap!" he joked. Jaime was also exciting to be around, fun-loving, and she had a dry sense of humor at times.

"She was a terrible tease and had a very quick wit," said Sam, who was impressed by her intelligence. "She was very sharp … She learned quickly and retained all she learned. That's why she was such a good pilot."

Although Jaime could be strictly business, she also had a soft side. She was sensitive and warm and looked for genuine and honest qualities in others.

Sam said no matter how tough and focused on work Jaime could be, her eyes always gave her away.

"I could see just who she was and what she was feeling by looking in her eyes. I would get lost in those beautiful blue eyes."

— *RP*

She Made Us Better

Jenny Powers had a feeling there was something wrong that gloomy Sunday morning when she pulled up to her parents' Ephrata, WA home.

"The house was empty, and I just started crying without knowing why," said Jenny. The next morning the family received the call that would change their lives.

On January 7, 2006, Army pilot Jaime Lynn Campbell died when her UH-60 Blackhawk helicopter crashed outside the Iraqi town of Tal Afar. She was 25 years old.

During her short life, Jaime served as an inspiration to her two younger sisters, Jenny and Jessica, and was the pride and joy of her parents, Sgt. Maj. Jeffery and Miki Krausse. Jaime was eager to start a family of her own with her husband of three years, Army Capt. Sam Campbell.

Jaime's mother will never forget how brightly the sun was shining the day her little girl was born. It was as if an extra ray had blessed the world with its presence. Jaime's whole life was like that — radiant.

Growing up in Ephrata, Jaime was an uncommonly-driven child who totally immersed herself in everything she did.

"When Jaime decided to do something, she was going to do it the best she could and give it her all," Miki recalled. "She loved being busy and feeling productive."

A passionate animal lover, Jaime's grade school agreed to excuse her one day a week so she could give local veterinarian Donald "Doc" Mustard hands-on assistance during his surgeries. Jaime also had her own animal practice: a family of dogs, cats, a ferret, a ring-necked dove and an abused horse she rescued named Shadow.

Jaime was even busier during high school. She was active in 4-H, maintained excellent grades, was student body president and won the title of Washington State Rodeo Queen.

"She achieved everything she put her mind to. She had a competitive, but generous spirit," said her father.

Although she was proud of her dad's military career, as a young girl Jaime resented the military for the time it took him away from her. His annual training for the National Guard fell on her birthday every year, so he always missed her celebration. But while studying for her bachelor's degree at Washington State University, she decided to join the National Guard to help fund her education. She quickly realized how rewarding the military was and joined the ROTC so she could become an officer and lead. Eventually, Jaime would pursue her dream of flying by becoming a helicopter pilot with the Alaska National Guard.

Everyone who met Jaime was inspired by her determination and spirit. Jenny remembers her sister's uncompromising nature. "She didn't take the standard; she always wanted to be above it and wanted everyone else around her to be above it as well," said Jenny.

Brian Johnson, a fellow flight school student, remembers Jaime as an inspiring person and friend. He said, "We could all feel her sincerity and genuineness. She made us better."

Sam Campbell would also be inspired by Jaime. The two first met at a national high school rodeo competition in Colorado. Initially unimpressed by Sam, fate would bring them to the same advance ROTC camp four years later.

"Sam said he didn't believe Jaime was a hard worker because her nails were too nice," her mother Miki recalled. Such a ridiculous assumption made Jaime mad, but love eventually grew between the two and they married on August 31, 2002 at Ephrata's Catholic Church. Three years later, on August 6, 2005, they were sealed (a Mormon marriage ordinance) as husband and wife in the Salt Lake City LDS Temple right before their deployment to Iraq.

Military families are not uncommon, but few families ever experience serving their country together in war. The young Campbells did just that. Shortly after Sam left for Iraq, Jaime followed. During their three years of marriage, they only lived together for 11 months. So, when Jaime received her assignment to the Middle East, she was excited to go because she would be near her husband. Although stationed at different bases, they were able to see each other about once a week.

Jaime's tour also overlapped with her father's, a command sergeant major. Jaime was stationed north of Baghdad: her father was south of the city. She would make refueling stops at his base.

"We would only get to see each other 10 or 15 minutes, but it was well worth it," he said.

On occasion, he would also accompany her on missions. "I was just really, really proud of her, sitting in the backseat of that helicopter," he remembered.

On their final flight together, Jeff Krausse never imagined that would be the last time he would see his daughter alive. "I didn't even get to give her a hug goodbye because she was flying," he said.

Jaime was laid to rest January 21, 2006 in Ephrata. Jeff was humbled and deeply moved by all the people who came to support the family and pay respect for his daughter's life. For her mother, it didn't seem real. She said she didn't really feel like she was there.

The Black Hawk that flew overhead served as a painful reminder of how much Jaime loved to fly. Jenny, a parent herself, recalls the unbearable anguish she felt watching her parents bury their child. Sam spoke of the beauty Jaime brought to his life and how instrumental she was in his reconnection to his faith. He then spoke of how their shared faith had become critical in dealing with the death of his wife.

Jenny misses her sister's incredible spirit. "You could be at the hardest point in your life and she had a way of making you smile and thinking it was okay," she said.

Miki remembers the last time they spoke. "Whenever she would call home she would always say, 'hey mom' and I always knew it was her. I just keep hearing her voice in my head saying, 'Hey, Mom.'"

On the day of Jaime's burial, the sun was shining brightly. Despite the cold, the gentle rays were insistent. Perhaps it was a final "Hey, Mom" from a fallen hero.

— Adrianna Belan
Independent writer

Sam
Dad

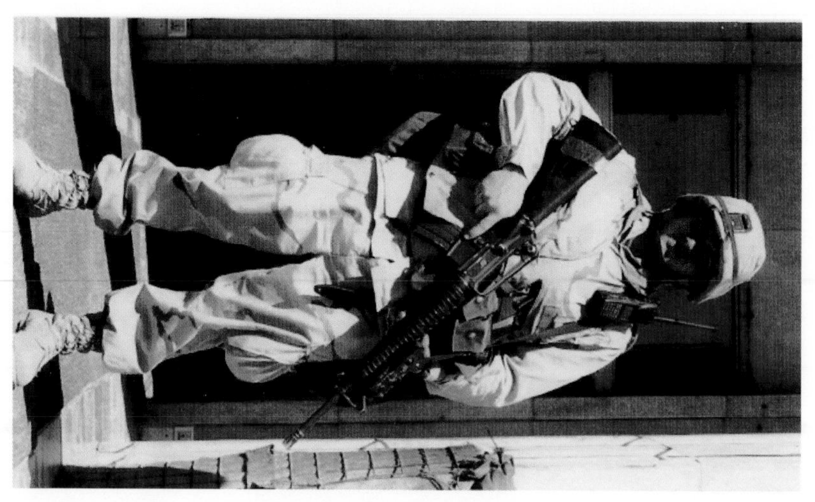

Lance Cpl. Juston Thacker
April 5, 1983 – June 24, 2004

If you were friends with Marine Lance Cpl. Juston Thacker, you were friends for life. And you'd never have to doubt that he'd always "have your back." "He'd be like a big brother to you," said his stepfather, Greg Bowling.

That's how Juston's 12-year-old cousin, Parker Meadows, felt about him. "He was my mentor — he's taught me a lot of things. He taught me how to shoot a bow, went fishing with me, wrestled with me. We always argued with each other, and we both loved it."

At one time, Parker felt like he wasn't quite measuring up at school when it came to the physical things like running fast and playing football, so he started bragging about his strong cousin, the Marine. When Parker's friends didn't believe his stories, Juston put on his Marine T-shirt and picked up his "little buddy" at school. "Then they believed me," smiled Parker. "He just looked so tough. He wasn't very tall, but all his height went into his muscles."

Despite Juston's intimidating appearance, those who knew him thought of Juston as more of a gentle giant who shied from attention. The last time Juston's mom can remember him actually relishing the spotlight was when he was 2 years old. His first complete sentence was "by the power of Grayskull, I am He-Man!" The performance, which was always accompanied by a turkey baster for a sword, made his mother, Sharon Bowling, laugh every time.

She just never imagined her little super hero would really grow up to be one.

— RP

Our Hero

It was hard to put into words, but Dixie Sisk knew it was the last goodbye. It's a thought no military family member likes to bring to the surface of his or her mind. Deep down inside, she just felt the end was near. The feeling of doom stayed with her when she hugged her beloved grandson, Juston Thacker, and sent him off to war.

The whole family was clouded in darkness. Sharon Bowling, Juston's mother, admitted, "This time it felt different." She did not want him to go.
Just days after Juston left, his aging pet collie took his last breath. Jake died less than a week after the departure of his playmate and his master.

It seemed even Juston had a premonition that he would not return. He explained to his mother that he wanted full military honors at his funeral. "He told me he knew he wasn't coming back, and he told me he loved me. And that's the last time I talked to my son," Sharon said, tearfully.

The night before officially hearing the news, Grandma Sisk says Juston visited her in a dream. It was as if he wanted her to hear it from him that he wouldn't be there to give her any more hugs. "I could see him walking down a rocky path in his military uniform ... so very, very tired."

Just three months earlier, Juston had celebrated his 21st birthday with family, wolfing down pepperoni rolls and Slush Puppies, and talking about the war and his need to go back. Grandma Sisk says he sat at her kitchen table while she sewed military patches on his shirt. She told him she did not want him to leave. He said he had to go.

Juston was particularly close with his grandparents. Growing up, he was the type of kid who would listen to their stories about their lives and history without ever getting bored.

One of his favorite places to spend time with his grandfather was a peaceful spot that included a 500-pound rock for a chair. "He would say, 'Come on, Granpop, let's sit on talking rock for awhile,'" said Tom Sisk. "He was small then. We had good talks there."

"He was like an old soul in a young body," explained Juston's stepfather, Greg Bowling. He called Juston a "sponge" because he was always absorbing all that he could.

Then there was the side of Juston that was difficult to take seriously; he was still the kid who never really grew up. His mother recalls the time, at 4 years of age, when he used her clothesbasket to slide down a flight of stairs. He broke his arm during that adventure, but his bigger concern was making sure his mom wasn't

upset. "He told me, 'It's summer and there's no snow,'" laughed Sharon. "His eyes would get really wide and he'd raise his eyebrows. His expressions were innocent, but you could see the mischief in his eyes."

He was a practical joker who loved playing in the mud, bobbing for apples with his younger cousin, Parker Meadows, and fighting battles with his water gun. But on September 11, 2001, the day America's tragedy changed his generation forever, Juston decided it was time to grow up.

He traded in the water gun for real ammunition. He put his dreams of going to college on hold and enlisted in the Marines.

During his first overseas tour of duty, Juston served as an embassy guard in Kabul, Afghanistan, in December of 2002. Six weeks into his second trip to the Middle East, Lance Cpl. Juston Tyler Thacker was killed in Bari Khout, Afghanistan. Military friends say he was caught in an ambush during a routine mission. There was heavy gunfire exchanged, and a long battle ensued. In the end, insurgents killed Juston and another Marine.

In a letter to Juston's mom, platoon commander 1st Lt. L.B. Hardison wrote, "By Juston engaging the enemy force, they were unable to detonate an improvised explosive device. We were able to find it. Many people could have been killed had Juston not fought those men [that day]."

In the small town of Princeton, WV, news of Juston's death spread fast, and the loss was felt by all. To friends and neighbors, it was as if they had also lost a son and brother.

"Juston was the kind of man who never met a stranger," said Sharon.

Hundreds turned up for Juston's funeral, including people whom the family had never met. One military wife drove with her children nearly five hours from Hickory, NC. She did not know Juston, but her husband was serving in the same company.

During the funeral procession, people lined both sides of the road, holding signs to thank Juston for his courage and sacrifice. The sight was unreal for the whole family. "There was an elderly man who stood at attention for more than five minutes," said Sharon, touched with surprise.

Juston wished to be buried in Arlington, but that's one wish family members could not bring themselves to grant. His body rests in Roselawn Memorial Garden, about five miles from the people he loved most and the streets he ran in — with a smile on his face and a T-shirt covered with mud. The spot is also just a few miles away from Princeton High School, where he played offensive tackle, guard and defensive tackle, and his retired jersey, number 68, is on display at the school.

Coach Ted Spadaro remembers Juston by wearing an armed forces pin on his shirt for every game. "He loved the game," said Spadaro. "He didn't start out as the best player, but he really worked hard to improve. He had a great desire to be the best."

At Ceres Elementary School, a memory garden blooms in Juston's name and students have planted a tree in his honor. Drivers traveling from Roanoke, VA into Princeton will cross the Lance Corporal Juston Thacker Memorial Bridge, and each year a brave student in Princeton will receive what family members have named the "Buddy Award" for courage. The Lance Corporal Juston Thacker Foundation has been established by Juston's family to raise scholarship money and increase patriotism and awareness for America's war heroes: War heroes like Juston, who are finally home.

— Sonu Wasu
Reporter for WATE-TV in Knoxville, TN

"The man who will go where his colors will go, without asking, who will fight a phantom foe in a jungle and mountain range, without counting, and who will suffer and die in the midst of incredible hardship, without complaint, is still what he has always been, from Imperial Rome to sceptered Britain to Democratic America. He is the stuff of which legions are made. His pride is in his colors and his regiment, his training hard and thorough and coldly realistic, to fit him for what he must face, and his obedience is to his orders. As a legionary, he held the gates of civilization for the classical world...he has been called United States Marine."

— Lieutenant Colonel T.R. Fehrenbach
U.S. Army (This Kind of War)

Spc. Michelle Marie Witmer
February 13, 1984 — April 9, 2004

Army Spc. Michelle Witmer of New Berlin, WI, was an identical twin. Both young women and their older sister served in Iraq together. Michelle, 20, and her older sibling were members of the National Guard's 32nd Military Police Company, based out of Milwaukee.

Michelle was killed during an attack on her Humvee in Baghdad. Her family was told she was trying to return fire when she was shot. She was the first female in the National Guard to be killed in combat, and the first Wisconsin National Guard member to be killed in combat since World War II. Her sisters accompanied Michelle's body home.

Michelle was a warm, spontaneous person who loved animals and children. She reached out to many Iraqi kids who were drawn to her outgoing personality. And it was no surprise to the Witmers when she insisted on adopting one of three puppies rescued by her unit. The dogs were on their way to the United States when Michelle died.

At a memorial service for her twin, Charity Witmer said, "Michelle was a loving, empathetic woman, more wonderful than words can describe. She loved the drama, she loved the cheese, she loved to tell stories."

Michelle is the recipient of a Bronze Star and a Purple Heart. In New Berlin, a road has been named in her honor. It is called Michelle Witmer Memorial Drive. For her own part, Michelle chose a road less traveled … and along the way she made a difference.

— RP

She Grew Up to be a Hero

When Michelle Witmer was 10 years old, she told her family she wanted to be a hero when she grew up — "even if I have to push someone off a bridge just so I can save them!" As it would turn out, all she would have to do was volunteer to ride shotgun one night instead of taking her usual position as driver, and she became that hero.

Born Feb. 13, 1984, Michelle Witmer and her twin sister, Charity, grew up in an amazingly close and loving family in New Berlin, WI. An older sister and brother, Rachel and Tim, and younger brother, Mark, would complete John and Lori Witmer's household. The children experienced both home school and public schools, but throughout, the family lived, learned and loved together on a daily basis.

"Michelle was creative, smart, sensitive and had the greatest sense of humor," her mother, Lori, recalls. "She just made me laugh!

One night when she and Charity were about 15, they came in late and were grounded. The next day, they made a video tape interviewing neighbors discussing whether or not the grounding was too harsh a punishment. Interspersed with the neighbors' opinions were the girls looking directly into the camera, pleading, 'I'm sorry!' It was hysterical!"

"Also," father John adds, "the girls were best friends, but extremely competitive. They'd wrestle — full out — on the kitchen floor, usually until one of them got hurt!"

That combination of toughness and humor would help Michelle and her sisters when all three found themselves in Iraq with the 32nd Military Police Company of the Wisconsin Army National Guard.

Rachel and Michelle had received their orders in March, 2003, and left that April. After spending part of their time acclimating in Kuwait, the two sisters were sent to Iraq in June. Charity received her orders in November, 2003, and left in December. Ironically, it was only after Rachel and Charity had joined that Michelle had decided to enlist.

"She had seen what a transformation the Guard had done for the less outgoing Rachel," Lori remembers, "and she wanted the same sense of discipline and self-confidence."

When Michelle arrived in Iraq that December of 2003, she was thrown into a world totally opposite from anything she had ever known.

Assigned to a military police unit — better known as "multi-purpose" to the troops — Michelle saw war horrors for the first time. At Assassins' Gate (an ornate gate leading to Saddam Hussein's former Republican Palace compound, now the headquarters of the United States-led occupation) she witnessed pools of blood and body parts everywhere. Once, she had to retrieve the body of an Iraqi daughter hanged by her father. Going into bombed buildings or streets to remove corpses became almost a daily duty.

However, alongside the horror was humor. One night, when a fellow guardswoman was depressed, Michelle jumped up spontaneously and yelled, "Let's salsa!" To everyone's amazement, she grabbed her compact disc player, ran up to the roof, and began to salsa with her friend!

The Iraqi children sensed this fun-loving openness and gravitated toward her. They would surround her, touch her and call out her name. One day, Michelle was ordered to accompany her commander, Scott Southworth, to provide security during a visit to an orphanage. Once there, Michelle was moved by the plight of the handicapped orphans and the tender hearts of the nuns caring for them. Consequently, she wrote a moving letter to her family explaining that the visit was a life-changing experience. Later, she shared with her mother how, after the war, she wanted to make a difference in the lives of women and children in countries like Iraq. After Michelle's funeral, more than $55,000 in memorials was presented to the Sisters of Charity by the Witmer family.

For Charity Witmer, the last time she saw her twin sister and best friend was an especially happy time. Both had a rare few days leave together, and they had ventured to one of Saddam Hussein's properties. Hussein's lions and cubs were still enclosed in a yard, surrounded by a metal fence.

"Michelle kept trying to attract the cubs over to us by running a stick along the fence," Charity laughs. "But the cubs, seemingly indifferent, never moved. At one point, Michelle tripped and fell, cutting her knee. Blood began to pour out, and in an instant, all the cubs ran to the fence. We looked at each other and laughed hysterically!"

On the night of April 9, 2004 — one week before she was due to go home — Michelle's unit was sent to patrol a particularly rough area. She took the gunner's position this time, instead of her usual spot behind the wheel. Maybe it was because the guardsman who usually took this spot was expecting his first baby in three months. Maybe it was just part of the squad's assignment rotation. The Witmer family will never know for sure.

But as the convoy moved along the road, an improvised explosives device (IED) exploded and forced the vehicles to stop. Michelle's unit was ambushed. In the ensuing battle, one bullet's path found the only opening — along her side — where no covering protected Michelle. She died instantly.

The National Guard lost its first female member ever to be killed in action; Charity lost her best friend; the Witmer family lost a vibrant, intense, funny part of their lives.

The circumstances of Michelle's death were quick, brutal and violent. But her life, far-reaching beyond that one moment, was full of love for family, siblings, children and fellow servicemen and women. And yes, she grew up to be a hero.

— Valerie A. Nichols
Author, English teacher
valerieanichols.com

Lance Cpl. Chance Russell Phelps
July 14, 1984 – April 9, 2004

Chance Phelps was named after John Wayne's character, John T. Chance in the western Rio Bravo. His mother rented the movie when she was forced to stay in bed while pregnant with her son.

"The name 'Chance' just hit me. I thought 'That's it!'" said Gretchen Mack.

The Dubois, WY native was a natural athlete. He was a wrestler, a linebacker (football was his favorite sport) and a pitcher — his fastball once clocked in at 92 miles per hour.

"He excelled at everything physical, even if it was the first time he tried something," said Chance's dad, John Phelps.

And in one way, Chance did live up to his name. While Sheriff Chance rallied others to protect a town from scoundrels in Rio Bravo, Chance decided to join the Marine Corps to help protect the country and to follow in the footsteps of his father, who served in Vietnam.

"Chance was obsessed with the military since before I can remember. We didn't know which service he'd be in, but we were sure he'd join when he was old enough," said his sister, Kelley (Phelps) Orndoff.

But she says his desire to protect and serve really came out after the 9/11 attacks.

"He joined the Marines to fight for our country," Kelley said. "I definitely know that my brother died fighting for something he truly believed in, and he had no doubts as to why he was sent to Iraq."

— RP

The Story of Chance

The Defense Department press release announcing Chance Phelps' death gave no details. In a compact paragraph, it just gave his name, age, hometown, unit and place of death. Nothing else. Nineteen years old. Killed In Action. Al AnBar Province, Iraq, 9 April 2004. It didn't say Chance was a courageous hero, a caring brother, a loyal friend and a beloved son. He was, but it didn't say so.

Chance: The Courageous Hero

Bronze Star Summary of Action, Lance Corporal Chance Russell Phelps, USMC
On 9 April 2004, Lance Corporal Phelps was performing duties as a 240G machine gunner for 2nd platoon, Battery L, 3D Battalion, 11th Marines. At approximately 1630 his convoy was heading southeast when it was attacked with an improvised explosive device (IED). This IED detonated approximately 100 meters in front of the convoy and caused the platoon commander's vehicle, which was the lead vehicle, to slow down momentarily. The convoy was immediately engaged with a high volume of accurate medium machine gun, AK-47, and RPG fire from three, seven-man positions approximately 200-300 meters from the east side of the road, behind a series of berms. The initial burst of machine gun fire disabled the lead vehicle and wounded all three occupants. The vehicle was caught in the kill zone. As Lance Corporal Phelps' driver moved his vehicle to a position of advantage, LCpl Phelps immediately began to suppress the enemy in order to relieve pressure from the Marines caught in the kill zone. The enemy, realizing that they were being engaged from two locations, shifted some of their fire to the rear of the convoy. The focus of enemy fire was clearly the HMMWV mounted crew-served weapons as they attempted to destroy them with machine gun and RPG fire. Lance Corporal Phelps, exposing himself to enemy fire to suppress their positions, continued to fire his weapon effectively despite receiving a high volume of intense and accurate machine gun, AK-47, and RPG fire at his vehicle. His fires were crucial to relieving pressure from those caught in the kill zone so that they could better orient on the enemy and the convoy leaders could call for the Quick Reaction Force from adjacent units and for Close Air Support. As this initial engagement ensued, Lance Corporal Phelps was mortally wounded. Lance Corporal Phelps was killed saving the lives of his fellow Marines. For his undisputed bravery and heroism during the heat of battle, bravery that saved the lives of others and cost him his own, he is enthusiastically recommended for the Bronze Star with Combat Distinguishing Device, posthumously.

Chance: The Caring Brother

Chance's big sister by two years, Kelley (Phelps) Orndoff, says it was rare to see Chance get serious. "He loved to impersonate people and do whatever he could do make you smile. My brother, without a doubt, was the funniest guy I've ever known. He'd make us laugh until we'd choke and couldn't breathe anymore. He loved to call us on the phone and pretend he was someone else, and my mom and I always fell for it," said Kelley.

She calls Chance the kind of person who was always in tune with people's needs. Kelley admits her brother was "the cool guy" in school. But she remembers that, despite his outward appearance as just another jock, Chance was incredibly deep and caring.

"I noticed he was more emotional than me, and I was supposed to be the girl. When we were little we fought constantly, but the instant I got sick or injured he would be right there at my beck and call, helping me with whatever I needed," she said. "He constantly got on my case for treating our mom badly; he would always pull me aside and tell me to just love her."

"The last time I heard Chance's voice was almost unbearable," said Kelley who remembers how badly her brother wanted to be at her wedding to Army Staff Sergeant Rob Orndoff. "It was late February and he was getting ready to ship out. He called and I wasn't able to answer the phone, so he left a message. On my voicemail he said he was turning off his cell phone for good and getting on the bus to take him to the airport for Iraq. He also said he was sorry for not being able to contact Rob and me, and he wished us both a great wedding; he started bawling and hung up the phone without a goodbye," said Kelley sadly. "That was the hardest thing I've ever had to listen to. He was scared and I wasn't there to say goodbye to him."

Chance: The Loyal Friend

To Chance's friends, he was fiercely loyal.
It's more than a thousand miles from the Marine Corps Base at Twenty-nine Palms, California to the cemetery on top of the hill in Dubois, Wyoming. The Marines all could have gone anywhere else on their four-day pass—the beach, Las Vegas, their own homes—but they came to Dubois. The trip took them nearly twenty hours.

When they got there, they put on their dress blues and stood silently in the wet snow at Chance's grave. Then they drove another twenty hours to get back to their base and the start of another week.
That's what you do for a friend like Chance. That's how you spend your Memorial Day weekend.

Chance: The Beloved Son

Chance's mother, Gretchen Mack, doesn't need Memorial Day to honor her son. For her, every day is Memorial Day. For her, each minute is a new milestone—a time to remember and, sometimes, to wonder.

"Chance....how could I possibly describe the way I felt the day you were born? You had my heart from the beginning, and I do believe you knew that, too."

She remembers things no one else knew."As he grew up, he just became more handsome, but he was a gentle soul inside, just managed to keep that part hidden away from everyone except me..." She is proud of his accomplishments. "I loved watching him play football and he liked showing off for me too! When he was 13 I was at a game watching and he intercepted the ball and took off down the field. When he got to the end-zone he took the ball and spiked it hard onto the turf and did a little dance. The ref said he got a little carried away and penalized them 5 yards. But Chance didn't care; he just grinned at me and ran it on in again!"And she is proud of his gentle heart.

"He hugged me after that game they won, in front of his friends. I loved it, but he looked a little sheepish after he did it because his buddies were laughing at him. He was just so damn excited he said later, 'I forgot they were standing there!'"

She is proud of what he did."That day he graduated from boot camp was the second most awesome thing I had witnessed; the first was the day he was born. He couldn't hide from me the tear that slipped down his cheek as he became a Marine. He caught my eye and grinned before the drill instructor noticed! What a day...What a man he had become." And she is proud of what he might have done."He told me once that he thought he would make a pretty good dad, just had to find the right girl. I had no doubts that he would make a great dad, and I was looking forward to that day...just never happened."

She will always be proud. *"He is still 'my Marine.'"*

And ours.

— Lt. Col. Mike Strobl
U.S. Marine

Afterword

By Maj. Gen. Thomas M. Sadler
United States Air Force (retired)

The phrase "freedom isn't free" is significant to many Americans. Freedom does not come cheap. It is not a gratuitous right, but a precious privilege that has to be earned over and over again. This book honors all those who have made the supreme sacrifice by sharing the names of a few.

Over 200 plus years ago, 57 men signed our constitution. Ben Franklin said, "You now have a Republic, we will have to sacrifice to keep it."

Because of the men and women in this book, the Republic still stands.

Faces of Freedom reflects the face of America; the rich diversity from all walks of life, every race and creed. Some were experienced combat veterans, others fresh out of training. All were warriors who willingly faced an enemy in combat for the good of our nation, laying down their lives in the supreme act of devotion to their countrymen.

Each one of us now should do our best to see they did not die in vain. We should never forget that this great country was built on faith in God, the family and the American flag.

John Stuart Mill wrote, "War is an ugly thing, but not the ugliest thing. A man who has nothing for which he is willing to fight ... is a miserable creature who has no chance of being free, unless made and kept so by the extortions of better men than himself."

The names in this book are some of those "better men."

— Maj. Gen. Thomas M. Sadler (U.S. Air Force, ret.) is the former commander of the 21st Air Force. His 37-year career took him to combat tours in three major conflicts: World War II, Korea, and Vietnam. Some of his many decorations include the Distinguished Service Medal, Silver Star, and the Purple Heart.

Sgt. 1st Class Paul R. Smith, U.S. Army

September 24, 1969 – April 4, 2003

Medal of Honor Citation

For conspicuous gallantry and intrepidity at the risk of his life above and beyond the call of duty: Sergeant First Class Paul R. Smith distinguished himself by acts of gallantry and intrepidity above and beyond the call of duty in action with an armed enemy near Baghdad International Airport, Baghdad, Iraq on 4 April 2003. On that day, Sergeant First Class Smith was engaged in the construction of a prisoner of war holding area when his Task Force was violently attacked by a company-sized enemy force. Realizing the vulnerability of over 100 fellow soldiers, Sergeant First Class Smith quickly organized a hasty defense consisting of two platoons of soldiers, one Bradley Fighting Vehicle and three armored personnel carriers. As the fight developed, Sergeant First Class Smith braved hostile enemy fire to personally engage the enemy with hand grenades and anti-tank weapons, and organized the evacuation of three wounded soldiers from an armored personnel carrier struck by a rocket propelled grenade and a 60mm mortar round. Fearing the enemy would overrun their defenses, Sergeant First Class Smith moved under withering enemy fire to man a .50 caliber machine gun mounted on a damaged armored personnel carrier. In total disregard for his own life, he maintained his exposed position in order to engage the attacking enemy force. During this action, he was mortally wounded. His courageous actions helped defeat the enemy attack, and resulted in as many as 50 enemy soldiers killed, while allowing the safe withdrawal of numerous wounded soldiers. Sergeant First Class Smith's extraordinary heroism and uncommon valor are in keeping with the highest traditions of the military service and reflect great credit upon himself, the Third Infantry Division "Rock of the Marne," and the United States Army.

Cpl. Jason L. Dunham, USMC

November 10, 1981 – April 22, 2004

Medal of Honor Citation

For conspicuous gallantry and intrepidity at the risk of his life above and beyond the call of duty while serving as Rifle Squad Leader, 4th Platoon, Company K, Third Battalion, Seventh Marines (Reinforced), Regimental Combat Team 7, First Marine Division (Reinforced), on 14 April 2004. Corporal Dunham's squad was conducting a reconnaissance mission in the town of Karabilah, Iraq, when they heard rocket-propelled grenade and small arms fire erupt approximately two kilometers to the west. Corporal Dunham led his Combined Anti-Armor Team towards the engagement to provide fire support to their Battalion Commander's convoy, which had been ambushed as it was traveling to Camp Husaybah. As Corporal Dunham and his Marines advanced, they quickly began to receive enemy fire. Corporal Dunham ordered his squad to dismount their vehicles and led one of his fire teams on foot several blocks south of the ambushed convoy. Discovering seven Iraqi vehicles in a column attempting to depart, Corporal Dunham and his team stopped the vehicles to search them for weapons. As they approached the vehicles, an insurgent leaped out and attacked Corporal Dunham. Corporal Dunham wrestled the insurgent to the ground and in the ensuing struggle saw the insurgent release a grenade. Corporal Dunham immediately alerted his fellow Marines to the threat. Aware of the imminent danger and without hesitation, Corporal Dunham covered the grenade with his helmet and body, bearing the brunt of the explosion and shielding his Marines from the blast. In an ultimate and selfless act of bravery in which he was mortally wounded, he saved the lives of at least two fellow Marines. By his undaunted courage, intrepid fighting spirit, and unwavering devotion to duty, Corporal Dunham gallantly gave his life for his country, thereby reflecting great credit upon himself and upholding the highest traditions of the Marine Corps and the United States Naval Service.

Fisher House

The Fisher House program is a unique private-public partnership that supports America's military in its time of need. The program recognizes the special sacrifices of our men and women in uniform and the hardships of military service by meeting a humanitarian need beyond that which is normally provided by the Departments of Defense and Veterans' Affairs.

Because members of the military and their families are stationed worldwide and must often travel great distances for specialized medical care, Fisher House Foundation donates "comfort homes," built on the grounds of major military and VA medical centers. These homes enable family members to be close to a loved one at the most stressful time — during the hospitalization for an unexpected illness, disease or injury.

There is at least one Fisher House at every major military medical center to assist families in need and to ensure that they are provided with the comforts of home in a supportive environment. Annually, the Fisher House program serves more than 10,000 families, and has made more than two million days of lodging available to family members since the program originated in 1990. Since Oct. 1, 2006, there is no longer a charge for families to stay at any Fisher House. Fisher House Foundation is now paying the daily fees for families at all military Fisher Houses. It is estimated that guest families save more than $10 million each year over the cost of commercial lodging; and approximately $100 million since the program began.

The Fisher House Foundation also supports: the Scholarships for Military Children Program; the Hero Miles program, which provides free airline tickets to military men and women and their families if they are undergoing treatment at a military or VA medical center owing to an incident that occurred during their service in Iraq or Afghanistan; and the Newman's Own Award, which challenges volunteer organizations that help our Armed Forces to present innovative plans in support of military families by offering grant money to carry out the plan.

Wounded Warrior Project

The Wounded Warrior Project (WWP) exists to provide tangible comfort and support to severely injured service members as they transition back to civilian life. WWP lets our veterans know that America has not forgotten them or their sacrifices. It brings a message of hope for the future to our troops in need.

Beginning at the bedside when they first arrive at a military trauma center with little more than the clothes on their back, WWP benefits liaisons — many of whom are wounded soldiers themselves — hand out backpacks full of necessities and talk to the injured and their families. They discuss the future, the challenges of transitioning, maximizing insurance benefits, and anything else. They are standing testimony that an injury does not have to prevent an active life.

Wounded soldiers must work everyday to regain lost strength and to learn to cope with a changed life. The road to recovery is measured in years, not days, and time in the hospital is only the first step in a lengthy healing process. WWP is there in the next phase of their recovery to continue where the hospitals leave off.

The Wounded Warrior Disabled Sports Project, a partnership between WWP and Disabled Sports USA, offers injured soldiers the opportunity to reconnect with family and friends through adaptive sports. It also provides a foundation for the development of a positive self-image and increased confidence — both crucial to the rehabilitation process. This program offers such sporting events as golf, cycling, skiing, and rock climbing.

Due to the popularity of the Wounded Warrior Disabled Sports Project, WWP has also developed WWP Outdoors. Through sponsor support, WWP Outdoors offers individuals adaptive outdoor sporting events and activities like hunting, fishing, dog sledding, boating, target shooting, and camping all across America. These opportunities provide the wounded with rehabilitation activities not confined to the hospital, and they gain a lifelong hobby that they can enjoy without the need for special equipment or ongoing training.

To learn more about WWP or to make a donation, go to woundedwarriorproject.org.

"When You Go Home
Tell Them Of Us And Say
For Your Tomorrow
We Gave Our Today"

—John Maxwell Edmonds